ABU DHABI

POWER AND POLITICS IN THE GULF

Christopher Davidson and Dirk Vanderwalle (editors)

After decades of sitting on the sidelines of the international system, the energy-exporting traditional monarchies of the Arab Gulf (Saudi Arabia, the United Arab Emirates, Kuwait, Bahrain, Qatar and Oman) are gradually transforming themselves into regional, and potentially global, economic powerhouses. This series aims to examine this trend while also bringing a consistent focus to the much wider range of other social, political, and economic issues currently facing Arab Gulf societies. Quality research monographs, country case studies, and comprehensive edited volumes have been carefully selected by the series editors in an effort to assemble the most rigorous collection of work on the region.

CHRISTOPHER M. DAVIDSON

Abu Dhabi
Oil and Beyond

HURST & COMPANY, LONDON

First published in the United Kingdom by
C. Hurst & Co. (Publishers) Ltd.,
41 Great Russell Street, London WC1B 3PL
© Christopher M. Davidson, 2009
All rights reserved.
Printed in India

The right of Christopher M. Davidson to be
identified as the author of this volume has
been asserted by them in accordance with
the Copyright, Designs and Patents Act, 1988.

A catalogue data record for this volume is available
from the British Library.

ISBN
978-1-85065-978-5

www.hurstpub.co.uk

CONTENTS

CONTENTS

CONTENTS

ACRONYMS

ADAC	Abu Dhabi Airports Company
ADAT	Abu Dhabi Aircraft Technologies
ADBIC	Abu Dhabi Basic Industries Corporation
ADCO	Abu Dhabi Company for Onshore Oil Investments
ADDF	Abu Dhabi Defence Force
ADFD	Abu Dhabi Fund for Development
ADFEC	Abu Dhabi Future Energy Company
ADGAS	Abu Dhabi Gas Liquefaction Company
ADIA	Abu Dhabi Investments Authority
ADIC	Abu Dhabi Investment Company
ADMA	Abu Dhabi Marine Areas Company
ADNEC	Abu Dhabi National Exhibitions Company
ADNOC	Abu Dhabi National Oil Company
ADSB	Abu Dhabi Shipbuilding Company
ADSI	Abu Dhabi Systems Integration
ADTA	Abu Dhabi Tourism Authority
ADWEA	Abu Dhabi Water and Electricity Authority
AGEDI	Abu Dhabi Global Environmental Data Initiative
AMD	Advanced Micro Devices
ARAMCO	Arabian-American Oil Company
ATIC	Advanced Technology Investment Company
BBME	British Bank of the Middle East
BCCI	Band of Credit Commerce International
BP	British Petroleum
CED	Campagnie Eolienne du Detroit
COM	Council of Ministers
CMN	Constructions Mecaniques de Normandie
DDF	Dubai Defence Force
EAD	Environmental Agency Abu Dhabi

ACRONYMS

EADS	European Aeronautic Defence and Space Company
EFG-Hermes	Egyptian Financial Group Hermes Holding Company
EIM	Emirates Internet and Multimedia
EMAL	Emirates Aluminium
ERWDA	Environmental Research and Wildlife Development Agency
FNC	Federal National Council
GASCO	Abu Dhabi Gas Industries
ILO	International Labour Organization
IPC	Iraqi Petroleum Company
IPIC	International Petroleum Investment Company
JODCO	Japan Oil Development Company
KHDA	Knowledge and Human Development Authority
NATO	North Atlantic Treaty Organization
NCC	National Consultative Council
NMC	National Media Council
OBAD	Office of the Brand of Abu Dhabi
ODERCO	Oilfield Drilling Equipment and Rig Company
OECD	Organization for Economic Cooperation and Development
OMV	Österreichischen Mineralölverwaltung Aktiengesellschaft
OPEC	Organization of the Petroleum Exporting Counties
SCR	Supreme Council of Rulers
SPC	Supreme Petroleum Council
TDIC	Tourism Development Investment Company
THAAD	Terminal High Altitude Area Defense system
TRA	Telecommunications Regulatory Authority
UAE	United Arab Emirates
UDF	Union Defence Force
UNFAO	United Nations Food and Agricultural Organzation
ZADCO	Zakum Development Company
ZCCF	Zayed Centre for Coordination and Follow-up

INTRODUCTION

A new economic superpower has emerged. In command of nearly 8 percent of global oil reserves,[1] with over \$1 trillion in sovereign wealth funds,[2] and with innovative new economic sectors being established according to a thoughtful master plan, Abu Dhabi—the principal emirate of the United Arab Emirates federation—will soon wield enormous influence across both developing and developed worlds. Moreover, with the hosting of Formula One's championship-decider in 2009, with the building of an entirely carbon-neutral 'green city' in the desert, with satellite branches of the Guggenheim and Louvre museums, and with campuses of New York University, La Sorbonne, and other premier academies under construction, Abu Dhabi will soon be poised to eclipse even Dubai—its ubiquitous UAE partner—as a household name.

With ninety years of remaining hydrocarbon production and with plans to increase oil output by 30 percent in the near future[3] Abu Dhabi will have the resources and surpluses it needs—regardless of the vagaries of broader economic trends—to extend considerably its historic strategy of building up petrodollar-financed overseas investments. With acquisitions across Asia, Africa, and increasingly in Western Europe and North America—including a major stake in Citigroup and ownership of the iconic New York Chrysler Building— the emirate's plethora of government-backed investment vehicles already control funds several times greater than those of Kuwait, China, Norway, and other prominent asset-managing states. Moreover, since the passing of its greatest patriarch—Sheikh Zayed bin Sultan Al-Nahyan—in 2004, Abu Dhabi has been stirred into even more inspired action by dynamic new leadership. A sleeping giant has

1

awoken, and a multi-dimensional domestic economy is being built up to provide employment and investment opportunities for citizens and an expanding population of skilled expatriates alike. Without the urgent need to diversify faced by Dubai and other Gulf economies coping with declining oil reserves, Abu Dhabi has introduced more carefully than its neighbours a variety of non-oil activities including high technology heavy industries, a 'future energy' sector, a luxury real estate market, and cultural tourism. With astute management and strong government backing, these should all be able to weather the looming global recession and will evolve steadily in the coming decade to form one of the most impressively vibrant economies in the Arab world.

Of no less significance has been Abu Dhabi's near complete political stability since the 1960s and the remarkable resilience of its preeminent Al-Nahyan dynasty: one of the world's few surviving traditional monarchies. As most political scientists would concur, without such a strong foundation, meaningful socioeconomic development is often difficult to achieve.[4] By drawing on a range of legitimacy resources, including massive wealth distributions to the indigenous population, the forging of a new national identity, abundant displays of public charity, and—perhaps ironically given its oil-exporting legacy—the championing of the environment, the ruling family has adjusted continuously, at least for the time being, its particular version of the 'unwritten bargain' with the broader citizenry.[5] Genuine political reforms have yet to take place, and democratisation, at least in the western sense, remains a distant prospect. By placing key representatives of other powerful families and loyal clans in directorial roles in the surfeit of new parastatals and private companies charged with overseeing the new economic sectors, the monarchy is now also pioneering a system of 'tribal capitalism.' The hybrid, semi-formal, political system of the oil era that witnessed family patriarchs becoming cabinet ministers or other officials at the helm of seemingly modern public sector institutions, has evolved once more. Impressively reinvigorated for the post-oil era, Abu Dhabi's elites, still forged from centuries-old alliances, have been reconfigured as development-focused boardroom executives alongside their roles as tribal sheikhs.

Threats have come from all directions and thus far Abu Dhabi has shielded its successes from a range of external and internal challenges.

INTRODUCTION

In many ways, despite the peculiarities associated with having great oil wealth,[6] the emirate is far closer to being a real state than many of the other Gulf monarchies, and especially Dubai. With valuable material resources and an extensive hinterland to protect, Abu Dhabi has never positioned itself as an autonomous post-modern city state that can rely solely on the inward investments and vested interests of international business partners to keep it safe and functioning as a global hub.[7] Instead, Abu Dhabi has been required to develop a comprehensive foreign policy, build up a military, and—by subsidising the five poorest emirates of the federation—preserve the integrity of the UAE. Furthermore, there are a number of deeper, structural problems that the emirate is currently faced with, many of which could eventually impede economic development and undermine political stability. These include a labour nationalization conundrum, an underperforming education sector, the absence of an adequate roadmap for future political reform should circumstances change, an increasing federal wealth gap, and—despite Abu Dhabi coming under an intensifying international spotlight—persistently invasive media censorship and a worrying human rights record.

Little has been written specifically on Abu Dhabi. Most texts have been broader studies on the UAE[8] or have been Dubai-centric,[9] given that emirate's meteoric impact on the world stage. There exist a few Abu Dhabi-related ruler biographies[10] along with state-sanctioned histories,[11] some fascinating memoirs,[12] and other short term, 'snapshot', accounts of the emirate's development.[13] But there has never been a study that has charted Abu Dhabi's dramatic trajectory from its origins as a desert sheikhdom in the eighteenth century to its current pre-eminence. The aim of this book is to provide such a comprehensive overview—in part so that Abu Dhabi's unique circumstances can be situated within their full historical context, and in part so that its many achievements and resounding successes can be appreciated by the wider audience they deserve. Similarly, the emirate's present shortcomings are discussed within a respectful, yet constructively critical, framework. If these weaknesses can be acknowledged, and if future obstacles are identified and discussed, then Abu Dhabi's potential is perhaps limitless.

3

1

THE EMERGENCE OF ABU DHABI

The early history of Abu Dhabi is a tale of two great patriarchs. The first confirmed his family's position at the head of a large tribal federation by the beginning of the nineteenth century, while the second—blessed with a long and uninterrupted reign—consolidated further the sheikhdom's influence over great tracts of territory including strategic hinterland oases, an island capital, and rich pearling grounds. These achievements took place against a perilous backdrop of domestic and regional threats, many of which could have eroded Abu Dhabi's power and irrecoverably curtailed the family's ambitions. Undoubtedly, there were enormous internal challenges, with consecutive rulers having to contend with repeated—and at times successful—breakaway attempts by secessionist tribes, several coups and counter-coups from close relatives, and frequent economic downswings. Even more pressingly, they had to navigate a careful path between the objectives of two hostile powers on both their eastern and western flanks and the gunboat-backed demands of the newly arrived British Empire. Nevertheless, with a mixture of military might, artful diplomacy, and good fortune, the sheikhdom's leadership repeatedly transformed danger into opportunity and prospered from the decline of their neighbours. This allowed Abu Dhabi to emerge as the pre-eminent regional power by the dawn of the twentieth century.

The forging of a dynasty

First referred to in early seventeenth-century Omani chronicles for their heroic role in assisting the Sultan of Muscat's operations against

Portuguese forts,[1] the tribesmen of the Bani Yas played an increasingly pivotal role in the centuries-old struggle for mastery of the lower Arabian Gulf. Of uncertain origin, with some attesting to an early migration from the Najd,[2] while others claim lineage from Oman's Yas bin Sasa,[3] it is most likely that the Bani Yas were not the descendants of any one ancestor but rather an ancient grouping of smaller tribes bonded together by common causes and shared circumstances. Certainly, with nearly thirty sub-sections today, some of which still consider themselves to be independent tribes in their own right,[4] it seems that the Bani Yas were never much more than a loose tribal federation. Nevertheless, by the early eighteenth century they were a sufficiently cohesive military and political force, united under the rule of Falah—a well respected elder, and in control of dozens of fertile oases at Liwa in the Dhafrah region. Sometime in the mid-eighteenth century, Falah was succeeded by his eldest son, Nahyan bin Falah. Named after the *wadi Nahyan* or Nahyan valley in the Yemen,[5] he became the first of the Al-Bu Falah sheikhs of the Bani Yas.

Having fortified their capital at the Liwa village of Al-Mariyah, Nahyan's sons and grandsons—notably Isa bin Nahyan and Diab bin Isa—saw the dynasty safely through several turbulent decades. For the most part they were assisted by other Bani Yas sections in addition to two friendly neighbouring tribes: the semi-nomadic Manasir (Al-Mansuri), who co-habited the Liwa with the Bani Yas; and the Dhawahir (Al-Dhaheri), who populated another grouping of oases at Buraimi,[6] to their east. Both of these tribes backed Diab when he was openly threatened by the descendants of one of Nahyan's younger brothers, led by Zayed bin Muhammad.[7] Diab was able to assassinate the usurpers and expel Zayed's only son—Hazza bin Zayed—to distant Bahrain.[8] In 1793 Hazza managed to return to Liwa and avenge his father's death by killing Diab. Once more, the Bani Yas and their tribal allies intervened, ensuring that Diab's only son, Shakhbut bin Diab, was able to force Hazza into a final exile and put his remaining opponents to the sword.[9] Thus, under Shakhbut, the progeny of Nahyan were repositioned as the *tama'im*, or supreme sheikhs, of the Dhafrah. And with few exceptions his Al-Nahyan descendants have held a firm grip on power ever since.

The founding of a sheikhdom

In about 1761, soon after the beginning of Diab bin Isa's reign, fresh water was discovered on a large island close to the shore and less than a week's camel journey away from Liwa. One version of events is that a Bani Yas hunting party had following the trail of a group of *dhabi*, or brown gazelles onto the island. After they set up camp one of their party discovered freshwater.[10] Another version has it that a fisherman wandered onto the island, dug a pit and found it full of drinkable water.[11] Indeed, even today, if one managed to find any open space on the island and excavated a hole a few metres deep this might still yield some brackish drinking water. Originally referred to as Mleih (perhaps because of the saltiness of the water),[12] or in some chronicles as Buzubbeh,[13] the island soon became known as the *abu*, or father, of the dhabi that had unwittingly slaked the hunters' thirst.

The strategic significance of Abu Dhabi soon became apparent to the Al-Nahyan, not only because of its water supply, but also because it commanded unbroken views of the coastline in both directions and was easy to defend from mainland attacks, courtesy of coral reefs around its perimeter.[14] As such Diab constructed a mud tower to protect the watering holes and encouraged the settlement of over twenty families, most of whom built *barasti*,[15] or palm frond houses. By the early 1790s, towards the close of Diab's reign, he had expanded his fortifications, laying the foundations for a large fort with a circular watch tower.[16] By this stage there were over 400 such houses on the island,[17] with many of Liwa's Bani Yas residents having decamped in favour of Abu Dhabi, where they were less likely to suffer from sporadic desert raiding parties.[18]

Thus, by the time of his son's succession, Abu Dhabi was already the sheikhdom's second largest town. Soon after, when Shakhbut bin Diab made further improvements to the fort between 1795 and 1798 and then built a watchtower at Maqta[19]—overlooking the channel between the island and the mainland—the island city had effectively become the Al-Nahyan's new capital.[20] Fresh waves of tribesmen arrived to populate the area, with many beginning to colonise other nearby islands, especially Dalma,[21] in an effort to break away from their former subsistence lifestyle to pursue a more versatile mode of production[22] where part of the year could be spent fishing, while other, cooler seasons could be spent husbanding animals or attending to long-established date farms in their original Liwa settlements.[23]

With this shift of the Bani Yas' centre of gravity from the hinterland to the coast, the Al-Nahyan and their subjects became considerably enriched, not only because of the newfound versatility and the obvious benefits of early economic diversification, but also because this was a time when international demand for pearls had begun to affect the shores of the Gulf. The waters of Dalma and many of Abu Dhabi's other islands were proving to be lucrative pearling beds, given their abundance of oysters.[24] Foreign merchants appeared in large numbers from as far afield as Bombay to buy up all of the best specimens for export to their affluent European clients.[25] As ruler, and the man responsible for the protection of all Abu Dhabi residents, Shakhbut could levy taxes on this new activity: the pearling crews had to pay collectively a *naub* tax on their boats in addition to royalties on any pearls valued at more than 1000 rupees;[26] while a *taraz* tax was taken from each of the two-men *qalta* pearling teams[27] to pay for guards to protect the town during the height of the pearling season[28] when many of the men were out at sea, or to watch over their boats which were left unattended along the coasts during the off-season.[29] As the economy grew, other lucrative forms of dues were introduced, including fishing rights,[30] the *nisab* date production fees,[31] and charges for the usage of the subterranean *aflaaj* water irrigation channels[32] near to the Liwa oases.[33] A salaried *amir* was appointed to collect the ruler's taxes from Dalma,[34] while a *wali*, or governor, was appointed to collect taxes from Liwa and other hinterland areas. In some cases Abu Dhabi families were paying between 5 and 10 percent of their incomes to Shakhbut's representatives, although in many cases they could make payments in kind in order to feed and clothe the increasing number of retainers, guards, and other officials employed by the ruler.[35]

External threats: Wahhabism, the Qawasim, and the British peace

By 1815, with over 2,000 residents in Abu Dhabi and over 3,000 in Liwa and the surrounding Dhafrah,[36] the sheikhdom was becoming a powerful entity and its patriarch—by this stage referred to as Sheikh

Shakhbut bin Diab Al-Nahyan—was one of the most dominant personalities of the region. In 1816 there was a brief period of instability following Shakhbut's deposition by his capricious eldest son, Sheikh Muhammad bin Shakhbut Al-Nahyan. However, with the help of his old tribal allies, Shakhbut kept his nerve and retreated to the Dhawahir's stronghold in Buraimi and built a new fort.[37] Two years later, with the added weight of Omani support, his coalition was strong enough to exile the renegade Muhammad to Qatar and place his popular second eldest son, Sheikh Tahnun bin Shakhbut Al-Nahyan, in the Abu Dhabi fort.[38] Assuming the role of chief advisor to Tahnun,[39] Shakhbut regained most of his former authority, and was frequently referred to as 'the sheikh of Abu Dhabi' for many more years.[40]

After quashing this filial coup, the remainder of Shakhbut's reign, or rather his proxy reign, was marked more by external interferences. Two powerful regional forces sharing religious and military ties had entered into a *de facto* alliance, seeking either the subjection of Abu Dhabi to tributary status, or if possible the complete dismantling of Shakhbut's expanding sheikhdom. For many years there had been waves of attacks on Bani Yas and Manasir settlements at Liwa, and on Dhawahir settlements at Buraimi. While some of these were perpetrated by disorganized desert raiders, most were part of a long-term campaign by the Wahhabis of the Arabian interior to reduce Al-Nahyan dominance in the Dhafrah and install a tax-collecting governor of their own. Moreover, as followers of Muhammad bin Abdul Al-Wahhab—who since the eighteenth century had preached a purified brand of Islam and a need to return to the golden era of the Prophet—the Wahhabis sought to convert all who lay before them to their austere religious tenets,[41] including the Bani Yas and their allies.

Backed by the military might of the Al-Saud family—whose sheikhs had been serving as Wahhabi rulers after Muhammad bin Abdul's death[42] and whose children had married into the Al-Wahhab family—Abu Dhabi's territory was repeatedly invaded. Refusing to acquiesce or convert,[43] Shakhbut was required to raise large, expensive armies and counter-attack on a number of occasions. By the 1820s the Wahhabis were in retreat, with Shakhbut having asserted greater authority over Buraimi—temporarily at least—by building a fort at Qattara village and forging an even closer relationship with the Dhawahir.[44] To achieve this victory, Shakhbut also had to negotiate a hazardous alliance with the Al-Bu Said rulers of Oman, with even his son Tahnun beginning to accept Omani subsidies in return for Abu Dhabi's military support.[45] This altering of the status quo exposed the Al-Nahyan to the wrath of Oman's traditional enemies, the Qawasim (Al-Qasimi) tribal federation of the northern coastline, especially after Tahnun twice assisted Omani forces in attacking the Qawasim capital of Ra's al-Khaimah.[46]

In many ways, conflict with the Qawasim was inevitable. With possessions as far west as the port of Sharjah, as far east as the Indian Ocean coastline, and as far north as the Musandam peninsula, the Ra's al-Khaimah sheikhs commanded the allegiance of several powerful tribes in close proximity to Abu Dhabi's settlements. Moreover, with Qawasim sheikhs also controlling the Persian coastline ports of Lingah and Al-Muhammarah,[47] Ra's al-Khaimah was greatly prospering from extensive maritime trade networks and undoubtedly held naval superiority in the lower Gulf. Thus, any further expansion for Shakhbut's sheikhdom, whether inland or seaborne would have had to come at the expense of the Qawasim.

Exacerbating the situation further, the Qawasim were also longstanding opponents from an earlier eighteenth-century civil war. Whereas the Bani Yas and their Manasir, Dhawahir, and Al-Bu Said allies were all members of the Hinawi tribal faction, the Qawasim were of the rival Ghafiri faction, having supported Muhammad bin Nasser Al-Ghafiri in the historic, but never forgotten conflict.[48] Worse still, those tribes aligned to the Ghafiri faction were for the most part adherents to the stricter Hanbali school of Sunni Islam,[49] while the Hinawi faction were usually followers of the more moderate Maliki school.[50] These significant differences may explain why the Qawasim, so unlike the Al-Nahyan, reached an understanding with the Wahhabis, eventually adopting some of their religious views.

In 1824 the ruler of Ra's al-Khaimah, Sheikh Sultan bin Saqr Al-Qasimi, made the first move. Supporting the exiled former ruler of Abu Dhabi, Sultan helped Muhammad bin Shakhbut to gather a smaller force to march on the capital. After plundering the town,

Muhammad sought to oust his father and younger brother, but failed after Tahnun launched a spirited counter-attack. Tellingly Muhammad fled to the nearest Qawasim stronghold, in Sharjah.[51] Only a year later the Al-Nahyan and Sultan were again at war through their proxies, with Shakhbut and Tahnun having supported the chief of the Suwdan section of the Bani Yas, Salim bin Nasser Al-Suwaidi,[52] in an attempt to take over a fort in Deira, on the border with Sharjah. For some years the small town of Dubai[53] had served as the unofficial border between Abu Dhabi and the Qawasim. Straddling a large creek, the western half of the town—Bur Dubai—had been nominally controlled by the Al-Nahyan, while Deira was under the protection of Sultan. When Shakhbut learned that Sultan had married the sister of his Dubai governor and duplicitous relative—Sheikh Muhammad bin Hazza Al-Nahyan—he feared a complete Qawasim takeover of Dubai.[54] When the Suwdan force arrived, fighting duly broke out, with neither side able to gain the upper hand. Only when the Deira fort was destroyed in 1827 as part of an Omani-brokered settlement, was peace restored. But Shakhbut kept supplying the Suwdan with weapons in an effort to re-assert his control over the area,[55] while Sultan refused to back down over his claims to Dubai. A cold war ensued, with Shakhbut fearful of a full scale Qawasim invasion, especially from the sea.

The attack never came, as simultaneous developments resulting from the arrival of the first major European power in the Gulf since the Portuguese in the early seventeenth century had effectively tipped the Qawasim into decline, and thus spared Abu Dhabi from any permanent defeat. Since the 1750s the British East India Company had established a monopoly over all overseas trade routes to the subcontinent, including the highly profitable sea lanes between Bombay and Basra.[56] By the 1760s they began to face a direct challenge from the Qawasim, who had set up an autonomous trading post at Basidu on the island of Qishm, close to the entrance of the Gulf. Despite the proximity of Qishm to the Persian mainland, the Afsharid and Zand rulers of Tehran were unable to intervene on behalf of their valued British commercial partners due to problems on their northern borders,[57] and the Qawasim soon ate into the Company's profits.[58] Determined to crush the Ra's al-Khaimah-based maritime trade network, the Company's directors built up a considerable, albeit contentious, body of evidence in an effort to demonstrate that the Qawasim were little more than common pirates. They then used this to convince London of the need to dispatch a Royal Navy task force to the region.[59]

Two ineffective coastal bombardments of Qawasim positions took place in 1809 and 1816,[60] but in 1820 the Royal Navy launched a major amphibious assault on Ra's al-Khaimah. A hail of shells broke down the walls of Sultan's forts and a force of over 7,000 Omani soldiers and British officers was landed on the beaches.[61] Outnumbered and ill-equipped, the Qawasim finally surrendered after several hours of close quarter combat. Subsequent attacks were then made on other suspect pirate bases in Qawasim dependencies, including Sharjah and the smaller towns of Ajman and Umm al-Qawain;[62] but fortuitously for Abu Dhabi the task force limited itself to its primary objectives and the British reprisals went no further down the coast.[63]

Without doubt the Al-Nahyan were the greatest beneficiaries of the conflict. As rulers of a sheikhdom with no real history of any maritime activity other than local pearl diving they were of no threat to the Company. Furthermore, given that Britain had no interest in interfering in hinterland disputes in a region it had no desire to colonise,[64] Abu Dhabi's terrestrial powers remained untouched. In contrast, the Qawasim's historic advantage of having a larger fleet and greater naval experience was effectively negated as Britain sought to impose and police a maritime truce on the sheikhs of the lower Gulf in an effort to prevent any further 'piratical depredations.'[65] Thus, fighting could still take place on land, but not by sea. Unsurprisingly, Shakhbut was at the forefront of brokering the post-war treaty with Britain on behalf of Tahnun,[66] who was immediately described as being a 'chief of superior talent'[67] by Britain's senior representative in the Gulf—the Political Resident.[68] The British negotiators also made clear that Abu Dhabi's involvement in these 'trucial agreements' was to be friendly and principally for its benefit and protection, rather than as the punitive measure that it was for Ra's al-Khaimah.[69] Reports were even filed stressing the usefulness to Britain of having Abu Dhabi develop into a 'powerful counterpoise to the restless habits of the Qawasim.'[70]

The struggle for supremacy

Despite the indubitably positive outcome of Britain's intervention, the Al-Nahyan found themselves unable to capitalize fully on the Qawasim's misfortunes and spent most of the 1830s mired in internecine squabbles and the unpleasant subjugation of attempted secessions. With Sheikh Shakhbut bin Diab Al-Nahyan entering old age, Sheikh Tahnun bin Shakhbut Al-Nahyan was unable to benefit from the same level of reflected authority from his father as he had done earlier in his reign, and in 1833 he fell victim to two of his younger brothers, Sheikhs Khalifa and Sultan bin Shakhbut Al-Nahyan. Tahnun had long distrusted his siblings and had always prevented them from entering his capital, however in a rare error of judgment Shakhbut persuaded Tahnun to relent in the interests of family unity. Khalifa and Sultan were thus allowed to return to Abu Dhabi:[71] the former duly shot Tahnun while the latter stabbed him to death.[72]

With little legitimacy given the fratricidal nature of their joint succession, Khalifa and Sultan were immediately vulnerable. Unable to rely on the Al-Nahyan's traditional tribal allies they controversially sought protection from the Wahhabis.[73] Although never converting, they nonetheless collected some 800 talas[74] and presented it as a tribute to the nearest Wahhabi representative,[75] thus enraging most of the Bani Yas, Manasir, and Dhawahir tribesmen who had fought alongside their father and elder brother against earlier Wahhabi incursions. As the first Al-Nahyan rulers to have voluntarily submitted to an external power,[76] Khalifa and Sultan's popularity declined even further and within months they were facing counter-coup attempts. The most serious of these was led by their still living eldest brother, the former ruler Sheikh Muhammad bin Shakhbut Al-Nahyan, who had made a pact with another of their brothers, Sheikh Hilal bin Shakhbut Al-Nahyan, in an effort to win Omani support for an attack on Abu Dhabi.[77] Crucially, and in what was probably one of his final acts, the elderly Shakhbut chose to openly support Khalifa and Sultan, presumably having chosen between the lesser of two evils.[78] Shakhbut travelled to Muscat and defused the situation, thus removing Muhammad's expected support.[79]

With his father's backing Khalifa soon assumed sole rulership, relegating Sultan to an advisory role, but his authority remained in question.[80] Another coup was attempted—this time led by a large group of cousins and other Bani Yas men.[81] Although Khalifa suppressed the rebellion, his revenge was so extensive that many of the perpetrators and their families had no option but to leave Abu Dhabi. Led by Maktum bin Buti Al-Falasi[82] and his uncle Ubaid bin Said Al-Falasi of the Al-Bu Falasah section of the Bani Yas,[83] they were joined by members of the Rumaithat (Al-Rumaithi) section and many others who remained disgusted by the dubious circumstances of Khalifa's succession. Marching up the coast and eventually settling in Dubai in the summer of 1833, they effectively reduced Abu Dhabi's population by over 20 percent—some 3,600 residents.[84] Moreover, given their strength in numbers, they immediately became the dominant power in the Al-Nahyan's distant outpost, and promptly claimed independence from Abu Dhabi under their new 'Maktum' sheikh.

With Khalifa severely weakened, the Qawasim seized the opportunity to support the Dubai rebels and launch a joint attack on Abu Dhabi. But with the British truces still in effect, Sheikh Sultan bin Saqr Al-Qasimi's fleet was unable to carry out a direct maritime assault and could do little more than maintain a naval blockade on Abu Dhabi island.[85] Khalifa gathered a force of over 3,000 Manasir and loyal Bani Yas tribesmen[86] and moved into the interior, cutting off Dubai's supply route from Buraimi.[87] Nonetheless, fighting raged on until the mid-1830s, with damaging consequences for Abu Dhabi's pearling industry, and only came to a stop when the Wahhabis—concerned over the economic decline of their tributaries—called for a ceasefire.[88] In return for the Qawasim lifting their blockade, Khalifa had little option but to acknowledge publicly the permanent loss of Dubai and the sovereignty of the Al-Maktum.[89] Described as a 'bitter concession for Khalifa to have had to make,'[90] in many ways most of the damage had already been done, as in 1835—in the midst of the conflict—Britain had gathered signatures for a fresh set of peace treaties. Little was different from the original 1820 trucial agreements, excepting an additional clause that strengthened the British prohibition on any form of maritime aggression.[91] But the new documents were also offered to Dubai, thus formalizing the new sheikhdom's separation from Abu Dhabi in the eyes of the Political Resident.[92]

As a further blow, at about this time Khalifa was unable to prevent Bani Yas boats—perhaps driven to desperation following the Qawasim blockade—from attacking British East India Company shipping.[93] A British warship[94] duly arrived off the coast of Abu Dhabi, and several of the Bani Yas' best boats were destroyed.[95] Fines were imposed on Abu Dhabi's wealthier residents—including a staggering 10,000 tala fine for Khalifa himself.[96] Many refused to pay, placing Khalifa in an impossible position with his British overlords, while some chose to replicate the Al-Bu Falasah's Dubai secession. Led by Khadim bin Nahman Al-Qubaisi[97] of the Qubaisat section of the Bani Yas—which had been heavily involved in the pearl trade and therefore particularly disadvantaged by the conflict and the fines—the absconders moved west and then north, before building a base at Khor al-Udaid, an uninhabited old camel station close to the Qatari peninsula.[98]

Diplomatic successes

With Khor al-Udaid's soon acquiring an infamous reputation as a pirate base[99] and with Abu Dhabi's population continuing to decline, Sheikh Khalifa bin Shakhbut Al-Nahyan sought to press home the advantages of the British treaties that had been so well understood by his father. Able to gain permission from the Political Resident for a strike on the Qubaisat in the interests of suppressing maritime depredations,[100] Khalifa attacked Khor al-Udaid in 1837.[101] As expected, he destroyed the settlement and the rudimentary port facilities, but then he proceeded to massacre the Qubaisat's men folk, allowing only their women and children to return to Abu Dhabi.[102] Outrage ensued, aggravated further by an ill-considered attempt by Khalifa to re-take Dubai in 1838. Notwithstanding the 1835 agreements and the almost certain British condemnation that would follow, Khalifa was convinced that some of the Qubaisat survivors had fled to Dubai, thus giving him the right to enter the town.[103] Although able to capture the fort in Bur Dubai from the Al-Maktum, he was soon ousted by the Qawasim, led by the governor of Sharjah, Sheikh Saqr bin Sultan Al-Qasimi.[104] In 1841 he tried once more, but was again thwarted, managing only to destroy some of Dubai's date gardens.[105]

14

By 1843 Khalifa had accepted the limits of Abu Dhabi's military capabilities and was beginning to make a determined effort to use diplomacy rather than force. Reminiscent of Sheikh Shakhbut bin Diab Al-Nahyan's manoeuvrings earlier in the century, Khalifa arranged to hold peace talks with the Al-Maktum in Buraimi. Having invited representatives from most major tribes, but excluding the Qawasim,[106] he effectively repaired the split within the Bani Yas and gathered support to evict Ghafiri tribes—including the Qawasim's close allies: the Bani Qitab (Al-Qitbi) and the Naim (Al-Nuami)—from areas they co-habited with Hinawi tribes allied to the Bani Yas. Most notably, Khalifa's younger brother and former co-conspirator, Sheikh Sultan bin Shakhbut Al-Nahyan, took a contingent of these new allies to Buraimi and expelled the Naim from some of the villages.[107] These actions were so greatly welcomed by the Buraimi-dwelling Dhawahir that Khalifa was in a position to buy large tracts of land in Buraimi and declare that the oases' date gardens were subsequently to be held jointly between the Al-Nahyan and the Dhawahir.[108]

With this stronger control over the strategic Buraimi region, his more cordial relationship with Dubai, and the allegiance of the majority of the lower Gulf's tribes,[109] by the mid-1840s Khalifa had affirmed Abu Dhabi's supremacy over the Qawasim. Quickly recovering from the double secessions, the capital's population grew to over 12,000 residents,[110] and with the British peace more closely adhered to and less fear of Qawasim attacks, the once lucrative pearl trade regained some of its lost momentum. Abu Dhabi soon boasted over 300 boats and over 2500 pearl diving crew.[111] Moreover, with Khalifa's earlier transgressions consigned to History, the Political Resident had warmed considerably to the Al-Nahyan. British reports described the 'population, trade, and resources of Abu Dhabi as having increased in a much greater ration than those of the Qawasim,'[112] and praised Khalifa for effectively policing the lower Gulf on Britain's behalf.[113] His family was referred to by residency staff as being 'delightful people and by far the most pleasant of any they had to deal with.'[114] And Khalifa was singled out for his 'gallantry, firmness and prudence, that had raised Abu Dhabi to be one of the most powerful of the communities of the Gulf,'[115] and his 'great attachment to the English both from inclination and interest.'[116] Perhaps most indicative of Abu

Dhabi's newfound status was that all visiting British warships had begun to fire a full five gun salute in Khalifa's honor, upgrading him from just three.[117] Previously, the only 'trucial sheikh' to receive this tribute had been the great Sheikh Sultan bin Saqr Al-Qasimi.[118]

Provocation and the renewed Wahhabi threat

As had so often happened before in Abu Dhabi's brief history, the relative tranquility that Sheikh Khalifa bin Shakhbut Al-Nahyan had eventually made possible was abruptly shattered by an internal power struggle. This time, unlike all previous and indeed all subsequent coup attempts, the opposition came from outside the Al-Nahyan family. In 1845 Khalifa and his brother, Sheikh Sultan bin Shakhbut Al-Nahyan, were unexpectedly attacked and murdered after a large feast. The killer—Isa bin Khalid Al-Falahi—although technically a relative of Khalifa was not a descendant of the eighteenth century ruler Nahyan bin Falah but rather the great-grandson of Khalid bin Falah, the youngest brother of Nahyan.[119] A number of tribal chiefs,[120] keen to restore the Al-Nahyan bloodline and maintain Abu Dhabi's stability and prosperity, soon managed to kill Isa and all of his sons.[121] Their real problem though was to whom they should hand over control of the ruler's fort.[122] Khalifa's eldest son, Sheikh Zayed bin Khalifa Al-Nahyan, was popular but deemed too young to succeed, so they looked to the sons of the former ruler, Sheikh Tahnun bin Shakhbut Al-Nahyan. Tahnun's second eldest son, Sheikh Said bin Tahnun Al-Nahyan, was well liked and duly installed, thus switching the ruling line back to the original 'legitimate' Al-Nahyan line as originally supported by Sheikh Shakhbut bin Diab Al-Nahyan in 1818.[123]

At first it seemed that the elders had chosen well. Said had the right lineage behind him and the British were happy to see the Al-Nahyan family reinstated.[124] A warship was even sailed close to the coast of Abu Dhabi to signal support for the new ruler.[125] But unfortunately for the sheikhdom, it quickly became apparent that Said possessed neither the military nor political acumen of his father, grandfather, or even uncle. Swayed by the prospect of glory he briefly—and naively—allied with his family's longstanding enemies, the Qawasim, to partition Dubai. As by this stage both Abu Dhabi and

Ra's al-Khaimah were increasingly frustrated by the Al-Maktum's 'often unscrupulous balancing act in the middle.'[126] But this was a mistake, as Khalifa had worked hard to find peace with Dubai and, ironically, Sheikh Maktum bin Buti had publicly condemned Isa and supported Said's succession.[127] Predictably the fragile pact collapsed and in 1847 Dubai brokered a new agreement with the Qawasim at Abu Dhabi's expense,[128] thus undoing his Khalifa's 1843 Buraimi accords.

Lacking in legitimacy and still hungry for a victory of some sort, in 1848 Said took the potentially fatal decision to 'liberate' one of the few Buraimi villages that was still under nominal Wahhabi protection. With the rare support of the Naim—who on this occasion stood to gain from the situation—Said easily overran the village's weak defences and then broke sieges in two forts before blocking off Wahhabi reinforcement routes from the interior.[129] But although there were short term gains for Abu Dhabi from these actions, this unprovoked action re-ignited all of the old Bani Yas-Wahhabi tensions that had lain dormant since Khalifa's accession.[130] Within a year the Wahhabis returned to Buraimi with a much larger force comprising both Qawasim and Dubai fighters.[131] Overwhelmed, Said had little choice but to retreat,[132] thus leaving the entire region open to Wahhabi invasion. Humiliatingly he also had to agree to collect tributary payments from his Manasir and Dhawahir allies on behalf of the Wahhabis, thus reducing his standing as ruler of Abu Dhabi even further.[133]

As Abu Dhabi teetered on the brink of decline once more, Said found himself facing the exact same problems—poor relations with Dubai, piracy, and secession—that his uncle had had to contend with early in his reign. In 1852, after repeated efforts to bring Dubai closer, Said supported Maktum's youngest brother, Sheikh Said bin Buti Al-Maktum, in a takeover bid. Unfortunately for Said bin Tahnun this was a premature manoeuvre as Said bin Buti failed in his attempt and fled to the Qawasim, who then took the lead role in supporting his succession when Maktum died later that year of natural causes.[134] In 1853, despite having just signed a new and 'perpetual' treaty with Britain that made permanent the 1835 maritime agreements and approved of Britain 'watching over [the trucial sheikhdoms] for ever more,'[135] Said suddenly found himself unable to prevent an outbreak

17

of piracy. Bani Yas boats had apparently attacked Qawasim vessels, prompting two British warships to sail into Abu Dhabi's makeshift harbour.[136] Said bin Tahnun was reportedly so terrified at seeing the ships' guns at such close range that he immediately apologized and complied.[137]

Against this troubled backdrop the reinvigorated Wahhabis encouraged the Qubaisat to attempt a second breakaway from Abu Dhabi, having helped them to rebuild their town at Khor al-Udaid.[138] Being as heavy-handed as Khalifa, Said bin Tahnun dealt with the renegade Bani Yas section by arresting all of the Qubaisat who remained in Abu Dhabi town and holding them hostage. He offered the Khor al-Udaid emigrants a safe passage home and guaranteed the release of their kinsmen. But this was a trick: when they returned they were heavily fined—including a penalty of 2000 talas for the Qubaisat chief[139]—and all of their boats were disabled until their debts could be paid. Denied access to their usual pearling activities, the Qubaisat had little option but to sell off their property, thus increasing tension within the community even further.[140]

Sheikh Zayed the First and the great consolidation

Although still suffering from the aftershocks of Sheikh Said bin Tahnun Al-Nahyan's misadventures, Abu Dhabi in the mid-1850s remained one of the great powers of the lower Gulf. Over 5,000 tribesmen could be called to arms, compared to about 3,000 men in Sheikh Sultan bin Saqr Al-Qasimi's territories and only about 1,000 in Dubai.[141] Moreover, with the 1853 treaties gradually serving to restore maritime peace, the sheikhdom's economy had resumed its growth. It was reported that dozens of shops had opened up in Abu Dhabi where there had previously only been two or three. And hundreds of traders, some of whom came from India and Bahrain, had established themselves in two different souqs—one for the South Asians and one for the Arabs.[142] The Al-Nahyan family just needed to find the right leadership qualities so that Abu Dhabi could withstand Wahhabi penetration, definitively eclipse the Qawasim, and recommence the expansionism first undertaken by Sheikh Shakhbut bin Diab Al-Nahyan and his sons.

In 1855 an opportunity suddenly arose when Said was ousted over a tribal matter. A Bani Yas man had been killed by his brother,[143] a tribal elder. But the executioner had not sought permission from the ruler, as was the custom, thus prompting Said to demand the death of the elder. The family in question refused to hand over the fugitive, indicating that they believed the original killing to have been justified. Said relented and promised to spare the life of the elder, but when he summoned him he stabbed him to death.[144] Revolt spread through the Bani Yas, and the deceitful Said fled to the Persian island of Qais,[145] leaving his younger brother Sheikh Saqr bin Tahnun Al-Nahyan to take control of the fort.[146]

Unable to claim any authority given his close association with Said, Saqr was soon expelled, thus presenting the Bani Yas with a second succession dilemma in the space of a decade. Fortunately Said had no sons, thereby allowing the mantle of rulership to pass smoothly back to the Khalifa line in the form of Sheikh Khalifa bin Shakhbut Al-Nahyan's son, Sheikh Zayed bin Khalifa Al-Nahyan,[147] who as described, could have succeeded in 1845 if it were not for his young age. Zayed, who had been sheltering in Dubai under the protection of Sheikh Said bin Buti Al-Maktum,[148] was promptly brought to Abu Dhabi, where he was widely fêted by the Bani Yas and their allies. Indeed, he was regarded as the perfect new ruler for the sheik-dom: he was in his early twenties, he was charismatic and astute, and his mother was from the Suwdan section, thus strengthening the bond between the Al-Nahyan and one of the most powerful Bani Yas clans.[149]

Zayed's teenage connection to Said bin Buti was to prove crucial the following year when Dubai joined forces with the Manasir[150] to head off a counter-coup by the exiled Said bin Tahnun.[151] In his absence from Abu Dhabi the latter had been brought back to the mainland by the Qawasim, who had given him land in Mamzar, on the fringes of Sharjah's territory.[152] The Qawasim then provided Said with the support he needed to remove Zayed. It would seem that Said also had British approval, at least in the first instance, as the Political Resident mistakenly believed Said's version of events that he was ousted because of his attempts to suppress piracy.[153] The attack was stealthy, before Said's army seized and looted one of the souqs while a smaller force led by his loyal elder brother, Sheikh Hamdan bin Tahnun Al-Nahyan, plundered the other souq. Said then laid siege to the fort and took the strategic Maqta watchtower first built by his grandfather. Fortunately, Zayed had been in Liwa at this time, avoiding capture and giving him the opportunity to bring together his many allies and then march on Abu Dhabi, eventually killing both Said and Hamdan in the reprisals.[154]

In late 1856, with his opponents in disarray, Zayed began the process of consolidation. With a keen appreciation of tribal politics, he sought to appease Said's surviving younger brother, Saqr, by marrying one of Said's daughters.[155] Mindful of the Al-Nahyan's fratricidal history he then installed his only brother, Sheikh Diab bin Khalifa Al-Nahyan, as his deputy ruler[156] and, as a further consolation, exempted him from all pearling taxes, thereby allowing Diab to become the wealthiest man in Abu Dhabi.[157] Zayed also married two of his daughters to two of Diab's sons—Sheikhs Muhammad and Shakhbut bin Diab Al-Nahyan—and refused to marry off any of his other daughters, thereby signifying the closeness of Diab's family to his own.[158] By 1870 Zayed had also reinforced his friendship with the Al-Maktum and Said bin Buti's successor, Sheikh Hasher bin Maktum Al-Maktum—by marrying a woman from Dubai.[159]

Zayed did make some miscalculations, including assisting Bahrain in an attack on their Qatari enemies in 1867. This was a gross violation of the maritime peace and prompted British warships to sail to Abu Dhabi and demand reparations.[160] It also destabilized the sheikhdom's northwestern borders, as Zayed had to fend off sporadic incursions from the Qatari ruler's son, Sheikh Jasim bin Muhammad Al-Thani.[161] Equally misjudged were Zayed's efforts in the 1890s to reprise his uncle Sheikh Tahnun bin Shakhbut Al-Nahyan's ambition of installing the Suwdan section in a position of power further up the coastline, beyond Dubai. As mentioned, Zayed's mother was an Al-Suwaidi, and he himself had taken a Suwdan wife—a daughter of the still living Suwdan chief, Sultan bin Nasser Al-Suwaidi.[162] These family connections may have clouded Zayed's sense of reason as he encouraged Sultan to build a fort at Zura—a sandbank close to the town of Ajman and therefore deep into Qawasim territory.[163] Unsurprisingly the settlement was soon terminated[164] following a successful Qawasim appeal to the British on the grounds that the close proximity of such a powerful Bani Yas section was likely to enrage all nearby Ghafiri tribes[165] and would soon plunge the region into conflict.

Overall, Zayed's reign was marked by several major diplomatic and military victories. The first of these great triumphs was the careful appeasement and permanent reintegration of the Qubaisat section. In 1869 the Qubaisat had seceded once again, and for the third time had tried to build up a settlement at Khor al-Udaid. Led by Buti bin Khadim Al-Qubaisi—the son of the former Qubaisat chief[166]—they were strengthened by the appearance of Ottoman agents in Doha in 1871 and duly claimed both Qatari and Ottoman protection.[167] Declaring Khor al-Udaid to be a sheikhdom independent of Al-Nahyan control,[168] the Qubaisat also claimed sovereignty over the lucrative pearling island of Dalma.[169] With great self-control, Zayed refrained from violence against a fellow Bani Yas section. Cancelling plans for a seaborne invasion, he began to negotiate with the British, arguing that the Qubaisat were undermining his ability to uphold Abu Dhabi's commitment to the maritime treaties. Although British assistance was not immediately forthcoming, Zayed's patience eventually bore fruit, when in 1879 a lawless Bedouin tribe of the interior—the Murrah (Al-Murri)[170]—appeared to be using Khor al-Udaid as a base from which to attack British shipping.[171] Keen to place Khor al-Udaid under Zayed's authority,[172] Britain sent a warship[173] to the area in advance of a small party from Abu Dhabi. Upon the ship's arrival the Qubaisat had already dismantled their houses[174] and had fled to Qatar where they were welcomed by Jasim. Crucially, Zayed then sent his cherished eldest son—Sheikh Khalifa bin Zayed Al-Nahyan—on a mission to Doha to persuade the exiles to return to Abu Dhabi.[175] Khalifa carried Zayed's personal guarantee that they would face no reprisals and would not suffer discrimination as they had done during his father's reign. Impressed by Khalifa's presence, most of the Qubaisat trusted Zayed's intentions and returned to Abu Dhabi where they were reportedly 'welcomed and well treated by their chief.'[176] Their leader was given pearling tax exemptions,[177] thus placing him on a par with Zayed's brother, and the pacified Qubaisat soon began to prosper. Khor al-Udaid, although remaining derelict, again came under Abu Dhabi's control, as evidenced by the building of a small outpost there later in the century.[178] Much to the Political Resident's satisfaction it ceased to serve as a pirate redoubt.

Another key accomplishment was Zayed's increased control of Buraimi and his strong stance against Wahhabi incursions which finally put an end to any tributary payments. Encouraged by the death of the Wahhabi ruler—Faisal bin Turki Al-Saud—in 1865 and the distant civil war being fought between Faisal's two sons,[179] in 1869 Zayed helped Omani forces to expel Wahhabi remnants from Buraimi.[180] With the path cleared he then resumed his father's efforts to reduce the influence of the Buraimi-dwelling Ghafiri tribes—the Bani Qitab and the Naim. With little prospect of Wahhabi or Qawasim assistance these tribes were easily restrained by Zayed's Manasir allies,[181] and all encroachments they had made during the reign of Said bin Tahnun were reversed. Once in control Zayed then skillfully defused any remaining tension by employing his usual marriage strategy to appease the defeated Ghafiri leaders. He took a daughter of the Al-Bu Khuraiban chief (Al-Kharabani)—the most powerful of the Naim sections—as a wife,[182] and then provided the Al-Bu Khuraiban with the same level of *shafiyah* or loyalty subsidies that they had been accustomed to under Wahhabi and Omani occupation.[183] By the late 1890s Zayed had also married off his second eldest son—Sheikh Tahnun bin Zayed Al-Nahyan—to the granddaughter of Ahmad bin Muhammad Al-Dhaheri, the chief of the Dhawahir.[184] In a further act of appeasement, Ahmad was then chosen to be the Al-Nahyan's first wali of Buraimi.[185] Although the Dhawahir had historically been in de facto alliance with the Al-Nahyan, Zayed was nevertheless keen to take these measures so as to repair a relationship that had stumbled under Said's collection of Wahhabi tributes; had again briefly broken down between 1887 and 1891[186] when the Dhawahir were concerned over the founding of a new village—Masudi—by Zayed's eldest son;[187] and had been strained by the Al-Nahyan's purchasing of land in several other Buraimi villages, including Qattara, Jimi, Hili, and Ayn al-Dhawahir[188]—the latter of which became the site for one of Zayed's new forts[189] and was even renamed 'Al-Ayn.'

Abu Dhabi as a regional power

In time these achievements earned Sheikh Zayed bin Khalifa Al-Nahyan the title of 'the great,' consolidated Abu Dhabi's status as the major regional power alongside Oman, and allowed the Al-Nahyan to fill even more of the void created by the rapidly declining fortunes of the Qawasim. In 1866 Sheikh Sultan bin Saqr Al-Qasimi died and Ra's al-Khaimah lost its great patriarch. Just three years later the Qawasim's territory was permanently partitioned, following an untimely warrior's death for Sultan's son, Sheikh Khalid bin Sultan Al-Qasimi.[190] And following the inability of Khalid's successor and younger brother, Sheikh Salim bin Sultan Al-Qasimi, to prevent a renegade cousin from establishing himself as an independent ruler in Ra's al-Khaimah, Sharjah and Ra's al-Khaimah were cleaved into two separate sheikhdoms.[191] Furthermore, with the chiefs of Ajman and Umm al-Qawain having long since signed independent peace treaties with Britain,[192] and with the Qawasim's principle Indian Ocean coastline dependency of Fujairah having also effectively broken away,[193] Salim was of little further consequence to Abu Dhabi's ambitions. By the close of the century there was no other sheikh in the region able to oppose Zayed, and he effectively represented all of the 'Trucial States' in discussions with Britain. Tellingly, in 1905 he presided over a meeting in Dubai to discuss tribal and border disputes[194]—an early glimmer of hope for future Trucial-wide cooperation. Zayed's performance and mastery over his neighbours prompted the Political Resident to report that 'Sheikh Zayed's influence now appears much stronger than even that of the Sultan of Muscat.'[195]

Since 1856 Zayed had also succeeded in preventing any internal rulership dispute, and for the remainder of his distinguished fifty-four year reign, especially during his latter years, he effectively provided Abu Dhabi with the stability it had long needed for its economy truly to flourish. Remarkably, he managed to maintain this prosperity despite the imposition of a second layer of British treaties in the early 1890s that enabled the Political Resident to control directly all aspects of the trucial sheikhs' foreign affairs—including their ability to contact and receive any foreign merchants from outside of the British-Indian network. Sparked by the Ottoman interference in the Khor al-Udaid affair and exacerbated by the interception of a letter written to Zayed in 1873 from an Ottoman officer offering political and commercial cooperation,[196] Britain was concerned that their low cost, essentially self-enforcing system of informal empire in the lower Gulf was under threat. The situation became even more urgent after 1888, when a Persian agent had visited Abu Dhabi, bearing gifts of Persian flags and a sword of honor for Zayed bearing the Shah's royal seal, and had read out a commendatory Persian epistle in front of an assembly of Al-Nahyan sheikhs and their allies.[197]

Britain's solution was to add three rather repressive clauses to the new treaties in 1892. These included the forbidding of all rulers from entering into agreements with non-British parties, the forbidding of all non-British parties from being allowed to visit their towns, and the forbidding of selling or mortgaging any part of their territory,[198] unless it was done via the Sharjah-based British agent.[199] Further restrictions were added later, including a prohibition on the importation of new pearling technologies, many of which could have led to even greater growth in the industry, but which would have risked the arrival of foreign entrepreneurs in the region.[200] Fortunately for Zayed and Abu Dhabi, pearling at this stage was still so lucrative that the enforced economic isolation was a manageable hindrance. By the time of Zayed's death in 1909, Abu Dhabi had by far the largest pearling fleet in the region—over 400 boats—and Dalma island was undoubtedly the pearling capital of the lower Gulf.[201] The price of pearls had quadrupled during his reign[202] and in the early twentieth century pearling was a multi-million pound sterling industry,[203] providing the ruler with over £60,000 per annum in pearling taxes alone.[204] In addition, the sheikhdom's agricultural output had increased markedly, courtesy of Zayed's commitment to renovating all of the aflaaj irrigation channels in Liwa and Buraimi,[205] and a host of newer and much sturdier dwellings were under construction across the sheikhdom. When British reports estimated the population of Abu Dhabi town to have risen to over 15,000 residents, including several dozen immigrant merchant families,[206] Zayed's capital had become one of the largest settlements in the Arabian Gulf.

2

SHEIKH SHAKHBUT AND THE
GREAT DECLINE

Inheriting a powerful and prosperous sheikhdom, hegemony over their neighbours, and a strong relationship with their British protectors, the children and grandchildren of Sheikh Zayed bin Khalifa Al-Nahyan nonetheless dragged Abu Dhabi into a mire of internal discord, poverty, and isolation. Their capital, which began the twentieth century as the most populous settlement in the lower Gulf, soon descended into obscurity and what had once been a thriving economy became an increasingly marginalized backwater. Decades of successful expansionism were coming undone as the ruling family's authority shrank so much that it commanded little authority beyond the most historic of its ancestral homes. By the mid-1960s, long after their more progressive and commercially-minded Bani Yas relatives in Dubai and the Qawasim of Sharjah had assumed leading roles in regional affairs, residents of Abu Dhabi found themselves on the sidelines of both important Gulf-wide political developments and a massive economic boom prompted by the discovery and exploitation of some of the world's largest oil reserves. In some ways, the sheikhdom's economic downswing was inevitable given the precariousness of its pearling industry and the impact of international recession. But even with the arrival of oil wealth little improved, as the Al-Nahyan still lacked a forward-thinking leader capable of harnessing the new economic opportunities and overcoming the factionalism that threatened to tear the monarchy apart.

25

The early successions

The many wives of Sheikh Zayed bin Khalifa Al-Nahyan—most of whom hailed from different Bani Yas sections or different tribes—underpinned the strength of his rule and the stability of Abu Dhabi during the nineteenth century. These marriage alliances served to appease previously hostile powers, often allowing the Al-Nahyan to wrest tribal loyalties away from other powers. They also provided Zayed with many sons: he had more than even the legendary Sheikh Shakhbut bin Diab Al-Nahyan.[1] Upon reaching maturity, these sons served as trusted lieutenants, often being deputized by Zayed and travelling on his behalf, thus extending his authority across scattered territories. After his death in 1909, however, the enormous hidden cost of having had such an extended family became apparent. With so many potential successors—most being only half brothers to each other and having grown up in separate households under different 'maternal blocs' backed by the tribe or family of their mothers' fathers—the sons of Zayed were faced with dynastic crisis.

The obvious candidate to take control was Zayed's eldest son, Sheikh Khalifa bin Zayed Al-Nahyan. With his mother[2]—who was probably Zayed's original wife[3]—being the daughter of the Manasir chief and considered to be Zayed's 'first lady,'[4] and with he himself having taken a Manasir wife,[5] Khalifa undoubtedly enjoyed strong maternal backing and a strong tribal pedigree with links to the Al-Nahyan's longest serving allies. Moreover, his aforementioned role in returning the Qubaisat to Abu Dhabi and his help with founding new settlements at Buraimi added further legitimacy to his claim, as did earlier visits to Bahrain and Muscat in place of his father.[6] He was duly encouraged by the Bani Yas elders to occupy the ruler's fort, but unexpectedly—and tragically for the sheikhdom's stability—he refused to succeed, perhaps having been discouraged by his mother and wife on the grounds of personal safety. After all, with the exception of his father, every ruler of Abu Dhabi since Isa bin Nahyan in the eighteenth century had either been killed in office or forcibly ousted.

The mantle of rulership was therefore passed down to Zayed's second eldest son, Sheikh Tahnun bin Zayed Al-Nahyan. With a pure blooded Al-Nahyan mother[7]—the daughter of Zayed's predecessor,

Sheikh Said bin Tahnun Al-Nahyan—and with a Dhawahir wife, Tahnun enjoyed some legitimacy amongst his father's allies, but was soon considered a weak and ineffectual leader. Probably suffering from polio, he failed to sire any sons and died of ill health in 1912.[8] The elders were again faced with a dilemma[9] and approached Khalifa for a second time. With Khalifa resolute,[10] Zayed's third and fourth sons were considered—Sheikhs Said and Hamdan bin Zayed Al-Nahyan. Both were the offspring of an Al-Bu Falah wife, the daughter of one of Zayed's most trusted advisors.[11] Hamdan, the younger of the two full brothers was deemed more popular and was duly installed.

Although without valuable Manasir connections, Hamdan could nevertheless still call upon powerful Bani Yas relatives, as he had married the daughters of a leading member of the Suwdan section[12] and of a wealthy Dubai-based member of the Al-Bu Falasah section.[13] Immediately after his succession he had also married Tahnun's widow, thereby bringing his line closer to the Dhawahir.[14] In some ways Hamdan's rule was successful, as he managed to solve a number of territorial disputes including a conflict between a number of small Hinawi tribes[15] and the Al-Bu Shamis (Al-Shamsi) section of the Ghafiri Naim tribe. He also forged a useful alliance with the Al-Mualla rulers of Umm al-Qawain, but wisely refrained from joining them in an attack on Sharjah that would have incurred the wrath of Britain and likely drawn Abu Dhabi into a prolonged tribal war.[16] By the early 1920s however, he was struggling. Having supported and harboured two exiled, conspiratorial cousins of the increasingly power Wahhabi ruler, Abdul-Aziz bin Saud Al-Saud,[17] he had increased the threat of renewed Wahhabi invasion and had broken the 1892 agreements that had guaranteed Britain exclusive control over all foreign affairs. Although a crisis was averted, following the arrival of a British warship that pressured Hamdan into expelling the fugitives,[18] he had by this stage also begun to face strong domestic opposition to his economic policies. Heavily criticized by his younger brothers for not paying out sufficient subsidies to either themselves or the Al-Nahyan's key allies,[19] and resented by Abu Dhabi-based merchants for having raised taxes, Hamdan was backed into a corner. Many of his subjects left the sheikhdom, and although he visited them in person and persuaded them to return, they remained disgruntled.[20] With the pearling industry having been in steady decline ever since the First World War and with the subsequent fall in international demand, there was little else Hamdan could do to ameliorate the situation.

The fratricides

In 1922 three of Sheikh Hamdan bin Zayed Al-Nahyan's younger brothers—including two full brothers, Sheikhs Hazza and Sultan bin Zayed Al-Nahyan, and a half brother, Sheikh Saqr bin Zayed Al-Nahyan—conspired to overthrow him. Sultan, who had emerged as the most powerful of the three, murdered Hamdan with the direct assistance of Saqr, and seized control of the ruler's fort.[21] Perhaps encouraged by materialistic wives,[22] the two usurpers raided the treasury only to be disappointed to find Hamdan's coffers almost empty.[23] Despite the atrocity, Sultan was able to garner some support.[24] Hamdan's family posed no further threat, having already fled to Dubai to join their maternal Al-Bu Falasah relatives.[25] Moreover, Abu Dhabi residents were keen for a change in leadership given their economic circumstances, and Sultan had gained reluctant approval for his succession from Khalifa—his non-ruling eldest brother.[26] Many also had respect for Sultan's earlier marriage to a daughter of the Qubaisat: this was thought to symbolize the full re-integration of the previously secessionist section into Abu Dhabi politics. Indeed, Sultan's wife—Sheikha Salama bint Buti Al-Qubaisi—soon became regarded as an astute *eminence grise*.[27]

Within a year, Sultan was already in difficulty. The region-wide pearling recession was deepening and he had no way of raising the additional revenues needed to restore former subsidies. Opposition within the family increased,[28] and in 1926 his earlier co-conspirator, Saqr, seized an opportunity to shoot both Sultan and one of his sons—Sheikh Khalid bin Sultan Al-Nahyan—after a large family dinner. Khalid was wounded and managed to escape to his Qubaisat relatives, but Sultan—who had been hit in the back—died.[29] Having killed two of his siblings, Saqr was disreputable, and many considered him to be something of an outsider given that his mother was from the Al-Bu Falasah and the maternal side of his family dwelt in Dubai.[30] To make matters worse, in his state of weakened legitimacy,

he invited foreign interference in Abu Dhabi's affairs by offering tributes to Wahhabi agents in return for support.[31] This was the first time
an Al-Nahyan ruler had paid the Wahhabis since the reign of Sheikh
Said bin Tahnun Al-Nahyan in the 1840s.

Disgusted by his fratricidal younger siblings, this was the point
when Sheikh Khalifa bin Zayed Al-Nahyan decided finally to intervene in politics. Khalifa was pressed into action sooner than expected:
in 1927 he uncovered a Saqr-engineered plot to have both himself,
his only son—Sheikh Muhammad bin Khalifa Al-Nahyan,[32] and Sultan's second eldest son—Sheikh Hazza bin Sultan Al-Nahyan,[33] assassinated. He quickly formed a secret pact against Saqr that included
members of the Al-Bu Shaar (Al-Shaari) section of the Manasir[34] and
even Saqr's disillusioned youngest son, Sheikh Muhammad bin Saqr
Al-Nahyan. Employing a Baluchi-origin servant from Sultan's
remaining household staff, the group ordered Saqr's assassination to
take place on New Year's Day, 1928.[35] Although this attempt was
unsuccessful, with Saqr managing to escape, the Al-Bu Shaar later
caught up with him and executed him.[36]

Khalifa accepted full responsibility for the latest killing[37] and banished Saqr's children from Abu Dhabi.[38] With Khalifa's wife reluctant
to have their son appointed ruler for the same reasons that she had
discouraged her husband from succeeding in 1909, Khalifa nevertheless installed Muhammad bin Khalifa as a temporary caretaker in the
ruler's fort and backed him with a powerful contingent of Manasir.
Deciding to restore Sultan's bloodline, of which Muhammad had
promptly married into by taking Sultan's daughter as a wife,[39] Khalifa
proceeded to contact the exiled sons of Sultan. The third of these,
Khalid, had sought sanctuary immediately after his father's death in
the interior, under the protection of the sheikh of Al-Ihsa.[40] While
the two eldest and the youngest—Sheikhs Shakhbut, Hazza, and
Zayed bin Sultan Al-Nahyan respectively—had fortuitously left Abu
Dhabi ten days before the killing[41] and were being sheltered in
Buraimi by their grandfather's elderly wali: Ahmad bin Muhammad
Al-Dhaheri.[42]

Many of the Bani Yas elders, including those of the influential Suwdan section, pressed Khalifa to appoint Hazza, believing him to be the
most capable candidate.[43] The British appeared to favour the simpler

customs of primogeniture, perhaps in reaction to the bloody episodes of the past six years.[44] Leaning towards this second option, Khalifa's secretary wrote to the older Shakhbut and encouraged him to return to Abu Dhabi and take over from Muhammad.[45] After being installed in the fort, Shakhbut's succession went smoothly and was followed by his three brothers swearing an oath of fidelity to their still influential mother, Salama. They promised to support Shakhbut and never resort to fratricide.[46] Britain then backed this by issuing a public statement that killing one's brother was ungodly and that the Political Resident would gladly assist the trucial rulers in bringing such activities to an end.[47] Much to the population's relief, the length of Shakhbut's ensuing reign was to bring at least some degree of political stability to Abu Dhabi—at least on the surface. However, as opportunities eventually turned to threats he soon began to make enemies.

Sheikh Shakhbut's opportunities

Sheikh Shakhbut bin Sultan Al-Nahyan had inherited all of the economic problems that his father and uncles had tried to grapple with before him. The decline in pearling that had begun during Sheikh Hamdan bin Zayed Al-Nahyan's tenure had continued unabated. And by the mid-1930s, with a full-scale global depression and a looming Second World War likely to involve most of the first world pearl-purchasing economies, the industry had all but closed down. Exacerbating the problem and preventing any future resuscitation of the activity was an increase in international competitors and their implementation of techniques and technologies not available to Abu Dhabi's merchants.[48] Sheikh Zayed bin Khalifa Al-Nahyan may have managed to survive the described economic isolation first imposed on the lower Gulf by the British in the 1890s, but at that time conditions were far more forgiving. Shakhbut's merchants, in contrast, had to contend with Mediterranean pearlers who had access to bleaching and drilling equipment to produce better-looking specimens,[49] and Japanese pearlers who had begun to develop pearl farms in order to harvest large quantities of cultured pearls at a low cost.[50] The situation became so bad that Gulf pearling crews often returned home to find either no merchants waiting for them or to be offered very low prices.[51] Soon, pearling expeditions ceased completely, as most had previously been financed by merchants who took loans from Indian moneylenders—the former of which had fallen into heavy debt by this stage while the latter had mostly left Abu Dhabi or were charging prohibitively high interest rates.[52] By the end of the Second World War the British estimated the trade to be worth less than one tenth of its value before the 1920s.[53]

In parallel to these developments, there was also considerable frustration over Abu Dhabi's failure to negotiate air landing rights with Britain. Unlike the pearling downswing, this was something that Shakhbut could have done something about, and such an income stream would have softened the impact of recession. With longer range aircraft and new air routes between Europe and India,[54] Britain's Imperial Airways sought to add to its existing facilities in Oman,[55] and the towns of the lower Gulf were well positioned to serve as alternative refuelling bases.[56] With the exception of Abu Dhabi's Bani Yas island—which was used by the British only for emergency landings[57] and paid Shakhbut a very small rent[58]—almost all of the region's air landing revenue had been secured by Sharjah and Dubai. Since 1930 the ruler of Sharjah, Sheikh Sultan bin Saqr Al-Qasimi, had been receiving 500 rupees per month and a further five rupees for every aircraft that landed.[59] Likewise, in 1937 Sheikh Said bin Maktum Al-Maktum of Dubai had arranged for Imperial Airways to land flying boats on the Dubai creek[60] in return an annual fee of 5000 rupees.[61]

Similarly, by the late 1930s there had been concern that Shakhbut was not moving quickly enough to secure oil exploration concessions. Although he had no real option other than to sign with Petroleum Concessions Ltd.—a subsidiary of the British-backed Iraqi Petroleum Company (IPC)[62]—given the ongoing British restrictions on foreign relations,[63] other rulers nevertheless wasted no time in extracting substantial rent from the IPC.[64] At least some of this was being channelled into developing their sheikhdoms, often by installing basic infrastructure, while nothing was happening in Abu Dhabi. Notably in 1937 the ruler of Dubai had concluded a twenty-five year deal that gave him 60,000 rupees upon signing followed by an annual income of 30,000 rupees. A massive 200,000 rupees would then be paid upon discovery.[65]

In 1939, the mood in Abu Dhabi changed. Shakhbut finally met with the IPC and agreed to a seventy-five year concession.[66] Given the relatively large size of the sheikhdom, he was given a much greater signing up fee of 300,000 rupees, and then began to receive an annual income of 115,000 rupees. In 1950—with Britain having relaxed some of its exclusivity restrictions[67]—Shakhbut followed this up with a concession with the Superior Oil Company of California that provided him with a signing on fee of 1.5 million rupees and an annual income of one million rupees until oil was discovered.[68] And in 1953 he signed a similarly lucrative deal with the D'Arcy Exploration Company[69] to set up the Abu Dhabi Marine Areas Company (ADMA) to explore for offshore oil.[70] Throughout this period Abu Dhabi's residents were optimistic that this enormous new stream of wealth would soon elevate their sheikhdom from its bankruptcy and poverty. Indeed, there were some glimmers of hope. In 1952 Shakhbut had financed the building of a bridge at Maqta to link Abu Dhabi to the mainland,[71] and by 1962 he had constructed two desalination plants and a power station.[72] As a further improvement to the sheikhdom's water supply he built a pipeline from Buraimi to Abu Dhabi, although in many ways he was fortunate that this was a success, as he had refused to pay for a geological survey.[73] In 1965, much to Britain's delight, he also set up an Abu Dhabi Defence Force. Unlike the British-officered Trucial Oman Scouts that had been established in 1956 to provide protection for the oil companies,[74] this new force would be entirely funded by Shakhbut.[75]

Sheikh Shakhbut's troubles

Despite these massive oil-related revenues and Abu Dhabi's huge potential, it soon became apparent that the early optimism was misplaced. For several reasons Sheikh Shakhbut bin Sultan Al-Nahyan was reluctant to spend. He had lived through the recessions of the 1920s and 1930s and favoured thriftiness on the grounds that he would be more capable of offsetting any future economic decline. Prophetically perhaps, he also feared that any rapid oil-financed development would have far-reaching socio-cultural consequences for Abu Dhabi, predicting that the resulting changes would soon erode the traditional way of life. With this line of thinking he was, however, in the minority. Consequently the final fifteen years of his reign were dominated by a pitched struggle between his own conservatism, the more adventurous members of his family, and what remained of the sheikhdom's business class.

In the early 1950s Shakhbut had banned all new construction, including roads, and he required prospective builders to seek his permission—which was rarely forthcoming.[76] Moreover, reminiscent of his nineteenth-century predecessors—who often prevented their subjects from building stone houses lest they became independent forts[77]—he blocked the importation of construction materials. Although for his personal benefit he spent money on expanding the ruler's fort,[78] and his house was the only residence in Abu Dhabi to benefit from air-conditioning.[79] At about this time he also began to obstruct the entry of foreign merchants. When the Bahraini entrepreneur Muhammad Kanoo visited Shakhbut in 1958, Kanoo was deliberately kept waiting before eventually being pressed for an enormous 20 percent share of all profits.[80] In contrast the rulers of Dubai and Sharjah quickly developed mutually beneficial arrangements with the reputable and experienced Kanoo Group.[81] Shakhbut's protectionism even extended to merchants from other trucial sheikhdoms. At one point, only a couple of Dubai-based businesses were allowed to open branches in Abu Dhabi each year, and even these were charged 'entrance fees.'[82] It would seem that Shakhbut had earlier caught members of his own merchant community in correspondence with their Dubai counterparts, and he feared this would lead to external interference in Abu Dhabi's affairs.[83]

Shakhbut also had a strong distrust of banks and modern accounting. Dubai and Sharjah had been hosting banks since the 1940s,[84] and Britain put pressure on Abu Dhabi to do the same. However, when a Dubai-based team from the British Bank of the Middle East (BBME) was finally granted permission to visit Abu Dhabi in 1958, Shakhbut reportedly refused to sign any of the contracts that had been drawn up and 'exasperated all concerned.'[85] Although—after a year of further negotiations—a branch was finally opened in Abu Dhabi and Shakhbut accepted the services of a personal financial advisor,[86] it soon became clear that the bank's methods were not understood by the ruler. On one occasion he had ordered a large consignment of rifles and an electricity generator, and had taken out a loan to pay for them. But when BBME officials oversaw the delivery they soon realized that Shakhbut had no intention of actually honoring any of the payments. He did not appreciate the concept of a loan and had assumed that the goods were to be a personal gift from Britain. When confronted, Shakhbut accused the officials of trying to steal money from him, and then blamed and fired his financial advisor. Only following the intervention of the British agent was Shakhbut persuaded to at least pay for the generator, if not the rifles. It was felt that unless such a compromise was reached then Shakhbut would have definitely expelled all BBME personnel from Abu Dhabi.[87]

Equally worrying for the sheikhdom's merchants and other residents was Shakhbut's opposition to the establishment of a proper municipality office in Abu Dhabi. Again, such an office for basic record-keeping and town management had existed in Dubai and Sharjah for years. In 1959 a Dubai national employee of the BBME[88] was asked by the British to help Shakhbut's youngest son, Sheikh Sultan bin Shakhbut Al-Nahyan, to set one up. When Shakhbut visited the site of this much-needed development he reportedly became so suspicious of all the written records he saw that he ordered the two men to purchase petrol from the souq and burn the office down, and never to open it again.[89] He also ordered that maps of Abu Dhabi were not to be produced, or if they were, then they were to feature no English. This made it difficult for the standardization of place names and indeed for the safe movement of visitors around the sheikhdom.[90]

Thus, by the mid-1960s, with ever greater numbers of oil company personnel arriving in Abu Dhabi, neither the town nor its merchants were able to capitalize on the situation as they lacked both the basic physical infrastructure and the necessary financial and commercial organization. A second power station project had been initiated due to chronic energy shortages in the sheikhdom, but remained incomplete on account of Shakhbut's reluctance to continue funding it.[91] And although the IPC was permitted to construct another desalination plant, the labour contract had to be awarded to a Dubai-based company, given the lack of basic equipment in Abu Dhabi.[92] Indeed, the oil companies had to purchase the bulk of their supplies in Dubai and then transport them to Abu Dhabi or its outlying islands.[93] British firms alone were thought to be losing 1,000 pounds sterling a month due to Abu Dhabi's inactive economy.[94] As a prominent businessman recalls, this was incredibly frustrating, especially when the exploration companies arriving in Abu Dhabi had to source their goods from elsewhere: '…the people of Abu Dhabi could see them importing cars, trucks, materials, and equipment but since nothing was being bought here, there was no benefit to the local economy. The local merchants could not provide the needed products and services nor could they accommodate the increasing number of oil workers because they lacked capital and were forbidden from building anything.'[95]

Disgracefully, Abu Dhabi was also lagging far behind its neighbours in basic social services. More than a decade after Shakhbut had signed the first concessions there was still no formal education system in the sheikhdom, thus delaying the emergence of a skilled indigenous population that could participate in the new industries. Shakhbut was scathing of the schools that had opened up in the other sheikhdoms, believing them to create unnecessary problems. In the early 1950s, when approached by the new ruler of Sharjah—Sheikh Saqr bin Sultan Al-Qasimi—for advice on how to settle a dispute concerning whether or not the sons of an exiled man should be permitted to remain in a Sharjah school, Shakhbut bragged that such a complication would never arise in Abu Dhabi because there was not even a single school.[96] Although Shakhbut eventually agreed to open a small school in 1958—Al-Falahia School—its administrators immediately encountered another problem: their ruler refused to employ foreign teachers or to accept the same Kuwaiti and other Arab curricula and teaching materials that had been offered to and used by the schools in Dubai and Sharjah.[97] At this stage there were only a handful of Abu Dhabi men who could qualify as teachers and no textbooks were available, so Al-Falahia had to close the following year.[98] Even when it reopened in 1961—along with another school in Al-Bateen— the new teachers were only allowed to teach subjects that related directly to Abu Dhabi, and no international history or geography lessons took place.[99]

Perhaps most tragically, Shakhbut also remained uninterested in introducing any kind of modern healthcare provision for his people. When a team of doctors arrived at Britain's behest from India in 1956, their suggestion of opening a new hospital in Abu Dhabi came to nothing.[100] And incredibly—after Britain had eventually forced the issue and dispatched the necessary construction materials for a new hospital in 1962—the packing cases remained untouched on the beaches for the best part of a year.[101] Incongruously, although probably unbeknownst to most of his subjects at the time, during this period Shakhbut's sons and daughters were paid to travel to India for medical consultations,[102] British doctors were flown in to treat Sheikha Salama bint Buti Al-Qubaisi—his elderly mother,[103] and he himself went to the United States to have treatment for an eye condition.[104] And a little later, while on a visit to Jordan he had donated over £700,000 for various projects, most of them healthcare-related—more than had ever been spent on social services in Abu Dhabi.[105]

In terms of region-wide cooperation, by the early 1960s Shakhbut's miserliness was also impacting on Abu Dhabi's relations with its neighbors. A proposal for Abu Dhabi to join a trucial postal system was immediately vetoed by Shakhbut, despite being favoured by all of the other rulers and seemingly without disadvantages.[106] Most controversially for the merchant community, an offer in 1966 from Dubai and Qatar for Abu Dhabi to join their new joint currency—the riyal—was also rejected, even though it would have undoubtedly facilitated trade between the three sheikhdoms.[107] Instead Shakhbut preferred to replace the rupees and talas that had been circulating in Abu Dhabi with Bahraini dinars, even though Bahrain could offer no meaningful currency cooperation.[108]

This track record of obstinacy greatly harmed Abu Dhabi's standing with Britain, which had understandably begun to channel its resources into those sheikhdoms where they would be most welcomed and most properly harnessed. Since 1952 there had existed a Trucial States Council presided over by the British agent in Sharjah which, among other responsibilities, supervised the aforementioned Trucial Oman Scouts.[109] By the early 1960s, with Britain increasingly keen to foster a greater sense of community amongst the trucial sheikhdoms in the eventuality that the declining British Empire would someday need to withdraw from the Gulf, the chairmanship of the Council was allowed to rotate amongst the rulers and a Trucial States Development Fund was established.[110] Predictably, when the Council's first five year plan for allocating this fund was announced in 1961, very little was earmarked for Abu Dhabi. In contrast Dubai, Sharjah, and Ra's al-Khaimah were assisted in setting up agricultural trials stations, touring doctor services, and scholarship schemes for students to study abroad.[111] Britain tried again and again to bring Abu Dhabi closer to the Council, but often Shakhbut failed to attend its scheduled meetings, or if he did he would remain obstreperous. The British agent even admitted that 'with Shakhbut present in meetings it is impossible to get many progressive ideas debated as he continually says that things are alright as they are now.'[112] Believing that Shakhbut could be made to feel more of a stakeholder if Abu Dhabi were a contributor to the development fund, Britain encouraged him to allocate at least some of his oil concession wealth to the project. But again cooperation was unforthcoming, with Shakhbut only agreeing to supply four percent of the fund's budget.[113] Nevertheless, at least this was something, and British administrators soon realized the irony of the situation: Shakhbut's meager contribution to the fund was still much more than he was spending on his own sheikhdom's development. Therefore the poorer sheikhdoms began to benefit from Abu Dhabi's potential oil wealth much earlier than Abu Dhabi's own population.[114]

Dissatisfaction and emigration

Unsurprisingly, Sheikh Shakhbut bin Sultan Al-Nahyan's reign was increasingly undermined by emigration. Immediately after his succession a number of Bani Yas families—including those from the Suwdan section who had hoped for Sheikh Hazza bin Sultan Al-Nahyan to become ruler—left Abu Dhabi and settled in Qatar.[115] Throughout the 1930s and the Second World War many more families departed, often simply to escape the difficult conditions of the recession.[116] But, unforgivably for Shakhbut, even during the early years of Abu Dhabi's oil boom the sheikhdom's population continued to shrink. As more and more residents realized that their ruler's attitudes were preventing any real prospect of economic recovery, they opted to move to those towns that were already prospering under much more astute leadership. Moreover, it was not only economic concerns that prompted these departures. Many were also appalled by some of the political views being expressed by Shakhbut and his brothers.

Since the early 1950s, and especially following the Suez Canal crisis of 1956, Arab nationalist sentiments had been filtering into the lower Gulf.[117] Spreading most rapidly through the region's schools, most of which were populated by expatriate Arab teachers—many of whom were Egyptian, Iraqi, or Syrian—such views soon began to take hold amongst the indigenous population.[118] If anything, the rulers of Sharjah and Ra's al-Khaimah embraced Arab nationalism: even if it risked their ultimate demise as traditional monarchs, a closer association with the Jamal Abdul Nasser administration and the Arab League was thought to offer an escape route for the Qawasim sheikhdoms from centuries of British control and humiliation. They accepted Arab League seed money, allowed Egyptian agents to enter,[119] and even set up an Egyptian educational office.[120] The reaction in Dubai was more subdued, as the Al-Maktum family unquestionably continued to benefit from Britain's presence—both politically and economically. Nevertheless, since 1953 there had been an active 'National Front' of sympathizers in Dubai,[121] and although they were at times a considerable nuisance to the new ruler[122]—Sheikh Rashid bin Said Al-Maktum—they were tolerated and eventually co-opted.[123] Conversely, in Abu Dhabi Shakhbut's citizens were discouraged from even discussing Arab nationalism. This was a cause for concern for the Political Resident who believed Shakhbut's stance was becoming dangerous: the latter needed to allow his people to at least feel involved in the politics of the wider Arab world. While the Resident had few doubts that the Al-Maktum family also wished for the demise of Nasser's movement,[124] at least they were not quite as brazen as the Al-Nahyan. He reported to London that the 'rulers of Abu Dhabi clearly welcomed Britain's intervention in Suez, and were hoping that Nasser would be taught a lesson and removed completely.' It was also reported that Shakhbut's youngest brother—Sheikh Zayed bin Sultan Al-Nahyan—had remarked to the British agent that 'Britain should do to Cairo what the Russians have done to Budapest.'[125]

These economic and political grievances, which were often combined with a personal quarrel with Shakhbut, cost Abu Dhabi some of its most notable families. In the 1950s a number of the Mazari (Al-Mazrui) Bani Yas section departed for Dubai,[126] while many from the Qubaisat and Rumaithat sections moved to Qatar.[127] In the mid-1960s about one hundred disgruntled Dhawahir opted to live under King Faisal bin Abdul-Aziz Al-Saud.[128] Another great loss to the sheikhdom was the astute Mani bin Otaibah Al-Murur from the Marar section[129]—one of Abu Dhabi's most distinguished figures. The capital's population was thought to have contracted to just 4,000, with only eight small retailers left in the souqs.[130] And the population of the entire sheikhdom was thought to number less than 17,000.[131]

Instability and Saudi-Wahhabi interference

Even in the diaspora communities, many remained committed to returning to Abu Dhabi. For this to happen, Sheikh Shakhbut bin Sultan Al-Nahyan needed to be overthrown, or at least sidelined by a more energetic relative. The first public challenge came in the 1930s—somewhat unexpectedly—from the ostracized sons of the deceased Sheikh Saqr bin Zayed Al-Nahyan. After Sheikh Khalifa bin Zayed Al-Nahyan had expelled them from Abu Dhabi in 1928, Saqr's offspring had moved with their families to Dubai, where they lived in ignominy with their Al-Bu Falasah grandmother.[132] Mindful of the influence that marriages had played during the fratricides, Shakhbut had then ensured that none of Saqr's five sons could marry back into the Al-Nahyan bloodline,[133] and insisted that no Al-Nahyan boys took the name 'Saqr.' He also ordered that any of Saqr's relatives who did visit the capital had to leave before sunset.[134] Nevertheless, in 1938, the eldest and third eldest of Saqr's sons—Sheikhs Diab and Zayed bin Saqr Al-Nahyan—moved to Bahrain, where they established contact with agents of Abu Dhabi's historic Wahhabi rivals in an effort to launch a coup against Shakhbut.[135]

Although the plotters failed to win full support, by the early 1950s they were in a much stronger position, courtesy of a renewed Wahhabi interest in the lower Gulf. By this stage under the overlordship of the Kingdom of Saudi Arabia and backed by the Arabian-American Oil Company (ARAMCO)—the operating company of Saudi's American oil concession holders: Standard Oil of California and the Texas Oil

Company—the Saudi-Wahhabis hoped to end permanently Al-Nahyan sovereignty over the disputed Buraimi settlements and at the same time extend the territory of their concession. Undoubtedly, they were catalyzed by reports that Britain's Iraqi Petroleum Company had begun prospecting close to Buraimi, thus raising expectations that there was a major onshore oilfield in the vicinity. A 'lost' Saudi exploration party on the border with Abu Dhabi was encountered in 1948,[136] and in late 1952, following a failed peace conference in Dammam, the situation deteriorated further. Saudi Arabia's Turki bin Utaishan arrived in Hamasa—one of the Buraimi villages that had remained on the periphery of Sheikh Zayed bin Khalifa Al-Nahyan's increasing influence in the 1890s. Turki brought with him an armed force of forty soldiers in addition to money, food, and presents for the local notables.[137] Proceeding to marry the daughter of the chief of the Al-Bu Shamis section of the Naim,[138] he then proclaimed himself governor of Buraimi.[139] Although Britain's Trucial Oman Levies—the predecessors of the Trucial Oman Scouts—were deployed and the trespassers were expelled, with Turki being shot by a British officer,[140] the situation remained tense.

In 1954, Saudi Arabia altered its strategy and began to pursue legal action, having astutely co-opted the sons of Saqr and other disgruntled families for its purposes. ARAMCO's research department in Dhahran had been compiling a history of tax payments in the lower Gulf, with the intention of proving that for much of the nineteenth century the residents of Buraimi had been in tributary relations with Wahhabi agents.[141] Shakhbut and the British soon realized that Saudi Arabia was also bribing several of the tribes in Buraimi, and had managed to gain an oath of loyalty from twenty-eight tribal leaders.[142] These even included members of two sections of the Al-Nahyan's long-serving Manasir allies—the Al-Bu Mundir[143] and the Al-Bu Rahmah[144] (Al-Mundiri and Al-Rahmi)—who were concerned that Shakhbut had stopped distributing the subsidies and gifts they were accustomed to.[145] Diab and Zayed bin Saqr—both still in Bahrain—were then asked to present evidence in favour of Saudi Arabia to international investigators, and were rewarded with funds to carry out Shakhbut's assassination.[146] Fortunately for Shakhbut the plot failed on both counts. When the tribunal was held in Switzerland later that year,[147] Abu Dhabi found broad support, and although Saudi Arabia was permitted to install a police post in Buraimi, it survived less than a year.[148] Similarly unsuccessful with their attempted coup, Diab and Zayed failed to find sufficient accomplices in Abu Dhabi.[149] Their anticipated Manasir support failed to materialize, with the Al-Bu Mundir chief actually betraying their intentions to Shakhbut.[150] With little choice but to resume their exile, they fled to Saudi Arabia.[151]

Family pressure and dynastic discord

Although surviving these hazardous external challenges to his authority, the latter years of Sheikh Shakhbut bin Sultan Al-Nahyan's reign were if anything even more unstable, with new threats beginning to emerge from within the inner sanctum of his family. By 1960 Shakhbut's extreme parsimoniousness had led him to cut back on the personal allowances given to key Al-Nahyan figures. Foolishly this retrenchment extended to influential relatives of Sheikh Muhammad bin Khalifa Al-Nahyan, who had held the fort for him in 1928, and even to Shakhbut's two surviving brothers, Sheikhs Khalid and Zayed bin Sultan Al-Nahyan (Sheikh Hazza bin Sultan Al-Nahyan having died in 1958).[152] Only following their mother's personal intervention were the allowances restored,[153] but even this was deemed an insufficient gesture as the payments were not enough to keep up with his siblings' legitimate expenses. In particular, Zayed, who had been serving as Shakhbut's wali in Buraimi since taking over the position from Ibrahim bin Uthman in 1946, complained that he was unable to meet his daily costs—including the vital provision of subsidies to local tribal chiefs—and therefore had to rely on gifts from their mother's Qubaisat family.[154]

Conceivably unable to find any alternative solution, and remaining adamant that he did not actively seek to oust Shakhbut, Zayed began a low intensity campaign to undermine privately his brother's credibility in front of the still powerful British agent. While the official and semi-official histories[155] of this episode tend to depict Zayed as merely seeking a way to help Shakhbut, it is also possible to interpret his conversations as being subtle suggestions that he was a capable yet peaceful ruler-in-waiting who was backed by the whole of his family and would be far more compatible with British interests than his predecessor. In 1962 Zayed had candidly discussed his difficulties with the agent, who then reported back to the Political Resident[156] that 'he [Zayed] was consistently bitter about Shakhbut, and openly so… he said that his brother has set his mind absolutely against development plans.'[157] In a separate conversation that same year with an employee of the agent, Zayed had then related an entire argument he had had with Shakhbut during which he had told his brother that 'under your rule there is complete chaos, and as you are unwilling, at any time, to take advice, the only alternative is to leave things in your hands.'[158] Significantly perhaps, Zayed afterwards asked the employee to relate the content of their conversation to the agent.[159]

In yet another of these frank conversations with agency staff, Zayed had shared details of more of the quarrels that had taken place between himself and Shakhbut. Zayed claimed he had told his brother that 'if you are sincere in your desire to work for the people in the state, you should not only seek but also take the advice of the [British] agent,' before Shakhbut then criticized him for spending money on irrigation and agricultural projects in Buraimi. Zayed then recounted the rather troubling statement made by his brother that if he [Shakhbut] were to prepare a budget for development it would mean that 'the people would be aware of the ruler's income, which would be very shameful and could not be countenanced.'[160]

More seriously, during a personal meeting with the British agent in mid-1966 Zayed described an incident in which he—together with Khalid and Muhammad—had collectively pressed Shakhbut once more about setting up a proper budget, but that Shakhbut had then accused them of forming a league against him. This conversation no doubt gave the impression that the whole Al-Nahyan family was united against Shakhbut.[161] In the summer of that year Zayed travelled to London, ostensibly to seek medical treatment for one of his sons. But while he was there he also met with Foreign Office officials. Although a transcript of the contents of this meeting does not exist, it has been reported that Zayed again made it clear that he had the full support of all the Al-Nahyan against Shakhbut. The meeting seemed to have taken place at Zayed's behest and—importantly—the Trucial States agent himself was present, also happening to be visiting

London at that time.[162] It is believed that Zayed then had a follow-up meeting with British agents at a hotel in Kuwait to discuss the same matter.[163] After returning to Abu Dhabi Zayed reported to the agent that he still found Shakhbut uncompromising. Furthermore, he emphasized that a number of tribal leaders in Buraimi were prepared to take matters into their own hands if nothing happened soon.[164] According to the agent, Zayed gave the impression that he was concerned that Shakhbut would be in personal danger from these men if there was no abdication.[165]

3

SHEIKH ZAYED THE SECOND
PROSPERITY AND UNITY

Following the succession of a dynamic new ruler and the careful removal of his predecessor, Abu Dhabi's fortunes in the latter part of the twentieth century improved dramatically. A rudimentary yet capable government was formed, and with access to ever-increasing oil export revenues from the late 1960s it was to oversee frantic socioeconomic development on an unprecedented scale. With generous distributions of the new wealth and the removal of all forms of taxation the Al-Nahyan family went far further than the tribal subsidies of the past and all but eliminated poverty in their sheikhdom. But most successful was the leading role played by Abu Dhabi in the region-wide efforts to finance and build a resilient federation out of the historically antagonistic territories of the lower Gulf. With the British Empire waning, one of its last remaining outposts had to contend with new challenges. With predatory neighbours and an uncertain future, the only solution for the old Trucial States was one of collective security. Although tested to its limits throughout the 1970s and 1980s—and thrice almost breaking apart—the new union of independent 'emirates' nevertheless held together. This was only made possible by the federal vision of the 'father of the nation': Sheikh Zayed bin Sultan Al-Nahyan—the seventeenth and perhaps strongest ruler Abu Dhabi had ever had.

A ruler in waiting

A string of British visitors to Abu Dhabi in the mid-1960s recorded their shock and dismay upon finding the capital in such an undeveloped state. The British agent remarked that 'it could hardly seem stranger that this potentially oil-rich town now consists of just barasti huts, a broken down market… and a few buildings put up by the oil company.'[1] Others reported that Abu Dhabi was a 'complete scandal,'[2] while the Political Resident's wife[3] noted in her diary that 'tarmac roads have been made in odd stretches… the road from the Agency is a sea of mud and the beach is still used as a public lavatory… at the moment everything remains at a standstill; and all those involved in trying to get a move on are being slightly driven around the bend.'[4] Although historically unwilling to embroil itself in domestic disputes and preferring to maintain as small an imperial footprint as possible, Britain was nevertheless pressed into action by Abu Dhabi's deplorable condition. It was simply unacceptable that so much impoverishment and the unravelling of a centuries-old ruling dynasty were the responsibility of just one man. Moreover, as evidenced by the Buraimi disputes of the 1950s, the security of the hinterland was becoming equally as important as the maritime peace in the new age of oil exploration and exportation: it was therefore imperative that Britain could rely on a strong ruler in Abu Dhabi who could command the full loyalty of his subjects. Thus it was decided that Sheikh Shakhbut bin Sultan Al-Nahyan, who had ruled since 1928, had to be replaced.

Fortunately, there was an obvious successor. With the once favoured Sheikh Hazza bin Sultan Al-Nahyan already deceased, and with Sheikh Khalid bin Sultan Al-Nahyan deemed unpopular, Shakhbut's youngest brother was without rivals. Indeed, quite apart from his aforementioned entreaties to the British agent and his visit to London, Sheikh Zayed bin Sultan Al-Nahyan's impressive administrative record over the previous decades was already well known to the British. On this subject British reports had described Zayed as being not only charismatic but also 'the only real man among the four brothers… a fine organizer with a clean liver.'[5] Since 1945, when their king-maker uncle Sheikh Khalifa bin Zayed Al-Nahyan had died, Zayed had effectively become Shakhbut's deputy.[6] And for the next three years, as Shakhbut's envoy, he played a key role in pacifying disputes between Abu Dhabi and Dubai-based tribes that were threatening to spiral out of control.[7] Most significantly, in 1946 he had been appointed wali of Buraimi. By 1966 he had therefore been *de facto* ruler of the sheikhdom's second largest town for nearly twenty years. During the latter half of this tenure he forgave and welcomed back many of the tribes that had earlier defected to the Saudi-Wahhabi cause, much to Britain's delight. He also succeeded in developing his domain beyond all expectations: a remarkable feat given that he had no access to his brother's oil concession revenues and was operating on very limited resources.

In 1950 Zayed had embarked on a decade-long project—'Al-Saruj'—to rebuild with *saruj* or mud plaster the old aflaaj irrigation system in Buraimi. Unable to hire labourers he had to persuade the elders of nearby tribes to provide the necessary manpower.[8] These improvements were so great that the flow of water trebled and agricultural output increased enormously.[9] With the British agent impressed by these results, in the early 1960s it was one of the few initiatives in Abu Dhabi that attracted support from the Trucial States Development Fund.[10] Trade also flourished in Buraimi, or at least as much as could be expected with so little activity taking place in the capital. Zayed had helped with the building of small shops and—perhaps in emulation of the laissez-faire attitudes being adopted by Dubai's pro-business Al-Maktum rulers[11]—he allowed his merchants to trade in the souqs without paying rent.

Zayed's greatest achievements in Buraimi were in the field of social development. In contrast to Shakhbut's distrust of education and foreigners, in 1958 Zayed had built a small school—Muwaiqih—and had happily employed Jordanian teachers to staff it.[12] Thus, Buraimi's children had access to formal education at least three years before their counterparts in Abu Dhabi town. Similarly, when the aforementioned team of Indian doctors arrived in the sheikhdom in 1956 they received a much warmer reception in Buraimi than in the capital,[13] and in 1960 two North American missionary doctors[14] were invited by Zayed to set up a clinic, with an offer even being made to build them a church if they needed one.[15] In 1963 their practice expanded into larger buildings and became Buraimi's Oasis Hospital—a development which again was far in advance of any comparable facilities available in Abu Dhabi at that time.[16] Although the townsfolk could rarely afford the hospital's consultations and medicines, Zayed would issue them with a *burwa* or permission slip that bore the stamp of his signet ring. On production of this they would receive the treatment and then Zayed would eventually try to foot the hospital bill himself.[17] Throughout this period the quarrels with Shakhbut intensified, and Zayed often found himself having to defend his social policies. In 1961 he supported a British initiative to employ Sudanese teachers—believing it to be of benefit to Buraimi's education system, even though it was against Shakhbut's wishes.[18] And in 1962, during one of Shakhbut's visits to Europe, Zayed seized the opportunity to order basic clothing and medicine—the bills for which would most likely not have been paid had the ruler been present.[19]

Installing Sheikh Zayed

The problem for Britain was how to replace Sheikh Shakhbut bin Sultan Al-Nahyan with Sheikh Zayed bin Sultan Al-Nahyan in such a way that it would not be viewed by international observers as the heavy-handed intrusion of an imperial power. This was, after all, a time of increasing intolerance for 'outdated' European colonial systems. In the words of a former Political Resident: 'by proceeding to extremes we certainly run a risk of antagonizing world opinion, which appears to be on the look-out for any stick which is offered for beating the British Empire with.'[20] Equally problematic was Zayed's own standing. He could not be seen by tribal elders and relatives to have relied on the support of an external power, as this would forever taint his legitimacy, both in Abu Dhabi and the entire Arab region. But nor could he oust Shakhbut by himself: on top of the oath he and his brothers had made to their mother, violence was clearly anathema to Zayed's character. Moreover, as a trusted deputy, and the only male relative that Shakhbut ever permitted to sleep in his house, an open coup would have been a personal betrayal.

The deposition had to appear to be a joint enterprise that enjoyed the full backing of the entire Al-Nahyan family and various tribal elders. And it had to take place swiftly and smoothly so that there was no opportunity for discussion and no power vacuum. Unfortunately, as with the motives behind Zayed's earlier conversations with British agents, there is little consistency in the historical records available, given that all of the parties involved either wished to take personal credit for the installment of the new ruler or preferred to distance themselves from the event. One version, which is perhaps the most palatable to Abu Dhabi's residents today, is that Zayed confronted Shakhbut personally in his fort and informed him that Britain would allow him to continue only as a figurehead ruler and that he would have to appoint Zayed as a grand vizier—in control of the sheikhdom's finances and development projects. It was only when Shakhbut rejected this rather generous offer that Zayed informed him that a contingent of the Trucial Oman Scouts was waiting outside to lead him away.[21] An alternative and perhaps equally plausible account is that the acting Political Resident[22] and the commander of the Trucial Oman Scouts[23] met with Shakhbut in the fort and politely but firmly asked him to abdicate in the interests of his people.[24] The bewildered Shakhbut was then given the opportunity to telephone Zayed—who was not present on the scene. Zayed then explained to his brother that it would be best for him to retire peacefully and that as the new ruler he would guarantee him a safe departure from Abu Dhabi with full ceremonial honours. When Shakhbut refused to leave the fort, the British commander's Scouts called upon the ruler's bodyguards manning the ramparts to come out with their hands up. The Scouts then courteously formed a guard of honour for Shakhbut as he was driven in his car to the airstrip and then put aboard an RAF aircraft bound for Bahrain and then Beirut.[25]

Regardless of the actual method, the deed was done, and 1966 came to a close with Zayed as the new Al-Nahyan patriarch, firmly in control of Abu Dhabi and its oil concession wealth. Importantly, he had the blessings of both the British and his subjects. His elder brother Sheikh Khalid bin Sultan Al-Nahyan remained on the sidelines and Zayed even had the support of Shakhbut's youngest son and heir apparent, Sheikh Sultan bin Shakhbut Al-Nahyan.[26] Shakhbut's eldest son, Sheikh Said bin Shakhbut Al-Nahyan, was similarly compliant, having earlier been implicated in family controversy and having then spent time in Europe receiving medical treatment at Zayed's expense.[27] In any case both of Shakhbut's sons were to die in the late 1960s due to their ill health and lifestyle complications,[28] and in 1970 Shakhbut was allowed to return from his travels in Lebanon and

Iran and was accommodated in Buraimi until his death nearly twenty years later.[29]

A new government

Sheikh Zayed bin Sultan Al-Nahyan lost no time in assembling a team of advisers to oversee the creation of a new administration that would supervise the many long overdue development projects in the sheikhdom. Muhammad bin Habrush Al-Suwaidi and Ahmad bin Khalifa Al-Suwaidi of the Suwdan section of the Bani Yas were placed, respectively, in charge of Abu Dhabi's finances and foreign relations. These were joined by another skilled Bani Yas man: Mani bin Otaibah Al-Murur of the Marar section, who Zayed had persuaded to return to Abu Dhabi after his described quarrel with Sheikh Shakhbut bin Sultan Al-Nahyan.[30] And selected to become Zayed's first oil adviser was Mana bin Said Al-Otaibi—a member of a wealthy merchant family that had begun to marry into the Al-Nahyan line.[31]

Zayed then installed his only mature son—the eighteen-year old Sheikh Khalifa bin Zayed Al-Nahyan—as the new wali of Buraimi, which by this stage was being referred to by the name of its largest settlement: Al-Ayn. Three years later, in 1969, he also placed Khalifa in charge of the Abu Dhabi Defence Force (ADDF). Keen to bring on board his most powerful relatives and placate them with major responsibilities and a role in the decision making process, Zayed appointed the only son of Khalid, Sheikh Muhammad bin Khalid Al-Nahyan—as his deputy finance advisor.[32] Most significantly, he sought fully to accommodate the sons of the still living Sheikh Muhammad bin Khalifa Al-Nahyan—who was once again the second most power-ful man in Abu Dhabi. Muhammad bin Khalifa's eldest son—Sheikh Hamdan bin Muhammad Al-Nahyan—was made wali of Das Island and then appointed chairman of the department for public works.[33] Muhammad's second eldest son—Sheikh Mubarak bin Muhammad Al-Nahyan—was made chief of police in 1966, and later in the year his sixth son—Sheikh Surur bin Muhammad Al-Nahyan—was appointed chairman of the new department for justice. When Zayed set up a more formal executive council in early 1971 it comprised his son Khalifa and five of Muhammad's sons.[34]

Planning and prioritizing

The unspent oil exploration rents that had been accumulating under Sheikh Shakhbut bin Sultan Al-Nahyan had been considerable,[35] but by the time Sheikh Zayed bin Sultan Al-Nahyan took office Abu Dhabi's revenues had increased dramatically. In 1958—some nineteen years after the signing of the first Iraqi Petroleum Company concession—oil had been discovered at Umm Shaif, and in 1962 a modest one million tons of offshore oil was exported from Das Island—the new centre for Abu Dhabi's oil industry. A year later onshore production had begun, with exports being shipped from Jebel Dhanna;[36] and in 1965—during Shakhbut's last full year as ruler—over nine million tons were exported, worth about £25 million.[37] In 1967, as Zayed was beginning to set up his government, the sheikhdom was exporting an enormous £63 million worth of oil.[38] Commendably, even during these heady boom times it was recognized that oil was a finite resource and that Abu Dhabi needed to identity its development priorities. To ensure judicious spending, a Council of Planning was set up to manage annual budgets, and in 1968 its first five year development plan was announced. Ardent that the planners would get the best value for money, Zayed made sure they always hired consultants independent of the many foreign companies seeking contracts in Abu Dhabi.[39]

One of the Council's first tasks was to expand the capital's primitive medical facilities, and 3 million Bahraini dinars were allocated initially for this purpose,[40] before soon increasing to an annual expenditure of 6.5 million dinars on healthcare and the building of hospitals. Education was similarly prioritized, with 12.4 million dinars being added to the 0.5 million dinars Zayed had already spent on the building of schools during his first two years as ruler.[41] Abu Dhabi's first secondary schools were built using this allocation, and—at a cost of nearly 3 million dinars—industrial training courses were provided to nationals so that they could find employment in the oil companies. Mindful of the need to keep the economy diverse and not entirely reliant on oil exports, the Council also ensured that the oil revenues were supporting the growth of pre-oil sectors, while also helping to establish a number of new ones.

In an effort to catch up with the agricultural developments that had been taking place in Dubai and Sharjah—both of which, as described, had been benefiting from Trucial States Council funding—13.4 million dinars were allocated to building trials stations in Abu Dhabi, including the Arid and Semi-Arid Lands Research Station on Saadiyat Island. The aim of these was to develop new strains of crops that would be more resistant to the harsh desert climate, and thereby improve the productivity of Abu Dhabi's farmers.[42] To kick-start trading activities in the capital and create a more business-friendly environment for merchants, new shops were constructed in the souqs,[43] and—to save goods from having to be dumped in crates on the beaches—over three million dinars were spent on constructing a new harbour, Mina Zayed.[44] Some basic manufacturing activities were also encouraged by the Council of Planning, especially those that required little expensive equipment or technology to function and could supply materials to the numerous foreign construction companies. The first of these new plants was a cement works,[45] and this was soon followed by factories to manufacture piping, bottles, and other 'import substitution' goods that were relatively easy to make in Abu Dhabi and would be costly and inefficient for contractors to import from elsewhere.[46] Over the course of the first five year plan, all of these activities—both old and new—were supported by a massive public works programme. 200 million dinars were spent on putting in the necessary physical infrastructure for the new economy, including paved roads, bridges, and basic airport facilities;[47] and 4 million dinars were spent on installing water pumps and a sewerage system.[48]

Distributing the wealth

Alongside building up Abu Dhabi's economic base and setting up a basic welfare state, it was vital that Sheikh Zayed bin Sultan Al-Nahyan began to distribute directly at least a portion of the oil revenues to the entire indigenous population. His subjects, many of whom had endured decades of recession and poverty under Sheikh Shakhbut bin Sultan Al-Nahyan, deserved to reap the rewards of the new wealth, and—with personal conviction—Zayed sought to improve drastically their everyday lives. Also, it was important that as the new ruler he needed to distance himself from his brother's thriftiness, and he had to meet the expectations of those tribes who had always supported his family while placating those of historically less consistent loyalty. Furthermore, despite the fast pace of the construction boom and the influx of thousands of foreigners, Zayed was still very much a traditional tribal chief, with his legitimacy—although robust—being derived from little more than his lineage and personality. Thus, if he could oversee the efficient distribution of wealth to families and individuals, and not just spend on large scale development projects, then the sheikhdom's lucrative natural resources could be effectively transmuted into his own personal generosity, thereby rendering the population eternally grateful for his munificence. Indeed, as discussed later in this book, this strategy soon led to the development of a full-blown allocative state that continues to provide important political capital for Zayed's sons today.

With these multiple objectives, as part of the first budget nearly 4 million dinars were spent on a housing project for more than 2000 of the most indigent families.[49] Many of these had been living in insalubrious conditions in settlements close to Liwa that had benefited neither from Zayed's earlier Buraimi-specific burwa system or from the economic upswing of the first oil exports. This project, at the very least, moved them into dwellings with basic amenities. Many of the keys to these new homes were handed out personally by Zayed; and on one occasion in 1968 his eldest son dispensed over 150 keys on his behalf.[50] As an alternative for more affluent Abu Dhabi nationals in Al-Ayn and the capital, some families received at least two plots of land: one to build a house upon and one to build a commercial or residential building that could then be leased out to a foreign company or its employees. For those with agricultural backgrounds, a plot of farmland was allocated and then they were assisted with the purchasing of all the necessary equipment.[51] Monetary values were assigned to each type of animal that was successfully husbanded, and payments were duly made each year.[52]

Underpinning this wealth distribution and considerably boosting the population's prosperity was the removal of all forms of taxation. Up until this point there had been several tax burdens on Abu Dhabi's residents and many of these, such as those imposed on pearling and agricultural activities, had existed for centuries, often being collected by salaried officials. Shakhbut's rule had done little to lessen these, with, by way of example, no fewer than six different forms of dues— some amounting to several hundred rupees a year—still being imposed on the fishing industry as late as the 1960s.[53] Thus, almost overnight, Zayed's oil boom government effectively ended his family's historic tax-raising role and provided fresh opportunities for his people's economic participation and self-enrichment.

Buoyed by these many positive developments, within just a few years of Zayed's succession Abu Dhabi had reversed its reputation for backwardness and—as it had been during his grandfather's reign—the sheikhdom once again became a relatively attractive destination for the more migratory of the lower Gulf's tribes. At a time when hinterland borders were becoming more rigid due to oil explorations and when the various housing projects were encouraging greater settlements and therefore engendering stronger notions of sheikhdom-specific citizenship, Zayed was swift to capitalize on his brief window of opportunity. Keen to boost Abu Dhabi's population and repair more of the damage done by his predecessor, he sent personal invitations to those tribes most likely to accept. In 1967 part of the Khawatir (Al-Khatri) section of the Naim tribe which was living near to Ra's Al-Khaimah accepted Zayed's offer and moved to join the rest of their section, who were living in Hafit, close to Al-Ayn.[54] But following a bitter reaction from the ruler of Ra's al-Khaimah—Sheikh Saqr bin Muhammad Al-Qasimi—they were obliged to return.[55] Nevertheless, the following year Zayed achieved the victory he sought when over half of the Zaab (Al-Zaabi) tribe, most of whom resided on the Jazirah al-Hamra near to Ra's al-Khaimah,[56] decamped en masse and moved to Abu Dhabi island, where Zayed had promised them prime plots of land. Although of the Hanbali religious school, and having historically settled in Qawasim territories, the Zaab were actually of the Hinawi faction—unlike the Ghafiri Qawasim and Khawatir, and therefore thought to be more compatible with the Bani Yas and their allies. This migration alone increased Abu Dhabi's population by nearly 3,000 and did much for the sheikhdom's status at a time when the entire indigenous population of the lower Gulf was still little more than 70,000.[57]

British withdrawal and the need for unity

In parallel to the impressive socio-economic developments taking place in Abu Dhabi, external events in the guise of rapidly changing conditions and attitudes in faraway Britain were soon to have a major impact on the Trucial States, and most especially on Sheikh Zayed bin Sultan Al-Nahyan, who was on the cusp of being transformed from tribal sheikh to international statesman. Although victorious in the Second World War, Britain's economy had been severely weakened, and the international competitiveness of its industries had declined ever since.[58] By the early 1960s, with public demands for a greater commitment to rebuilding the domestic economy and improving the welfare state, British parliamentary politics were understandably dominated by the issue of imperial retrenchment. Its armed forces had already been recalled from all outposts 'east of Aden' and it seemed likely that a retreat from the lower Gulf was imminent, especially given the several hundred million pounds sterling that it was costing London to maintain its remaining bases in the Middle East.[59]

The announcement came much sooner than expected. In late 1967 a Westminster white paper was published that called for a complete British extraction from the region within four years.[60] The time frame alarmed the local rulers and wrong-footed the resident British administrators. Moreover, the many foreign companies—both British and non-British—that had begun to establish themselves in the lower Gulf were deeply concerned. At best, the sheikhdoms had rudimentary governments, and security services were in their infancy. Most worryingly, defensive capabilities were practically non-existent, and a number of threats from larger and militarily superior neighbours persisted. The consensus was that the withdrawal of British protection would immediately expose these former protectorates to intimidation or invasion.

In nearby Oman the Dhofar Liberation Front's leader—Mussalim bin Nafl—had already declared that, should he succeed in deposing the Sultan of Muscat,[61] then his attention would turn to the other Gulf monarchies, including those sheikhdoms that were 'founded on principles that served British interests as well as western oil interests in the region.'[62] Similarly, there was an ongoing threat from Iran, which had long coveted a cluster of strategically situated islands belonging to the Qawasim and the Al-Maktum. Ever since the reign of Mozzafar Al-Din Shah Qajar at the turn of the century, the four islands of Henjam, Abu Musa, Tunb al-Kuhbra and Tunb al-Sughra had been contested.[63] In 1928 Reza Shah Pahlavi's soldiers had occupied Henjam and expelled its Al-Maktum ruler,[64] and in the 1960s Reza's son—Muhammad Reza Shah Pahlavi—renewed Tehran's claims to the remaining islands.[65] Most pertinent to Abu Dhabi, however, there remained considerable tension with Saudi Arabia. No formal peace agreement over the Buraimi territories had been made following the crises of the 1950s, no official border existed, and as Saud and Faisal bin Abdul-Aziz Al-Saud jockeyed for kingship, both continued to dispute Al-Nahyan authority in some of Abu Dhabi's westernmost extremities.[66]

Thus, there was an urgent need for the sheikhdoms of the lower Gulf to be drawn closer together so that they would enjoy at least some level of collective security after Britain's departure. Furthermore, given that their individual populations were still so small and that the opportunities for cooperation on socio-economic development projects were so manifest, the establishment of a federal government and a federal army seemed the most logical solution. Importantly for Britain, which by this stage had been guardian of the region for nearly 150 years and whose companies controlled the majority of the oil concessions, it was important that any such move towards unification would take place on its terms. Indeed, at this time the British agent remarked that it was important for Britain to help Abu Dhabi 'find its proper place... in a wider Arabian group, [this] will be to our political advantage in the long-term, when the time comes for Her Majesty's Government to retire from its special position in the Gulf.'[67] If Britain did not remain in control there was a fear that either the Arab League or even another superpower—most likely the Soviet Union—could become the architect of the proposed federation. Despite humiliation in the 1967 Arab-Israeli conflict, Arab nationalist sentiments remained strong in the Gulf, and as British Foreign Office reports warned '…if the rulers were prepared to admit the League to their territories it would be difficult, if not impossible, for the British to oppose an Arab organization, accepted throughout the world as representing the Arab states collectively, from taking over many of the functions which Britain had reserved for itself.'[68] It was also admitted that 'a failure to keep the Arab League out of the Trucial States would be a turning point in the history of the Gulf and our [the British] position here… leaving a chaotic situation behind.'[69] This threat of external interference was compounded following a 1968 statement by the Kremlin that called for 'regional defence alliances in the Gulf in order to protect its southern boundaries.'[70] As with the Arab League, if Moscow were to gain a foothold in any newly independent Gulf state, then western oil concessions and remaining British interests would be jeopardized.[71]

Fortunately, given the trucial-wide institutions that had been set up in the 1950s and early 1960s—including the Trucial States Council, the Trucial States Development Fund, and the Trucial Oman Scouts—Britain had already been allowing the local rulers to assume some of the functions of modern heads of state and had provided them with a forum for formal cooperation. Thus, it was decided to build upon these existing institutions, but in such a way that the long-standing historical differences between the sheikhdoms were respected and that the old balances of power remained in place.[72] In 1967 Britain had tried to establish a federation among the various sheikhdoms and sultanates of south-western Arabia—the Federation of Yemeni Emirates of the Arab South—but after British withdrawal this had soon unravelled due to the heavy centralization of power in Aden and swiftly re-emerging parochial interests.[73] It was imperative that any federal state in the lower Gulf would not repeat these mistakes, and that it would remain flexible enough to accommodate old, sheikhdom-level powers alongside any new central government.

From sheikh to president

For such a federation—or rather loose confederation—to succeed, Britain needed to appoint a strong leader who commanded respect far beyond his own sheikhdom and who had the necessary vision and energy to continue building up the new state long after independence. The first, and most obvious choice for this undertaking was Sheikh Rashid bin Said Al-Maktum. As ruler of Dubai—by that time the largest and most developed town in the lower Gulf—and having effectively been the leading voice in the Trucial States Council since its inception, he had already been approached by Britain to draw up a federal strategy. Although preferring to be supplied with a British crafted plan,[74] he nevertheless accepted the role and the first tentative federal discussions were held in his palace.[75] In February 1968 he invited Sheikh Zayed bin Sultan Al-Nahyan to meet with him at a campsite in Sih Al-Sumayh, close to Ghantoot, and the two rulers agreed to an initial two member union between Abu Dhabi and Dubai. Though little more than a symbolic accord, with most of the discussion dwelling on a joint teacher training programme and unresolved border disputes,[76] the transcript of the 'Dubai agreement'[77] was nonetheless regarded by Britain as being an important first step, not least because it mentioned the need for future common defence and foreign polices.[78]

Within months, Rashid had raised concerns about his suitability to lead such a union. In his earlier meetings with the British he had already admitted that Dubai would only be able to serve as a temporary capital given Abu Dhabi's much greater oil wealth and its superior potential to finance a federal state.[79] Indeed, with its boom in exports, Abu Dhabi was by this stage able to increase considerably its contributions to the Trucial States Development Fund, and by mid-1960 it was providing over 80 percent of the total budget.[80] Agreeing with Rashid, Britain was quick to acknowledge this shift, with their special envoy concurring that Dubai did not have sufficient revenues to support a new federal state and that in any case, the centre of the lower Gulf's economy would soon gravitate to Abu Dhabi.[81]

The presidency of the future union was therefore handed to Zayed, who—as with Rashid—met with British approval given his widespread influence and strong standing throughout the region. Moreover, his impressive state-building in Abu Dhabi had not gone unnoticed and, unlike his elder brother, it was known that he had always demonstrated a commitment to the Trucial States Council.

Even though not a ruler in the 1950s and early 1960s, he had nevertheless still attended most of the Council's meetings in his capacity as wali of Buraimi,[82] and was believed by the British to have been responsible for encouraging Sheikh Shakhbut bin Sultan Al-Nahyan to make greater contributions to the Fund.[83] Also—on those occasions when his brother had been absent—he had strongly supported initiatives such as a joint passport system and Trucial-wide traffic control.[84] Tellingly, following one of these meetings Rashid had confided to the British agent that in the future he would much prefer to do work alongside Zayed than Shakhbut.[85]

Fighting for federation

With Sheikh Zayed bin Sultan Al-Nahyan at the helm, the next round of meetings aimed to broaden the February 1968 union to include the other Trucial States. Given that the original Abu Dhabi-Dubai agreement was little more than an alliance of Bani Yas ruling sections that governed predominantly Hinawi faction tribes, it was a challenge for him to then incorporate Ghafiri sheikhdoms into the federation, most notably the Qawasim-ruled Sharjah and Ra's al-Khaimah. Furthermore, Britain was keen that its other Gulf protectorates—Qatar and Bahrain—were also brought into the union, despite their much larger populations and more mature economies. Zayed's proposed solution to these historical divides and obvious imbalances was to create a mini-union—the United Arab Coastal Emirates. This was to consist of the five poorest prospective members: the two Qawasim sheikhdoms and three of their former dependencies—Ajman, Umm al-Qawain, and Fujairah. The latter of which had only been upgraded to sheikhdom status in 1952.[86] This grouping would have allowed these territories—none of which were receiving oil revenues—to have a combined voice alongside the much wealthier Abu Dhabi, Dubai, Qatar, and Bahrain.[87] Unsurprisingly, given the Qawasim's proud history and erstwhile supremacy in the lower Gulf, Sharjah and Ra's al-Khaimah rejected the plan, and by the spring of 1968 the federation had moved no further forward.

Nevertheless, by the end of the summer relations had improved and representatives from the nine sheikhdoms met together in Qatar to hold the first session of the new federal 'Supreme Council of Rulers.'[88] A Kuwaiti-drafted and British-approved constitution was tabled, and the new Council began to discuss the creation of a federal consultative chamber and the setting up of various commissions to consider specific federal issues. Given Qatar's relatively more advanced government institutions it was to host three of these commissions—responsible for labour, real estate, and health care; while the commission for foreign policy was to be based in Bahrain, given its historic hosting of Britain's Political Resident. The two other commissions—for communications and commerce—were to be based in Abu Dhabi and Dubai respectively.[89]

But again, the federation failed to advance. Within a few months of these negotiations significant complications had arisen, and the future involvement of Qatar and Bahrain came into question. Bahrain claimed that the proposed commissions gave too much power to Qatar,[90] while Qatar was concerned that the planned consultative chamber would give Bahrain—with an indigenous population of over 200,000—too much influence, especially if it were based on proportional representation.[91] Although Zayed convened a further conference of the nine members in late 1969—which led to his appointment as president, Sheikh Rashid's appointment as vice-president, and the selection of Abu Dhabi as the federation's temporary capital[92]—the Qatar-Bahrain issue resurfaced, and the meetings began to unravel. Despite the personal intervention of the Political Resident—who warned of Britain's disappointment if differences were not overcome—the nine member union collapsed.[93] In any case, it was perhaps inevitable by this stage that the federation would be reduced to seven members, as in addition to their original misgivings Qatar and Bahrain were worried that a closer association with the lower Gulf sheikhdoms would become a security liability. Both were keen to build good relations with their larger and more immediate neighbour—Saudi Arabia; and Abu Dhabi's outstanding disputes with Riyadh were thought to be an obstacle to this. Similarly, both were anxious to cooperate with Tehran, especially Bahrain—which the Shah had persistently claimed was one of Iran's historic provinces.[94] With Tehran's concurrent claim to the aforementioned Qawasim-controlled islands, a union with Sharjah and Ra's al-Khaimah was therefore deemed hazardous. Indeed, while these federal meetings were taking place the Iranian foreign minister had even issued a warning to Bahrain not to join the British-engineered union.[95] The impetus for a union was gone and for the next two years Zayed was a president without a state. Qatar and Bahrain had declared themselves independent in the summer of 1971, after signing unilateral peace treaties with Saudi Arabia and Iran.[96] The seven remaining members were thus left with only a few months before Britain's scheduled withdrawal in December. Incredibly, during the final few meetings of the Trucial States Council the issue of federation was no longer even on the agenda,[97] and both Zayed and Rashid had privately admitted to the Political Resident that any form of union was unlikely.[98] They even offered to pay for the upkeep of a permanent British military presence, with a British report claiming that Zayed 'would be happy to contribute the funds himself from his oil revenues to secure the continuance of the benefits he and his fellow rulers derived from the British presence in the Gulf.'[99] Nonetheless, perhaps spurred on by pressure from the new British foreign secretary[100]—who had earlier cautioned Zayed that any future British 'friendship treaty' would only be offered to a federal state[101]—a makeshift union was established, and on 2 December 1971 a British-drafted provisional constitution was signed.[102]

Declaring itself the 'United Arab Emirates' (UAE), Zayed's federation was born and Britain completed its elegiac retreat. Immediately, there were serious problems to contend with. Only hours before, Iran had invaded the three disputed islands and Ra's al-Khaimah had refused to join the union. Even so, Iran was soon appeased and—as will discussed below—although the occupied islands have remained a bone of contention, further encroachment into UAE territory was avoided. Failing to gain sufficient foreign backing to establish itself as an independent emirate,[103] Ra's al-Khaimah agreed to join the union in early 1972—after the promise of generous Abu Dhabi aid and an equal standing in the federation with Sharjah.[104] The UAE was soon recognized by the United Nations, the Arab League, France, Germany, and—after all remaining British personnel were removed from the Sharjah airbase—even the Soviet Union.[105] Command of the Trucial Oman Scouts was handed over to Zayed and the force was renamed the Union Defence Force (UDF). The Trucial States Council was renamed the Supreme Council of Rulers, a 12 member federal Council of Ministers was swiftly appointed, and a consultative body—the Federal National Council—was established. Although these rudimentary new bodies were to remain in their infancy for many more years, they nonetheless succeeded in their first objective: they provided Zayed with the immediate minimum institutional legitimacy he needed to launch a federal government. Of equal if not more significance for the nascent state was the flurry of further federal symbols introduced over the next eighteen months. A distinctive UAE flag was created out of the colours of the original sheikhdoms' flags, and a set of commemorative postage stamps was produced. These were followed by the setting up of a federal postal service and a currency board, the latter of which effectively replaced the previous mixture of circulating monies with the new UAE dirham. Perhaps most memorably for the UAE national population, a competition was held to compose a UAE national anthem, and the winning entry was performed in Abu Dhabi on the first anniversary of 'UAE National Day'—2 December 1972.

The 1970s: constitutional crises

Mindful of Britain's desire to keep the federation as flexible as possible and conscious of London's earlier failures to create a union of Yemeni emirates,[106] Sheikh Zayed bin Sultan Al-Nahyan tried to avoid any significant centralization during his first few years as president. As such, while the United Arab Emirates' temporary capital of Abu Dhabi—as per the 1969 negotiations—was made permanent in 1971 and it was accepted that the new federal ministries should assume responsibility for foreign policy, immigration, and other matters of 'supreme national interest,' it was also recognized that each of the individual emirates should maintain their own local administrations and should keep control over their own natural resources and individual economic development paths. Fortunately for Zayed this need for flexibility had been built into the provisional constitution that the seven rulers had signed. A clause that had existed since the 1968 agreements permitted each member emirate to field their own militias and security services, despite the parallel creation of federal ministries

for the interior and defence.[107] Moreover, article 13 of the 1971 constitution allowed for emirate-level health and education departments,
while article 23 guaranteed that the emirates would continue to manage independently their own hydrocarbon industries.[108]

While these clauses must be credited with maintaining the early
integrity of the UAE and preventing 'opt-outs' during the first oil
boom, there was soon a growing concern that these same clauses were
holding the federation back.[109] In 1976 the provisional constitution
was five years old and many felt it needed to be expanded and made
permanent. A committee of twenty-eight men from across the
federation was appointed to debate the next step.[110] While many of
these—undoubtedly supported by Zayed and most Abu Dhabi
nationals—pressed for more centralization and the removal of article
23 on the grounds that it was keeping the rich emirates separate from
the poor, there was strong opposition, particularly from Dubai, which
was reluctant to allow any federal input into its economic decision-
making.[111] Although the committee finally opted to keep article 23,
there was a request that each emirate would in future need to contribute 25 percent of its oil revenue to the federal budget, so as to ensure
a more even distribution of wealth.[112] Sheikh Rashid bin Said Al-
Maktum—who by this stage had become the chief opponent to any
tightening of the federation—refused to submit to this. The UAE was
left divided and—according to a Bahraini newspaper report—Zayed
tendered his resignation and offered to move the capital away from
Abu Dhabi.[113]

As all were keenly aware, a UAE without Zayed was unimaginable,
as devoid of Abu Dhabi's bankrolling of the federal budget, the federation could not survive.[114] Thus, after four months of negotiation
between Zayed and Rashid an agreement was reached in which Dubai
would increase its budgetary contributions modestly in exchange for
Zayed keeping the constitution in a provisional state for at least
another five years[115] and allowing the federal ministry for the interior
to assume greater control over UAE-wide security.[116] This rapproche-
ment did not, however, solve the matter of the separate militias and
the need for stronger federal armed forces. As with the drive to
increase federal budgetary contributions from other wealthy emirates,
there was a consensus in Abu Dhabi that the Union Defence Force

needed to be far more than simply the old Trucial Oman Scouts and that each emirate should contribute to its growth. Controversially this would mean that both equipment and personnel belong to emirate-level forces would need to be reassigned to a central federal command. The Dubai Defence Force (DDF) had over 1,000 soldiers, the Sharjah National Guard fielded several hundred, and Ra's al-Khaimah had its own 'Badr Brigade;' while Abu Dhabi itself still had its own defence force.[117] Indeed, by this stage the Abu Dhabi Defence Force was staffed by over 10,000 soldiers and supported by several aircraft, armoured cars, and artillery: it was therefore much larger than the UDF.[118]

In 1978 the matter came to a head when Zayed merged the ADDF into the UDF and then installed his twenty-three year old second eldest son—Sheikh Sultan bin Zayed Al-Nahyan—as the enlarged UDF's first commander-in-chief. Although Sharjah immediately backed this move—perhaps given the precariousness of its ruler at that time and his reliance on Abu Dhabi support[119]—an alliance comprising of Dubai, Ra's al-Khaimah, and Umm al-Qawain expressed their outrage and announced their secession from the UAE.[120] Their rulers believed that independent militias were an important symbol of status for their respective emirates[121] and that Abu Dhabi's ambitions were unfaithful to the zeitgeist of 1971. For the second time in two years Zayed threatened to resign from the presidency,[122] but once again his opponents softened their position. The secessionist alliance was brought back into the fold, but only on the condition that no further amalgamation of armed forces would take place.[123] Much to Zayed's frustration, the DDF and the other militias continued their expansion outside of the UDF.[124]

With little respite, the following year Zayed was thrust into another constitutional crisis. This time, supporters of a much stronger federation—of which there appeared to be many—had submitted a petition to the Supreme Council of Rulers calling for greater action. Specifically, they voiced their concerns over the increasingly uncertain regional security environment resulting from the concurrent revolution in Iran, the Soviet buildup on the borders of Afghanistan, and the controversial Camp David Accords of the previous year. In short, they urged Zayed to resume his attempts to build up proper federal armed forces—regardless of his opponents' concerns;[125] they called for the Supreme Council of Rulers—which met infrequently and somewhat informally—to devolve more of its decision-making powers to the more formal Council of Ministers; and they demanded that the Federal National Council be given more control over the ratification of legislation.[126] Seeking to avoid a fresh confrontation with Dubai, Zayed set up a committee to consider the petitioners' demands and appointed Sheikh Muhammad bin Khalifa Al-Nahyan's respected eldest son—Sheikh Hamdan bin Muhammad Al-Nahyan—as chairman.[127] Deliberately perhaps, the contents of the petition became public and led to the first real demonstration in the UAE's history. Nationals across the federation, including many schoolchildren, came out in support of the demands and in de facto support of Zayed's vision.[128] The Dubai-led three emirate opposition pact again pulled out of the Supreme Council of Rulers and the federal government.[129] Only following the diplomatic intervention of the seemingly neutral Kuwaiti Minister for Foreign Affairs—Sheikh Sabah bin Ahmad Al-Sabah—was the UAE able to reunite.[130] Although Abu Dhabi welcomed the symbolism of Rashid's agreement to become the new prime minister of the federal government—with Hamdan as his deputy[131]—it was with bitter regret that Zayed and Hamdan then had to guarantee Dubai and its allies that they would face no further demands for federal integration.[132]

1979 to 1996: the long struggle

The 1980s and early 1990s afforded Sheikh Zayed bin Sultan Al-Nahyan no opportunities to break the deadlock. As each emirate pursued its own objectives, they lacked even basic federal coordination over the building of physical and financial infrastructure. And, more seriously, even unified security and foreign policies—the erstwhile bastions of federal control—began to give way to parochial interests. Most tangibly, as late as 1980 there was still no wide, modern highway connecting the United Arab Emirates' two largest cities of Abu Dhabi and Dubai.[133] Yet at the emirate-level Abu Dhabi had already built an impressive four lane highway connecting the capital to Al-Ayn,[134] and Dubai had built a paved road from its eponymous city to

Hatta—a sparsely populated mountainous enclave of the Dubai emirate. As individual planning departments failed to share their master plans, the UAE was also plagued by overbuilding and a duplication of investments. Similar factories were built in different emirates, leading to over-capacity,[135] and—most infamously—the UAE soon found itself with a surplus of 'international' airports. Perhaps as prestige projects, airports were built in Ra's al-Khaimah, Al-Ayn, and even Fujairah. All this in spite of the UAE's relatively small population and the close proximity of these facilities to the existing airports in Abu Dhabi, Dubai, and Sharjah. For years, the new airports were to remain under-utilized, and at one point even the Sharjah facilities became little more than an air freight terminal due to heavy Dubai competition.[136]

Federal regulation of the banking and financial sector also remained elusive. Although the currency board was replaced in 1980 by the UAE Central Bank, this federal body rarely had sufficient authority to intervene in emirate-level financial matters. The many mergers between commercial banks that took place throughout the 1980s were entirely the work of the emirate-level governments involved, since it was they rather than the Central Bank that put up the necessary funds.[137] More damagingly, the federal authorities were unable to investigate or even assist the Ra's al-Khaimah National Bank when it collapsed in 1985,[138] nor were they able to prevent the collapse of Sharjah's four commercial banks in 1989 after the Sharjah government had defaulted on loans in excess of $500 million. In this latter instance, the Central Bank's inability to deliver a rescue package allowed a foreign consortium to step in and shore up Sharjah's banking system.[139] But the Central Bank's greatest failure by far was in 1991 when it was relegated to being little more than a bystander role during the collapse of the Bank of Credit Commerce International (BCCI). The Central bank was unable to launch a proper investigation, which was ironic given that the majority shareholders were resident in Abu Dhabi and included some of the greatest champions of federal integration. Indeed, at the time of the BCCI's collapse some $750 million of its shares were held by members of the Al-Nahyan family. And although the bulk of these shares had been acquired on their behalf by financial middlemen keen to create an illusion of 'royal

65

backing' for the bank, it was unfortunate and embarrassing for Abu Dhabi that Zayed appeared to have provided the BCCI with its initial capitalization in the early 1970s.[140] Foreign investigators could not be thwarted and British and American teams[141] duly lifted the lid on a world of fake investments, secret financial havens, and kickbacks—mostly set up and perpetrated by Pakistani expatriate BCCI employees in Abu Dhabi. Conscious of their exposure to international lawsuits, the Al-Nahyan family ensured that most global BCCI investors were repaid in full and set up a new bank in Abu Dhabi—Union National Bank—to honor domestic BCCI account holders. Nonetheless the damage done to the ruling family's reputation, the Central Bank's legitimacy, and the UAE's international standing was enormous.

Of perhaps even greater concern to Zayed during this period was the UAE's inability to pursue a unified foreign policy. Much to the embarrassment of the federal government, during the late 1970s and early 1980s Ra's al-Khaimah again tried to gain superpower backing in an effort to form an autonomous state.[142] Although its intended sponsor—the Soviet Union—eventually backed out, having opted to build its warm water port elsewhere in the Gulf,[143] within a few years Ra's al-Khaimah had nevertheless resumed its unilateral overtures. Offering Iraq the opportunity to build airbases in its territory that were within range of Iran, the emirate was hoping to seek greater independent recognition in the Arab world from the major Arab military power.[144] More broadly, the Iran-Iraq War was to engender significant disagreements across the UAE. While Abu Dhabi publicly backed its Arab League colleagues and followed the newly formed Gulf Cooperation Council's pro-Iraqi line,[145] Dubai and Sharjah remained conspicuously neutral. With large naturalized Persian populations and historically lucrative trade links with Iran, these emirates ensured a steady flow of goods into Iran's ports and maintained cordial relations with Tehran.[146]

Although the protagonists had changed, by 1991 a UAE-wide federal foreign policy had still not emerged, with only Abu Dhabi and Dubai openly supporting the US-led 'Desert Storm' coalition against Iraq while the other emirates remained silent, perhaps fearful of future Iraqi reprisals.[147] Moreover, what may have been one of the root causes of Iraq's annexation of Kuwait could have also provoked an attack on the UAE. Since the late 1980s the struggling Iraqi economy had been seeking higher oil prices so that it could rebuild after the war, but widespread disregard of production quotas in several OPEC states—not least the UAE—was an obstacle to this.[148] The problem for Zayed's federal government was that because Dubai had never joined the Organization of the Petroleum Exporting Counties (OPEC) and continued to control its own oil industry—as was its right given article 23 of the constitution—this meant that the UAE's OPEC membership only really applied to Abu Dhabi, which had been a member since 1967.[149] Thus, although encouraged by OPEC's secretary-general[150] to curtail oil output so that prices could rise, Zayed was incapable of implementing any federation-wide oil policies.[151] A federal ministry for petroleum did exist, but it soon became apparent that the only institution with any real power was the Abu Dhabi-specific Supreme Petroleum Council (SPC). In 1994 the federal minister—an Abu Dhabi national[152]—was transferred to the secretary generalship of the SPC: in most states this would be considered a demotion, but in the UAE it was a significant promotion.

By the mid-1990s there were glimmers of hope, as changing domestic economic and political circumstances were inadvertently leading to a strengthening of the federation. Dubai, which had always been the primary defender of the original loose confederation of 1971, was running low on oil and gearing up for a massive indigenous economic diversification programme. If some of the more costly aspects of its autonomy—most notably its independent armed forces—could be handed over to federal control, then the emirate could channel its remaining resources into building the infrastructure needed for its new economy. Furthermore, with Sheikh Rashid—the chief confederalist—having passed away in 1990, his successors—a triumvirate of his three eldest sons led by Sheikh Maktum bin Rashid Al-Maktum—were without inhibitions. Thus, in 1996 the new generation of Al-Maktum rulers handed over the Dubai Defence Force to the Abu Dhabi-based commander-in-chief of the Union Defence Force[153] and thereby publicly accepted Abu Dhabi's supremacy in the federation. Dubai also agreed that the provisional constitution—which had been perpetually renewed since 1971—could be made permanent.[154] As such, many Abu Dhabi and other UAE nationals consider 1996 rather than 1971 to be the real beginning of the union, as only then did the second most powerful emirate begin to integrate. Also, by holding firm to his federal vision for twenty-five years, it is why 1996 should be considered one of the highest points of Zayed's reign.

4

OIL AND BEYOND
ABU DHABI'S NEW ECONOMY

At the helm of a strengthening federation, Abu Dhabi powered into the twenty-first century on the back of ever-increasing oil revenues, well established petrochemical industries, and massive oil-financed overseas investments. For the foreseeable future and despite worsening global conditions these sectors and strategies will remain the central pillars of the emirate's economy: Abu Dhabi will continue to be a major oil producer and to control the world's greatest sovereign wealth funds. And since 2004 its dynamic new leadership has also begun to diversify the economy. By maximizing Abu Dhabi's competitive advantages and reaching out to the most capable foreign partners, a plethora of new sectors have been launched. These include high technology heavy industries, a pioneering renewable energy sector, extensive real estate projects, and up market 'cultural tourism.' Having been carefully selected and nurtured, within a few years these sectors will be responsible for a potent and vibrant new economy providing plentiful employment and domestic investment opportunities. Unlike the more urgent and seemingly problematic diversification that has taken place in Dubai and elsewhere in the Gulf, the nature of Abu Dhabi's astutely managed economic developments should allow the emirate to carve out a high profile and sustainable global niche.

The oil and gas economy

With several major discoveries since the 1970s—both onshore and offshore, Abu Dhabi's share of global oil serves has continued to grow and now stands at about 8 percent: some 98 billion barrels, which represents about 94 percent of the United Arab Emirates' total.[1] Production currently stands at 2.7 million barrels today, but the Supreme Petroleum Council has recently invested over $20 billion in oil infrastructure with a view to expanding Abu Dhabi's output capacity by 30 percent to nearly 3.5 million barrels per day by 2010. Almost all of this excess will be sold to Asian buyers.[2] Even at this higher rate—and assuming no further discoveries—it is estimated that Abu Dhabi's reserves will still last another ninety years.[3]

The early days of one or two major concession holders are now long gone, and several foreign companies currently hold stakes in Abu Dhabi's oil industry. These include British Petroleum (BP)—the inheritor of the old Iraqi Petroleum Company's Abu Dhabi interests, Campagnie Française des Petroles, Royal Dutch Shell, Exxon-Mobil, Total, and the Japan Oil Development Company (JODCO). Most of the foreign companies keep having their stakes renewed, with some already having been extended up until 2026.[4] It is believed that their expertise and technological input continue to be welcomed. Since 1971 a 'national' oil company—the Abu Dhabi National Oil Company (ADNOC)—has always held the controlling stake in the various concessions. ADNOC holds a 60 percent stake in the largest onshore concession—the Abu Dhabi Company for Onshore Oil Investments (ADCO); a 60 percent stake in the largest offshore concession—the Abu Dhabi Marine Areas company; and a 51 percent stake in the Zakum Development Company (ZADCO)—another major offshore concession holder.[5] In any case, there are handsome profits for all concerned, with Abu Dhabi's total oil exports in 2007 estimated to have been worth over $260 billion.[6] Of this, it is thought that ADNOC's share was $67 billion—a figure likely to have risen to nearly $90 billion during the oil price hikes of 2008.[7] Even in 2009, with prices predicted to average little more than $50 a barrel, it thought that ADNOC revenues will still be in excess of $45 billion.[8]

Although incomparable to gas reserves elsewhere in Gulf—especially those of Qatar—Abu Dhabi nevertheless controls 3.4 percent of the world's natural gas: some 200 trillion cubic feet.[9] Much like the oil industry, the major offshore concession holder—the Abu Dhabi Gas Liquefaction Company (ADGAS)—is majority owned by

ADNOC, which holds a 70 percent stake, while the remainder is divided between BP, Total, and Mitsubishi Gas.[10] Similarly the major onshore concession holder—Abu Dhabi Gas Industries (GASCO)—is majority owned by ADNOC, which holds a 68 percent stake, while the remainder is divided between Total, Royal Dutch Shell, and Partex.[11] In the near future a new concession to be shared by ADNOC and ConocoPhillips will exploit untouched areas of the Shah and Bab onshore gasfields.[12] Although controversial, given the reportedly high sulfur and carbon dioxide content of Shah's gas,[13] this will boost Abu Dhabi's current daily gas production of about 4.5 billion cubic feet per day[14] to nearly 6 billion cubic feet per day. And by 2009 GASCO will have completed the final phase of the Habshan Gas Complex—one of the world's largest gas plants.[15] Despite these increases, Abu Dhabi will still face gas shortages, as some 85 percent of the emirate's power plants are gas fuelled.[16] These shortages have already stalled major development projects, including the construction of an Abu Dhabi-financed desalination plant in the poorer emirate of Umm al-Qawain,[17] and it seems that construction projects in the capital itself have been slowed down because of this. Hopes for a solution had been pinned on the massive Dolphin Gas project, which established Qatar as a co-supplier and committed Abu Dhabi to the large scale transportation and marketing of Dolphin gas to Dubai, Oman, and other net gas importers in the region.[18] However, despite two billion cubic feet per day of Dolphin gas now being piped in from Qatar,[19] the problem has not yet been solved.

The long term plan is the acquisition of, or at least access to, gas from much further afield. By doing so, Abu Dhabi will export its hydrocarbon expertise, satisfy its own energy needs, and perhaps even re-export non-Gulf gas to its more resource-scarce neighbours. Notably, following closely in the footsteps of an Omani deal to exploit Iranian gasfields,[20] Abu Dhabi's Mubadala Development Corporation has acquired the Singapore-based Pearl Energy, which in turn holds concessions to exploit Indonesia's Sebuku gasfield and the Jasmine field in the Gulf of Thailand. And through its Liwa Energy subsidiary company, Mubadala has also bought into hydrocarbon exploration companies in Algeria and Libya.[21] Similarly, other Abu Dhabi entities have bought into overseas explorations, including the Abu Dhabi

National Energy Company (referred to as 'Taqa'[22]), which now has a stake in North Sea and Canadian operations,[23] and the International Petroleum Investment Company (IPIC), which has developed an interest in Kazakhstani gas discoveries.[24]

Oil-related industrialization

In addition to the aforementioned agricultural developments and the small-scale import substitution industries—most of which concentrated on producing basic construction materials, since the first oil boom Abu Dhabi also established heavy, state-owned export-oriented industries. Most of these have concentrated on the production of metals, plastics, fertilizers, and petrochemicals. These all require abundant energy to manufacture and therefore best capitalize on Abu Dhabi's competitive advantages. The most prominent of these downstream industrial companies are Fertil (established in 1980 and co-owned by the Abu Dhabi National Oil Company and Total),[25] the Abu Dhabi Polymers Company or Borouge (established in 1998),[26] and Emirates Aluminium (EMAL), the latter of which operates the world's largest aluminium processing facility on Abu Dhabi's manmade Taweelah island. Most of these exports are believed to be destined for India, Bangladesh, Sri Lanka, and Malaysia.[27]

As with the hydrocarbon industry, over the next few years the sector will continue to expand—gas shortages notwithstanding—with both the Mubadala Development Corporation and the Abu Dhabi Basic Industries Corporation (ADBIC) planning to build massive new aluminium plants.[28] By 2013 the International Petroleum Investment Company will have built a new Chemicals Industrial City: capable of producing 7 million tones per year of aromatics and ammonia derivatives it will be the world's largest such complex.[29] Also, ADBIC is planning to invest a further $4 billion into its Abu Dhabi Polymers Park: by 2011 it is expected this will have led to a doubling in the emirate's polymers production.[30] Other projects will include those belonging to the new Emirates Iron Company, the Emirates Cement Factory, and the Al-Nasser Industrial Enterprises parastatal.[31] The government has put its full weight behind these developments, having increased spending on industrial infrastructure by over 400 percent since 2001.[32] Soon it promises the completion of the $10 billion Khalifa Port and Industrial Zone on Taweelah and has committed a further $8 billion for other sector-specific infrastructure projects.[33] A new unit—ZonesCorp—has been set up to administer these new districts, provide organizational support, and build residential camps for labourers.[34]

Overseas investments and sovereign wealth

Of equal if not greater importance to Abu Dhabi's economy since the 1970s has been the channelling of surplus oil revenues into long term overseas investments, rather than simply gold or short-term paper. Conceived as a means of buffering the domestic economy should the international oil industry falter, most of these investments have been made through a handful of government owned authorities or government backed companies. Indeed, of the latter, most simply state that their sole shareholder is 'the Government of Abu Dhabi.' Today, their combined assets are thought to be in excess of $1 trillion, generating some 10 percent in interest per year.[35] This compares very favorably with the world's other sovereign wealth managing countries, notably Singapore and Norway—with $490 billion[36] and $390 billion[37] respectively; and places Abu Dhabi far ahead of other Gulf investors such as Kuwait with $260 billion,[38] Dubai with about $100 billion,[39] and Qatar with a modest $60 billion.[40]

By far the most prominent of Abu Dhabi's sovereign wealth funds is the Abu Dhabi Investments Authority (ADIA). Founded in 1976, it reached about $100 billion in overseas assets by the mid-1990s[41] and about $360 billion by 2005.[42] Now symbolically housed in the tallest building in Abu Dhabi—the Samsung-ADIA complex,[43] it was estimated that ADIA reached nearly $900 billion in early 2008.[44] Although there may have been a slight drop by the end of the year as the global recession continued to worsen,[45] it is likely that that ADIA is still the world's largest sovereign wealth fund. Following Sheikh Khalifa bin Zayed Al-Nahyan's succession as ruler in late 2004 its chairmanship formally passed from Khalifa to a younger half brother, Sheikh Ahmad bin Zayed Al-Nahyan. Although since 2006 ADIA technically came under the umbrella of a new entity called the Abu

Dhabi Investments Council,[46] in practice it appears to remain fairly autonomous with Khalifa, Ahmad, and a long serving French banker[47] in full control of the purse strings. Housing teams of foreign experts that scour the globe for a variety of opportunities, it is thought that ADIA has historically favoured index-linked blue chip investments in the developed world. These fairly conservative investments are believed to still make up about 60 percent of ADIA's portfolio, the most recent example being the acquisition of a 5 percent stake in Citigroup. This $7.5 billion investment in 2007 made ADIA the largest shareholder in the largest US bank, and came just months after it had taken a 9 percent stake in Apollo—a leading US management firm. Moreover, as part of the same strategy the authority has been long been building up considerable investments in mature, western real estate, with its UK portfolio alone being valued in excess of $6 billion.[48] About 30 percent of the portfolio is in emerging markets, including South East Asia and some parts of the Arab world. Recent examples include ADIA's acquisition of an 8 percent stake in the Egyptian Financial Group Hermes Holding Company (EFG-Hermes) and a large stake in the giant Prince Abdul-Aziz bin Musaid Economic City in Saudi Arabia.[49] Of the remaining 10 percent of the portfolio, little information is available, although it would seem that most falls under the control of ADIA's new strategic investments department which is headed by the same astute manager as the emerging markets division.[50] Examples of ADIA's strategic 'wild card' investments may include a reported $5 billion investment in Libya's tourism infrastructure.[51]

Also now nominally under the Abu Dhabi Investment Council is the Abu Dhabi Investment Company (ADIC). Established in 1977 it is the second oldest and second largest sovereign wealth manager in Abu Dhabi, believed to be in control of over $15 billion in overseas investments.[52] Historically it has been under the control of the Suwdan section of the Bani Yas,[53] and today this remains the case with Khalifa bin Muhammad Al-Kindi and Nasser bin Ahmad Al-Suwaidi serving, respectively, as its chairman and deputy chairman. ADIC specializes in North African investments,[54] but in the last few years it has begun to diversify its interests and has, much like ADIA, seen value in depressed western real estate. Notably, in July 2008 it bought out Prudential's 75 percent stake in the iconic Chrysler Building in New York. Valued at about $800 million, the deal was reported in the international media as being brokered by ADIC,[55] although confusingly on this occasion it appeared that the acronym referred to the parent Abu Dhabi Investment Council.[56]

Abu Dhabi's third sovereign wealth fund is managed by the International Petroleum Investment Company. Originally founded in 1984 as an expertise-combining joint venture between ADIA and the Abu Dhabi National Oil Company, it remains co-owned by the two entities, but now falls under the umbrella of the Supreme Petroleum Council. Nevertheless it has an independent board of directors[57]—now chaired by Sheikh Mansur bin Zayed Al-Nahyan, which has successfully built up IPIC's overseas oil-related investment portfolio to nearly $14 billion. Some of its biggest investments include a 17 percent stake in Österreichischen Mineralölverwaltung Aktiengesellschaft (OMV)—a major Austrian petrochemicals company,[58] and a 65 percent controlling stake in Borealis[59]—a plastics company also based in Austria that has links with the Abu Dhabi Polymers Company. More recently, IPIC has invested in Japan's oil refining industry by purchasing a 21 percent, $780 million, stake in the Cosmo Oil Company.[60] And, in addition to its abovementioned interests in Kazakhstani explorations, in 2008 IPIC announced plans to invest $5 billion in a petrochemicals plant in the Central Asian country.[61] Over the next five years it is estimated that IPIC will have increased its portfolio of investments to $40 billion.[62]

Capturing many more headlines than either ADIC or IPIC has been Abu Dhabi's fourth largest but probably fastest growing sovereign wealth manager. Founded in 2002 by the soon-to-be crown prince, Sheikh Muhammad bin Zayed Al-Nahyan, the Mubadala Development Corporation is staffed by members of the same team involved in the early stages of the Dolphin Gas project. Many of these were handpicked for the purpose by Muhammad, most notably Mubadala's esteemed managing director, Khaldun bin Khalifa Al-Mubarak, and its CEO, Waleed bin Ahmad Al-Mokarrab Al-Muhairi of the Al-Bu Mahair section of the Bani Yas. Although Mubadala still serves as Dolphin's majority shareholder,[63] and—as evidenced by the described Pearl Energy acquisition—it clearly keeps an interest in hydrocarbon projects, since 2005 it has diversified considerably into a variety of other overseas investments. Most of these are overseen by its investment management group[64] and are already believed to be worth over $10 billion.[65] Most conspicuously, in 2005 Mubadala purchased a 5 percent stake, worth $130 million, in Italy's celebrated Ferrari car manufacturer. But other, much larger, investments have included a 7.5 percent stake, worth $1.3 billion, in the Carlyle Group—a US-based private equity giant, an 8.3 percent stake in the Guinea Alumina Corporation—whose refinery is adjacent to one of the world's highest quality bauxite reserves, an 8.1 percent stake, worth $620 million, in Advanced Micro Devices (AMD)—the world's second largest microprocessor manufacturer, and a 35 percent stake in Piaggio Aero—an Italian manufacturer of turboprop aircraft.[66] In summer 2008, Mubadala made its biggest single investment when it bought up $3.3 billion of shares in General Electric.[67] This has made Muhammad's corporation one of the top ten shareholders in one of the US' oldest firms. Further diversifying its portfolio, in late 2008 Mubadala moved fast to acquire a $165 million stake in Finnish wind turbine manufacturer WinWinD[68] and a 25 percent, $50 million, stake in the ailing US property company John Buck.[69] Soon, it will boost its stake in AMD to 20 percent at an additional cost of some $310 million over the original investment.[70]

Although dwarfed by the big four investment vehicles, there are numerous other sovereign wealth funds being operated by Abu Dhabi parastatals. Much like IPIC, the abovementioned Abu Dhabi National Energy Company or Taqa has a range of overseas energy and petrochemicals investments. Most recently it has acquired a 50 percent stake in a subsidiary of the French renewable energy company Theolia in an effort to develop Moroccan wind farms.[71] Under the chairmanship of Hamad bin Muhammad Al-Hurr Al-Suwaidi, it has built up about $9 billion in assets since its establishment in 2005,[72] although some reports place its assets much higher.[73] Although a publicly listed company, the government maintains control through a 51 percent stake courtesy of the Abu Dhabi Water and Electricity Authority (ADWEA) which in turn is chaired by Sheikh Diab bin Zayed Al-Nahyan.[74] Other, smaller funds include those operated by the Abu Dhabi National Exhibitions Company (ADNEC), which recently purchased the Excel Building in London for $600 million,[75] and Al-Mibar International, which has announced a $600 million joint venture with a Libyan company to develop real estate and tourism projects in Libya. This has been followed up with investments in farmland and agricultural business in Kazakhstan, Pakistan, and the Sudan.[76] Little is known of Al-Mibar, but it may fall under the umbrella of the Mansur-chaired Abu Dhabi Fund for Development (ADFD)—Abu Dhabi's primary dispenser of foreign aid, thus giving Mansur a second means of access to major overseas investments alongside the IPIC.

These formal sovereign wealth entities have very recently been joined by a number of consortia, often made up of leading Abu Dhabi businessmen and members of the ruling family. In some cases these groups have made direct investments independently of the parastatals, most notably the Abu Dhabi United Group for Development and Investment's purchase of Britain's Manchester City football club for about $360 million in summer 2008.[77] Amongst this group's members are Mansur and Sulayman Al-Fahim, the CEO of Hydra Properties. In another high profile case the ubiquitous Mansur has even acted as an individual, investing some $5.2 billion in November 2008 to gain a 16 percent stake in Britain's Barclays Bank.[78] Although not strictly speaking a sovereign wealth investment, the deal should nonetheless be classed as such given his status as a senior member of the ruling family.

The new economy

Notwithstanding the enormity of Abu Dhabi's oil reserves and its overseas investments, for some time there has been recognition of the need to diversify the economy or, more specifically, an effort to launch genuinely non-oil related sectors alongside the existing energy-reliant petrochemical industries. Thus far, Abu Dhabi's diversification has lacked the pace and, as most impartial observers would concur, the desperation evident in resource-scarce Dubai—where oil production began to decline as early as 1991.[79] However, an increasing concern over domestic employment prospects, unhealthy trade balances, and inflationary pressures has indubitably made the 'new economy' a development priority.

The issue of employment for Abu Dhabi's growing population of educated young nationals is complex and will be discussed later in this book; nevertheless the present makeup of the emirate's economy is not well suited to the population's future needs. Only a limited number of jobs requiring a narrow range of skills are ever likely to be available in government departments, oil companies, or investment vehicles; and those nationals with alternative aspirations, abilities, and qualifications will remain frustrated. Moreover, since 2003 it is thought that over $350 billion of Abu Dhabi's total non-oil trade of about $500 billion has been made up of consumer imports. Most of these have been cars and electronics purchased from Japan, Germany, the US, and Italy. Another $140 billion of the total trade has been made up of re-exports (mostly destined for Iran and India),[80] and only the tiny remainder has been genuine exports (mostly destined for Saudi Arabia and India).[81] Thus, imports have exceeded exports by about fifty-fold as the emirate has never had a strong non-oil manufacturing base. Closely connected to this problem, with little domestic economic activity and few domestic investment opportunities, the oil economy has increasingly burdened Abu Dhabi with excess liquidity. Although reliable data is rarely available, there is no doubt that the United Arab Emirates has been suffering from very high levels of inflation for the past five or six years. This has been exacerbated by an inability to increase interest rates, as the UAE—along with other Gulf states—has historically pegged its currency to the US dollar, with one dollar having been worth about 3.67 dirhams since 1997.[82] In 2008 the Central Bank estimated that the UAE's money supply was growing at its fastest ever rate (by about $50 billion per annum), and that inflation was at 11.1 percent.[83] This prompted one informed observer to comment that '...the need for opening new investment outlets is dire in order to control inflation and maintain economic growth earnings.'[84] In reality, the rate of inflation is much higher in Abu Dhabi than elsewhere in the UAE, given that it is the emirate in which liquidity has most dramatically outstripped investment opportunities. Food prices have been rising by between 15 and 20 percent per annum, and accommodation costs are undoubtedly hyperinflationary, aggravated by an increasing expatriate population and a shortage of housing stock in the capital. Despite a rent rise cap of 7 percent being introduced in late 2006,[85] well appointed two bedroom city centre apartments can no longer be acquired for less than $50,000 per annum, compared to just $16,000 per annum five years ago. The reformers, epitomized by Sheikh Muhammad bin Zayed Al-Nahyan, wished to diversify Abu Dhabi's economy in the late 1990s in the wake of nearby developments in other economies such as Dubai, Bahrain, and Qatar. However, through no fault of his own, the latter years of Sheikh Zayed bin Sultan's reign were ones of stagnation, with no sufficient concentration of power in any one individual's hands and—as with all long-serving administrations—a lack of motivation, initiative, and appetite for risk in the decision-making ranks. Indeed, during Zayed's final year there were weeds growing in prominent public places and a general atmosphere of sleepiness and inactivity hanging over the capital. In late 2004, however, everything changed. As demonstrated in the following chapter, a new generation of rulers was empowered and an arrangement made that saw Muhammad installed as the new crown prince and, more importantly, given almost supreme executive powers over Abu Dhabi's domestic affairs. Spearheaded by a new Executive Affairs Authority and his flagship Mubadala Development Corporation—which even set up a new operations department alongside its existing investment management group—Muhammad inspired Abu Dhabi's captains of industry to begin focusing on the emirate's domestic economic development.

Many of the new sectors that have been prioritized by Mubadala and the other Abu Dhabi developers are ones identified for long-term sustainable growth, and the consensus is that they are well placed to withstand the global recession, regional instability, and other vagaries of the international system. Although there are new foreigner-focused real estate and tourism sectors—which are vulnerable to downswings and likely to decline in the event of nearby wars, terrorist attacks, or the emergence of more attractive alternative destinations—these activities will serve merely to add vibrancy to Abu Dhabi's economy. They are by no means intended to be bedrocks of the emirate's diversification or barometers of its success, as seems dangerously the case in Dubai. Indeed, the tourist industry alone may now account for 17 percent of Dubai's GDP.[86] Moreover, as detailed below, Abu Dhabi has been more cautious with the location and nature of these activities than some of her neighbours. This should keep to a minimum the political and social costs of a potentially culturally incompatible residential or touristic expatriate population. Equally commendably, Abu Dhabi's new economic sectors and all of the new buildings, plants, and facilities that they will require are being incorporated into an all-encompassing emirate-wide master plan. Mindful of the disorganization that has resulted from rapidly diversifying economies elsewhere in the Gulf, where government-sponsored plans have often been introduced too late to have any real impact, Abu Dhabi has been quick to introduce its 'Plan Abu Dhabi 2030.' With long term objectives and considerations, the plan is pioneering, as it breaks the mould of the usual short and medium term plans extant elsewhere in the UAE, most notably the Dubai Strategic Plan (which only extends up to 2015).[87] Drafted by the Muhammad-chaired Abu Dhabi Urban Planning Council, the plan will see the new economy expand into carefully earmarked areas of the emirate and will ensure that the necessary infrastructure is already in place. Already Plan Abu Dhabi 2030 has initiated infrastructure projects costing in excess of $400 billion, and $175 billion of these should be complete by 2012.[88] By 2015 there will be a network of tramlines in place, and by 2020 there will be a metro system and a regional train service. In contrast, Dubai's diversification began without a plan: the city regularly grinds to a halt with traffic congestion, a mass transit system is still not finished, power outages are not infrequent, and luxury residential neighbourhoods have been built adjacent to major industrial zones and other high air and noise pollution areas. Crucially, the global recession is unlikely to slow down Abu Dhabi's 2030 ambitions, with government officials having already hinted that Abu Dhabi's sovereign wealth funds and oil revenues could be drawn upon should conditions deteriorate much further. Indeed, one spokesman claimed 'The reserves are available, I'm not saying we will dip into them, but if we need them they are there... the government will always intervene if delays to the project will affect the credibility and sustainability of business in Abu Dhabi.'[89]

High technology heavy industries

The centerpiece of Abu Dhabi's new economy has been a select range of high technology heavy industries. In most cases, these have involved the setting up of specialist subsidiary companies within the Mubadala Development Corporation or other big parastatals. The new companies have then been turned into joint ventures as international partners have been brought on board. The latter provide the technology, the market contacts, and credibility; while the parastatals provide the capitalization and ensure easy access to the necessary skilled labour by offering high, tax free salaries. Moreover, in some instances the parastatals have then strengthened the ventures by making direct investments in the foreign companies. Thus, the sovereign wealth component of the old economy has been reinvigorated and applied to the new economy. This is thought to have been a particularly persuasive method of recruiting reputable yet beleaguered western companies. As such, Abu Dhabi is using its surplus revenue to leapfrog decades of research and development and propel itself into the first world. With little subtlety, Mubadala's own media relations department confirms the strategy, stating that 'Mubadala is making capital intensive long term investments... By partnering with top companies, we are leveraging the required expertise to build businesses in Abu Dhabi that have a global reach. Mubadala is analyzing the latest international trends and technologies as well as importing knowledge and expertise. We are also providing the facilities needed to attract and develop talent to support the growth of the sector.'[90]

With little time lost since 2004, the sector has already had a major impact. For the first two quarters of 2008 it was estimated that the emirate's non-oil exports had risen by over 50 percent while imports had risen by only 25 percent.[91] Non-oil contributions to the gross domestic product also seem to be rising: currently they are thought to stand at about 40 percent, and it is predicted they will rise to 50 percent by 2015 and 60 percent by 2025.[92] One of the most prominent examples of this new high technology manufacturing is Abu Dhabi's aerospace industry.[93] As Mubadala's CEO has explained '...you can only make a studied play in five or six different sectors that you can ultimately become internationally competitive in, and we believe aerospace happens to be one of them.'[94] Out of the remnants of the Gulf Aircraft Maintenance Company—originally formed in 1977 and owned by Gulf Air—Mubadala has recently crafted a new subsidiary: Abu Dhabi Aircraft Technologies (ADAT).[95] While maintenance remains at the core of its business strategy, in summer 2008 ADAT achieved a double victory when it was awarded a contract to manufacture wing parts and other components for the European Aeronautic Defence and Space Company's (EADS) flagship A380 Superjumbo. Also, ADAT was approved by EADS as the only company in the Middle East permitted to service A380 engines.[96]

The former would not have been possible without Mubadala's $500 million investment in an Abu Dhabi-based carbon fibre plant, as this will provide ADAT with ready access to the materials it needs. While the latter would not have been possible without technological input from Rolls Royce as part of a deal brokered by Mubadala earlier in 2008. In the near future ADAT will also be supported by a new $8 billion high technology joint venture in Abu Dhabi set up by Mubadala and General Electric[97]—the abovementioned recipient of a large Mubadala sovereign wealth injection. Over the next five years ADAT plans to increase its annual revenues to $1 billion, expanding its maintenance operations from existing Gulf customers such as Etihad Airways and Qatar Airways into the Indian market;[98] and by 2013 it hopes to win contracts to manufacture parts for EADS' forthcoming A350. In the long term ADAT intends to export its components to other buyers—with Italy's Finmeccania having already signalled an interest—and it has even stated that it eventually intends to assemble entire aircraft in Abu Dhabi.[99]

In the near future Abu Dhabi will move into the manufacture of computer microprocessors, with Mubadala's stake in AMD having unsurprisingly led to a new joint venture in the emirate between AMD and another new Mubadala subsidiary: the Advanced Technology Investment Company (ATIC). The venture, tentatively named 'The Foundry,' is now 66 percent owned by ATIC, and will produce video cards, mobile phones, and consumer electronics, in addition to processors.[100] Other key examples of high technology heavy industries include Abu Dhabi's manufacturing and export of oil rigs. Since 2005 the Oilfield Drilling Equipment and Rig Company (ODERCO) has been selling rigs to other Gulf states and to Singapore. Impressively, in 2008 it won a $135 million contract to supply rigs to a Texas-based oil company, beating heavy European competition.[101] Shipbuilding has been identified as another priority area, with the Abu Dhabi

Shipbuilding Company (ADSB) having recently begun manufacturing entire ships. Originally set up in 1996 by Sheikh Muhammad bin Zayed Al-Nahyan for the purposes of repairing UAE Navy and UAE Coastguard vessels, it is now 40 percent Mubadala-owned and holds a $1 billion contract to build six new Baynunah Class corvettes for the UAE Navy.[102] This has been made possible by a Mubadala-arranged joint venture with a British naval defence company—BVT Surface Fleet,[103] and with France's Constructions Mecaniques de Normandie (CMN).[104] ADSB has already manufactured several naval landing crafts, some of which have been sold to the Royal Navy of Oman.[105] It is thought that the ADSB has also teamed up with another French manufacturer to build some small amphibious craft and mini-submarines, although these may be far from completion.[106] The new shipping industry will be complemented by the manufacture of integrated naval defence systems by Abu Dhabi Systems Integration (ADSI)—a joint venture between ADSB and Selex Sistemi Integrati, which in turn is a division of the aforementioned Finemeccanica.[107]

Further connecting Abu Dhabi's new industries to the military and thereby fulfilling two purposes—economic diversification and improved security—has been a spate of joint ventures with western arms and security equipment manufacturers. These include a three way partnership between Emirates Advanced Investments, Raytheon, and Lockheed Martin to produce Javelin portable anti-tank missiles. Significantly, these will be sold to both the UAE military and international customers.[108] Other projects include the joint manufacture with European companies of military motorcycles, jeeps, and reconnaissance aircraft.[109] Further examples include Biodentity—an Abu Dhabi-based company set up by the Abu Dhabi Investment Company and Canada's Cryptometrics, after the latter reportedly received an investment from ADIC. Biodentity will manufacture biometric face scan systems that will be sold to Abu Dhabi International Airport and other airports in the region.[110] Most recently, and on a much larger scale, Mubadala has set up a $1.2 billion subsidiary—Al-Yah Satellites—that will build military and commercial satellites. Its technology partner is Astrium—a division of EADS, and the pair intends to launch the satellites from Kazakhstan and sell them to the UAE military and other customers in southern Europe, Africa, and South East Asia.[111]

Future energy industries

Alongside the aerospace industry, the various military manufacturers, and other areas of non-oil diversification, there has also been an effort to build up 'future energy' and other green industries. As one spokesman[112] has explained: 'Abu Dhabi knows the energy business rather well. It also enjoys competitive advantages allowing it to successfully establish these new industries, while simultaneously diversifying its economy and providing high-quality job opportunities.'[113] Moreover, as the following chapters will reveal, despite the irony of Abu Dhabi being one of the largest hydrocarbon exporters, support for nature and improving the environment have historically been key legitimacy resources for the emirate's rulers. Also, there has long been a concern over the environmental impact of Abu Dhabi's rapid economic development. The World Wildlife Fund recently announced that the United Arab Emirates has the worst carbon footprint in the world—over five times greater than the global average and some six times greater than the carrying capacity of the Earth's biosphere.[114] In Abu Dhabi specifically, waste per capita has been estimated at over 2.3kg per day—most of it dumped into pits in the desert[115]—which is much more than the 1.5kg average for Organization for Economic Cooperation and Development (OECD) countries.[116] Therefore the launching of this new sector is actually serving three purposes: economic, political, and environmental.

In 2006 the Mubadala Development Corporation established yet another subsidiary to pioneer these developments—the Abu Dhabi Future Energy Company (ADFEC). The plan was for $4 billion of the new company's budget to come directly from Mubadala, while the remainder of its anticipated $22 billion budget would be drawn from international partners through joint ventures, thereby making the entity an excellent (and wholesome) foreign direct investment vehicle. ADFEC's first major project has been Masdar City, a large carbon-neutral development in Abu Dhabi's hinterland. Sheikh Muhammad bin Zayed Al-Nahyan laid the virtual cornerstone in 2008 on Masdar's website[117] and the project is expected to reach completion in 2016.[118] The aim is for ADFEC to provide the infrastructure for a 'free zone' that will allow up to 1,500 renewable energy and other environment-related international companies to base themselves in

Masdar, or at least have their regional headquarters there. Some of these will be focused on carbon capture technologies and it is expected that they will export their services to nearby countries still relying on outdated hydrocarbon extraction technologies. For every ton of captured carbon, the Masdar-based company will receive 12 Euros as per the carbon credit market established by the Kyoto Protocol, which will help to offset the rent they will pay to ADFEC.[119] Moreover, ADFEC itself is also hoping to benefit directly from carbon credit schemes should the United Nations' proposed Clean Development Mechanism be introduced. This system will provide remuneration for those companies that store captured carbon gas underground, and ADFEC plans to pipe captured gas from existing power plants in Abu Dhabi to disused underground oil wells in the desert.[120]

ADFEC is also hoping to attract research and development focused companies to Masdar in an effort to make Abu Dhabi the region's capital for green technologies. As another result of the Mubadala-General Electric agreements, one of these will be a joint venture that will also involve investments from Siemens and Credit-Suisse. This company will employ more than a hundred experts and manage a $50 million 'clean technology fund.'[121] Similarly, Mubadala's described investment in WinWinD is likely to lead to a wind power joint venture in Masdar.[122] In support of all these companies will be a new research centre—the Masdar Institute, and it would appear that the Massachusetts Institute of Technology, Imperial College London, the Toyko Institute of Technology, Columbia University, and the German Aerospace Centre have all agreed to assist.[123]

In the near future, ADFEC will build a number of non-hydrocarbon power plants in Abu Dhabi. The first of these—a $350 million solar plant in cooperation with the German Aerospace Centre—should be completed by 2009.[124] The next big step will be nuclear energy, with the company having announced plans to construct three nuclear power plants at a cost of $7 billion each. Two will be on Abu Dhabi's coastline, most probably in the western region, while the third is likely to be in Fujairah. Together, it is expected these plants will meet 30 percent of Abu Dhabi's energy needs by 2012, and perhaps all of the energy needs of partner emirates such as Fujairah. As with Masdar, a range of foreign expertise will be brought on board—with cooperation agreements already having been signed with French and US nuclear companies[125]—and, given the enormous expense and sensitivity of the project, there will probably be some element of sovereign wealth 'sweetening' involved. Certainly, the plan at present would seem to be that the uranium required by these plants will not be enriched in Abu Dhabi, but will instead come from a proposed international 'nuclear bank' that will cost $150 million to set up. Orchestrated by the Nuclear Threat Initiative—a non-governmental organization, the bank's financial backers already include Warren Buffet, the Norwegian government, and the US government. Unsurprisingly, in 2008 the federal minister for foreign affairs—Sheikh Abdullah bin Zayed Al-Nahyan—pledged that the UAE would also make a sizeable contribution.[126]

Exclusive real estate

The issue of foreign ownership of real estate is highly sensitive, as since their respective dates of independence the Gulf states all prohibited foreign ownership by law, on the grounds that certain activities—most notably landlordship—were to be exclusively for nationals. In recent years, certain parts of the Gulf—led by Dubai since 1997—have relaxed their rules: at first permitting long leaseholds, and then granting freeholds. In the summer of 2005 Abu Dhabi finally followed suit, allowing renewable 99 year leases for foreigners.[127] Although the sector is far from being a central component of Abu Dhabi's new economy, it is nevertheless viewed as an additional stream of domestic investment and employment opportunities for Abu Dhabi nationals, a useful foreign direct investment tool, and undoubtedly a means of improving the emirate's international reputation and visibility.

Abu Dhabi's new real estate sector cannot be compared easily with the developments in its neighbours, in part because the motivations behind its creation are very different: there is no desperation to bring in foreign money. Almost all of the emirate's real estate projects are at the very highest end of the market: despite being an immature industry, its prices are far higher on average than those in Dubai, Qatar, Ajman, Ra's al-Khaimah, and other areas. There are no middle or low end developments, and none seem to be planned. Moreover, all the major real estate projects—as per Plan Abu Dhabi 2030—have been carefully corralled into specified areas of the city. Keen to avoid embarrassing overlaps of non-Muslim residents with more conservative Abu Dhabi nationals and other Gulf Arabs, most of the emirate's 'Dubai-style' properties, complete with bars and nightclubs, will be situated on Reem—a large island off the main island's eastern coast. Whereas most of the properties targeted at Gulf Arabs (and in some cases restricted to Gulf Arabs) are being built either on the main island or on the hinterland approaches to Abu Dhabi. Also, it is notable that the authorities have been keen to market Abu Dhabi real estate in a more discreet fashion: rarely will one see large advertisements featuring alcohol imbibing western or Levantine women in revealing attire—as is often the case in Dubai—but rather scenes depicting family life, perhaps with small children and modestly dressed women covering their hair. Furthermore, for those projects clearly targeting Gulf Arabs the advertisements invariably stress the 'community facilities' that will be available: namely mosques. Abu Dhabi does not want a repeat of Dubai Marina, where many of the community's Muslim residents are appalled to find no mosque on the entire 150,000 inhabitant development.[128]

Abu Dhabi needs also to avoid an oversupply of property and the inevitable price correction that is taking place in the other nascent real estate sectors elsewhere in the Gulf. Although there are now many property developers operating in Abu Dhabi, some of which have even brought on board foreign backers,[129] and some of which have offered securitized sharia compliant Islamic bonds (*sukuk*) to raise capital,[130] there are nonetheless only a few master developers which control the main zones and are responsible for the necessary real estate infrastructure. These master developers are all either majority-owned by parastatals or are companies with ties so close to key members of the ruling family that they are still effectively under the government's control. In contrast, only 50 percent of Dubai's real estate stock is controlled by government entities, and it is predicted that Dubai will soon have as many property units reaching completion as Shanghai—a city with 13 times Dubai's population. The scale of this impending glut, and the government's inability to scale it back, led market analysts and ratings agencies to predict in summer 2008 that '...the magnitude of price corrections [in Dubai], should they occur, could be substantial.'[131] Certainly as the global downswing finally reached Dubai's shores in October 2008 prices plummeted. As will be discussed in the final chapter, the value of most Dubai properties has continued to fall drastically, with several planned developments being suspended and employees at major developers being made redundant.[132] Significantly, although Abu Dhabi expects to deliver 160,000 units by 2010[133] and has real estate projects totaling over $20 billion underway,[134] this is a mere trickle compared to its close neighbour. In early 2008 Abu Dhabi house prices increased at double the rate of anywhere else in the Gulf,[135] and by the end of 2008 they appeared to be holding up much better than elsewhere in the region.

Aldar Properties was the first of Abu Dhabi's new real estate companies, and its pioneering role can be compared to that of Dubai's Emaar Properties. With the Mubadala Development Corporation and the Abu Dhabi Investment Company as its two major shareholders (each with 17 percent stakes),[136] and with the managing directors of both Mubadala and the International Petroleum Investment Company sitting on its board,[137] Aldar is synonymous with the establishment, and probably accounts for over $4 billion of the sector total.[138] Thus far, it has specialized in developments aimed at Abu Dhabi nationals and other Gulf Arabs. Its first project—Raha Beach—is now close to completion, and most apartments and villas have sold for $800 per square foot.[139] Its other developments include Al-Gurm Resort—a collection of luxury chalets close to the emirate's mangrove swamps—and Coconut Island, which will consist of villas exclusively for Gulf nationals. Aldar has also ripped out the city's fire damaged old souq district and is building the enormous Central Market. This multistory complex straddling Khalifa Street will feature a shopping mall topped by luxury apartments.

The Reem Island developments are being master planned by Tamouh, Al-Reem Investments, and Sorouh. Together, the three companies have divided the island into different zones, with Tamouh's 60 percent share consisting of the City of Lights and Marina Square; with Al-Reem building Najmat village; and with Sorouh building the Al-Shams and Saraya resorts. The largest of the three—Tamouh—is owned by the Royal Group, which in turn is owned by Sheikh Tahnun bin Zayed Al-Nahyan, a younger full brother of the crown prince. Tahnun is also chairman of Al-Reem, and although Sorouh has a large number of shareholders it is nevertheless believed to be under the patronage of the ruler's two sons—Sheikhs Sultan and Muhammad bin Khalifa Al-Nahyan. Further developments on Reem by smaller companies—which should bring the island's population up to 200,000 upon completion[140]—will include Plus Properties' Skygardens project and Hydra Properties' 'Hydra-Trump Tower.' As for the latter, when asked why the tower would not simply be named after Donald Trump, as has been the case with Dubai's Trump Tower, Hydra's CEO—the aforementioned Sulayman Al-Fahim—insisted that Hydra's name needed to be alongside Trump 'because Hydra is not less than Trump.'[141] Indeed, Al-Fahim hosts the UAE's version of Donald Trump's 'Apprentice' television show: 'Hydra Executives.' He has even coined his own Trump-like catchphrase: 'impress me.'

Blessed with several small islands close to the main island, Abu Dhabi has had no need to resort to costly land reclamation (although some does take place), and over the next few years these too will be developed. Mubadala will focus on Sowwah Island, where it intends to build both commercial and residential real estate, and a new headquarters for the Abu Dhabi Securities Exchange.[142] Most of the development will be undertaken by John Buck International, a joint venture born out of Mubadala's abovementioned investment in the eponymous US property firm.[143] Most ambitiously, on nearby Nurai island a new company—Zaya—will initiate a $1 billion project comprising of only villas. Each will retail for over $25 million, and will only be reachable by private yacht or helicopter. Soon, even the giant 1000 acre manmade Lulu Island, which since its completion in 1992 has stood undeveloped off the Abu Dhabi corniche, will be built upon, with Sorouh recently having its masterplan approved.[144]

Luxury and cultural tourism

Although again secondary to the main thrust of Abu Dhabi's new economy, the emirate's tourism industry is rapidly expanding. Today there are a modest 10,000 hotel rooms available, but by 2012 it is expected there will be 25,000, and by 2030 there will be 75,000. As with the real estate sector, much of the industry will be in the hands of a few major developers, with Aldar alone planning to construct over 40 of Abu Dhabi's new hotels.[145] Moreover, Abu Dhabi is again aiming at the highest end of the market, perhaps in an effort to ensure more culturally compatible visitors to the emirate. In summer 2008 the capital's flagship hotel—the Emirates Palace—submitted itself to the *Guinness Book of Records* for offering the most expensive package holiday deal in History: $1 million for seven nights.[146] Among the biggest projects already underway are a 200 room 'eco-tourist' hotel and marina being built in the mangrove swamps, and a $3 billion 600 room MGM Grand Hotel being constructed in association with Las Vegas' MGM Mirage group.[147] Most of these new hotels will be clustered in specific areas, thereby keeping potentially unpalatable community overlaps to their minimum, and segregation will increase dramatically, with even public beaches charging fees for unaccompanied men and having exclusive areas for families and more obvious tourists.[148] Abu Dhabi clearly does not relish a repeat of Dubai's beach sex scandal of summer 2008 which resulted in two British nationals being arrested for alleged indecent conduct on a public stretch of Jumeirah beach.[149]

The big parastatals are supporting the sector by planning a wide range of cultural tourist activities, and these should help position the emirate as a distinct alternative to the more mid-market sun and shopping tourist trade of Dubai and other Gulf states. Much of the emirate's strategy has been developed by the Office of the Brand of Abu Dhabi (OBAD), which falls under the umbrella of the Abu Dhabi Tourism Authority (ADTA). The latter tends to hire well known publicity firms in the five or so countries where it has branch offices, and these in turn place advertisements in high brow publications.[150] Soon, ADTA expects to have ten additional overseas offices, and it is likely these will adopt the same tactic. The Mubadala Development Corporation is, naturally, also heavily involved. A Mubadala subsidiary,[151] the Tourism Development Investment Company (TDIC), has already organized several high profile exhibitions at the Emirates Palace. One such event—a Picasso exhibition—was thought to have brought 40,000 visitors to the capital.

Most famously, at a total cost of over $27 billion, TDIC is developing Saadiyat—'the island of happiness'—into Abu Dhabi's major cultural hub. Linked by ten bridges to the main island, by 2012 Saadiyat will be home to branches of the Louvre and Guggenheim Museums in addition to a new Sheikh Zayed National Museum, a performing arts centre, a maritime museum, and a nineteen pavilion cultural park. The Louvre Abu Dhabi will alone cost $110 million to build, and TDIC has agreed to pay a further $520 million for the Louvre brand name and the loan of various exhibitions and collections. As a further incentive, it is thought that Abu Dhabi will finance a new art research centre in Paris, pay for the restoration of Chateau Fontainbleau's theatre—to be renamed after Sheikh Khalifa bin Zayed Al-Nahyan, and provide $32 million to help the Louvre repair a wing of the Pavilion de Flore. When complete, the latter will host a new gallery of international art named after the late Sheikh Zayed bin Sultan Al-Nahyan.[152] The Guggenheim Abu Dhabi will be the sixth international branch of the renowned New York museum: to be designed by Frank Gehry, the new building will cover over 30,000 square metres and will become one of the world's largest exhibition centres.[153] Equally impressively, the building for the new national museum will be the result of an international architecture competition. It is likely to feature at least four different galleries focusing on Abu Dhabi's heritage, its environment, Zayed's leadership, and the region's economic transformation.[154]

Alongside culture and the arts, the sector will also be boosted by a series of high profile sporting events and world class leisure facilities. Building upon ADTA's staging of the world's first Formula One festival in 2007,[155] in something of a coup for Abu Dhabi the emirate will begin hosting the championship-decider Formula One Grand Prix in 2009. A circuit is being constructed on Yas Island by Aldar, and it is intended that there will be facilities to host over 100,000 spectators. Elsewhere on the island there will be other motor racing and sports-related developments totalling $40 billion, including hotels, restaurants, golf courses and a giant Ferrari theme park.[156] Building upon its described acquisition of a stake in the Italian company, Mubadala has effectively made Ferrari Abu Dhabi's 'home team,' and has cemented the relationship further by signing a three year sponsorship agreement that will see Ferrari F1 cars featuring the Mubadala logo prominently on their nosecones.[157] Bizarrely, skiing will also become possible in Abu Dhabi, with Tamouh building a giant indoor ski slope on Jebel Hafit—the United Arab Emirates' second highest mountain. Tamouh promises this development will be aimed at both leisure seekers and professionals, and will therefore escape the criticisms of gimmickry that are often levelled at Dubai's indoor slope at the Mall of the Emirates.[158] Music too features prominently in Abu Dhabi's tourism strategy. Mubadala has already staged Bon Jovi, Justin Timberlake, and Christina Aguilera concerts at the Emirates Palace and has promised several further high profile acts within the next few years. And it is thought that negotiations are in an advanced stage with leading opera and theatre companies.

Also in support of tourism, and indeed all of Abu Dhabi's new sectors—especially the new aerospace industry—has been the highly successful launch of a new international airline. Having withdrawn in 2003 from the loss-making Gulf Air partnership with Bahrain, Qatar, and Oman, Abu Dhabi unilaterally set up Etihad Airways.[159] Rather daringly the new Sheikh Ahmad bin Saif Al-Nahyan-chaired airline immediately declared itself to be the 'official national carrier of the UAE,' despite Dubai's award-winning Emirates airline being in its eighteenth year of operation. Nevertheless, Etihad has been able to prove itself very quickly, and over the last few years Ahmad has purchased several billion dollars worth of aircraft.[160] While Emirates undoubtedly stole most of 2008's headlines by taking receipt of its first A380s, Etihad was quietly placing a $43 billion order for over 200 new aircraft, including a mixture of A380s and Boeing 787 Dreamliners.[161] As the largest single order in civil aviation history, this will soon transform Etihad into one of the world's largest carriers, thereby making its growth trajectory even more impressive than Emirates and its other principal rival—Qatar Airways. Underpinning Etihad's phenomenal expansion, the Abu Dhabi government has also committed to a massive upgrade of air infrastructure, with the new Abu Dhabi Airports Company (ADAC) spearheading the redevelopment of Abu Dhabi International Airport at a cost of $6.8 billion. By 2012 two new terminals will have been added, expanding the airport's annual capacity from about 7 million to over 20 million passengers, most of whom will be tourists and transit passengers. Elsewhere in the emirate ADAC will also expand the old Al-Ayn airport and will redevelop the former military airport in Bateen to become 'City Airport': the first dedicated airport for private jets in the Middle East.[162]

5

THE TRADITIONAL MONARCHY
AN EVOLVING DYNASTY

No amount of careful planning and astute management can sustain
Abu Dhabi's economy should there be serious political instability.
Although the bloody fratricides of the nineteenth and early twentieth
centuries are unlikely to be repeated, the uncertainties of traditional
monarchy nevertheless remain, with three coups having taken place
in neighbouring emirates since 1971.[1] Should such an event take place
in Abu Dhabi its impact would be enormous: the emirate's international reputation would falter, undoubtedly denting the credibility of
its sovereign wealth funds and jeopardizing several of the new domestic sectors—especially those that rely on foreign direct investment or
sensitive technological inputs, such as the real estate and future energy
industries. Fortunately, Abu Dhabi's current rulers are in a stronger
position than any of their predecessors. Although not without its
problems, the Al-Nahyan family has evolved into a resilient and
dynamic dynasty whose leading members draw upon enormous personal resources and have successfully co-opted their historic tribal
allies and the emirate's business community into an extensive network
of distributed powers and 'tribal capitalist' positions.

Lessons from History

Abu Dhabi's political history is predominantly one of violence and
intrigue, but there have been certain periods of calm. Notably, the long

and relatively peaceful reigns of Sheikh Shakhbut bin Diab Al-Nahyan and Sheikh Zayed bin Khalifa Al-Nahyan brought much needed dynastic stability. More recently, Sheikh Zayed bin Sultan Al-Nahyan's thirty-eight year rule of Abu Dhabi and concurrent thirty-three year presidency of the United Arab Emirates provided the sheikhdom-cum-emirate with the consistency of leadership it needed to exploit fully its resources and embark upon a far reaching programme of socio-economic development. Time and again, the periods following the passing of Abu Dhabi's greatest patriarchs have witnessed upheaval, dynastic disintegration, and—often as a result—economic recession. Part of the problem has been that these long-serving rulers, in an effort to surround themselves with loyal deputies and cement tribal alliances, often sired many sons, usually from numerous wives representing differing powerful factions. As such, following the patriarch's inevitable death, future rulers have had to contend immediately with a large number of opponents, many of whom were only half brothers who had grown up in different households under different mothers. This was certainly the case for Shakhbut bin Diab's eight sons, and equally so for Zayed bin Khalifa's eight sons, many of whom were from different mothers. In both cases their fathers' deaths or depositions resulted in years of uncertainty and multiple killings within the family. Thus, for the nineteen contemporary 'bani Zayed' or sons of the late Zayed bin Sultan, there is an understandable fear that history may repeat itself, especially given that some of them have no full brothers, while others can be grouped into at least four distinct maternal blocs.

So far, trouble has been avoided, with one peaceful post-Zayed succession having already taken place and with the future ruling line seemingly established. Much of this stability can be attributed to Zayed's careful management of the dynasty during his final years. With formalized governmental, military, and economic posts to distribute to his most ambitious sons and other relatives—something which his predecessors never had the luxury of—Zayed fashioned his family into something comparable to a large political party operating within a single party system. Rival claimants, even in large numbers, could thus be kept within the network by being consoled with mini-fiefdoms and meaningful responsibilities. Favoured, popular sons who proved their abilities and demonstrated their worthiness as potential successors could then slowly be allowed to build up sufficient power-bases incorporating their less powerful siblings. Conversely, renegade sons who attempted to remove their adversaries or seize too much power would effectively be ostracized by their peers[2]—most of whom would stand to lose in the event of instability given their stakeholder status in the dynasty.

The bani Zayed

At the apex of the bani Zayed has always been Sheikh Zayed bin Sultan Al-Nahyan's eldest son: Sheikh Khalifa bin Zayed Al-Nahyan. Khalifa has been able to draw considerable legitimacy from his mother's[3] status as Zayed's first 'official wife'[4] and the purity of her Al-Nahyan bloodline: as a daughter of the kingmaker and ruler-that-never-was, Sheikh Khalifa bin Zayed bin Khalifa Al-Nahyan, her only son was to symbolize a political union between the two most powerful family lines. Now sixty-one years old, Khalifa bin Zayed has also held the important advantage of seniority over his brothers. Being Zayed's most mature son at the time of the 1966 succession meant that he was well placed to quickly gain administrative experience. He was able immediately to take over from his father to become the fifth wali of Al-Ayn,[5] and in 1969 was also put in charge of the Abu Dhabi Defence Force. In 1971 Zayed felt strong enough to install Khalifa as his crown prince—a newly devised monarchical position that seemingly guaranteed Khalifa's future succession and, within a few years, effectively made him his father's official deputy. Indeed, as chairman of the new Abu Dhabi Executive Council, Khalifa soon took over the day-to-day affairs of the emirate, thereby freeing his father to concentrate on broader regional and international issues. At the federal level, between 1971 and 1973 Khalifa was briefly the United Arab Emirates' prime minister, minister for defence, and minister for finance,[6] as his father lacked suitable candidates and Dubai had yet to be properly brought on board. Between 1973 and 1977 he then served as the federal deputy prime minister, but more significantly he was to become the deputy supreme commander of the Union Defence Force in 1978 and then later of the amalgamated

UAE Armed Forces in 1996. These long term positions, which he took very seriously,[7] gave Khalifa de facto control over all aspects of both Abu Dhabi's and the UAE's military given that his father—the supreme commander—was frequently preoccupied with other matters, and that the eventual assignment of the federal minister for defence portfolio to Dubai's Sheikh Muhammad bin Rashid Al-Maktum was largely nominal.[8] Similarly, given the limitations of the federal Ministry for Oil and Petroleum Resources, Khalifa's chairmanship of the hastily established Abu Dhabi-specific Supreme Petroleum Council also effectively gave him control over the emirate's oil policies.[9] Closely connected to oil and perhaps of even greater significance was his chairmanship of the Abu Dhabi Investments Authority, which effectively placed the emirate's surplus oil revenues and the bulk of its overseas investments within his hands. Other highly influential Khalifa positions were to include the directorship of Abu Dhabi's Department for Social Services and Commercial Buildings:[10] given that it, and more specifically its constituent 'Khalifa Committee,' were to distribute most of the government's wealth distributions to Abu Dhabi's citizens, this brought Khalifa enormous respect, gratitude, and loyalty from families and individuals. On the international stage, Khalifa's wealth-dispensing capabilities were similarly impressive, given his 1972 appointment to the chairmanship of the Abu Dhabi Fund for Development, which soon became the emirate's primary conduit for overseas aid programmes.

The second eldest of Zayed's sons—Sheikh Sultan bin Zayed Al-Nahyan—has not had the advantage of such powerful maternal relatives. His mother[11] was from a small section of the Bani Yas—the Mishaghin (Al-Masghuni)—that lived in the disputed Buraimi area.[12] Although this may have been a useful tribal alliance at the time, Zayed divorced her at an early age, and Sultan was subsequently brought up in the household of his uncle, Sheikh Hazza bin Sultan Al-Nahyan.[13] Now in his late fifties, Sultan enjoys a senior position amongst the bani Zayed, and is often regarded as having one of the most approachable personalities in the ruling family. Moreover, he is also considered to live a fairly frugal life and has had little interest in property ownership or material wealth. These character traits have endeared him to many tribal elders, with whom he has always regularly consulted. In the pursuit of power—if that was ever his intention—he has been far less successful, having repeatedly failed to maintain the positions that were conferred upon him. As mentioned above, in 1978 Sultan was controversially appointed commander-in-chief of the UDF. Despite the ensuing federal dispute, he kept his post, but suddenly lost it four years later, along with several lesser responsibilities he had accumulated. The exact reasons for his dismissal remain unclear,[14] but it is possible this was not a federal issue and that Sultan may have lost support from within Abu Dhabi. After a brief period away from Abu Dhabi he did return, but since then has remained outside of the loop. He has been something of a ceremonial deputy prime minister in the federal Council of Ministers, has chaired the politically marginal Abu Dhabi Department for Public Works,[15] and has occupied a seat in the SPC, although he has since lost the two latter positions.[16]

Although a decade younger than Khalifa and Sultan, Zayed's forty-nine year old third eldest son—Sheikh Muhammad bin Zayed Al-Nahyan—has had the advantage of full brothers, and together these men represent the most powerful bloc within the bani Zayed. Despite their mother—Sheikha Fatima bint Mubarak Al-Qitbi—being of the Ghafiri / Hanbali Bani Qitab tribe,[17] she was always considered Zayed's favourite wife and even today continues to be regarded as Abu Dhabi's 'First Lady,' with events having been held recently to honour her as 'Mother of the Nation.'[18] Muhammad spent his early years building an impressive career in the military: after graduation from Britain's Sandhurst military academy he went on to qualify as a pilot and in the late 1980s became commander of the UAE Air Force. In 1993 he was then appointed commander-in-chief of the UDF and subsequently the UAE Armed Forces,[19] thus placing him directly underneath Khalifa. Crucially, in the Gulf-wide military build up following the Kuwaiti crisis it was his signature that appeared on many of the UAE's multi-billion dollar arms procurements. In addition to taking an active role in the SPC, Muhammad also very capably oversaw Abu Dhabi's Offsets Group, which was responsible for ensuring that foreign arms contractors ploughed at least some of their revenue back into the emirate's economy.[20] Later he then supervised successfully the Dolphin gas negotiations with Qatar. Fully aware of his third son's emerging track record, obvious talent, and abundant energy, the aging Zayed took the unprecedented step of announcing Muhammad as his deputy crown prince in early 2004. This decision may have taken place as early as 1999 at a meeting in Geneva attended by members of the Al-Nahyan and Dubai's Al-Maktum rulers.[21] Regardless of the exact circumstances, Zayed had undoubtedly recognized a future ruler and had decided to find a compromise solution that would strengthen Muhammad yet protect Khalifa in equal measure.

The second eldest of the six 'bani Fatima' is the forty-six year old Sheikh Hamdan bin Zayed Al-Nahyan. In 1992, at the same time Muhammad was beginning his ascendancy, Hamdan was appointed federal minister of state for foreign affairs. Although this officially made him the deputy of the Ajmani-origin minister for foreign affairs, Rashid Abdullah Al-Nuami, the latter was not a member of Ajman's ruling Al-Nuami family and Hamdan was considered to be second only to his father in formulating the UAE's foreign policy. Increasing his standing even further, both domestically and internationally, he also became chairman of the UAE's Red Crescent Society—one of the largest and most generous charitable organizations in the Middle East. The third bani Fatima, forty-four at the time of writing, is Sheikh Hazza bin Zayed Al-Nahyan. After following Muhammad into the military he became a general in 1996—at the age of just thirty-one—and for some time afterwards served as the chief of Abu Dhabi's Security and Intelligence Services, thereby providing the bloc with access to another important powerbase in the emirate. The younger three of these full brothers have been no less influential, and made similarly rapid progress in their careers. Sheikh Tahnun bin Zayed Al-Nahyan, now approaching forty, served as the director of the ruler's private department. This gave him direct access to his father and made him a primary interface to the core of power. Sheikh Mansur bin Zayed Al-Nahyan, now thirty-nine, became chairman of the International Petroleum Investments Company in 1994, and then took over the well funded ADFD from Khalifa. Significantly, in 2001 his father created a new federal cabinet position for Mansur: minister of state for the Presidential Office. This effectively made him the federal-level interface for Zayed.[22] Sheikh Abdullah bin Zayed Al-Nahyan, now thirty-six years old, has enjoyed a similarly meteoric rise to power: in 1995, at age twenty-two he was made undersecretary to the federal minister for information and culture,[23] and soon after he became the actual minister. Among other responsibilities, this position gave him control over domestic media output and the censorship of imported foreign media.

The second most powerful bloc within the bani Zayed are the five sons of Sheikha Mouza bint Suhail Al-Khaili from the influential Al-Bu Khail section of the Manasir tribe, which has historically been the closest of the Al-Nahyan's allies. The eldest of these 'bani Mouza' is Sheikh Saif bin Zayed Al-Nahyan. Now forty-one, he began his career in the military, rising to the rank of lieutenant general before rising to head the Abu Dhabi police force in 1995. Afterwards he joined the federal cabinet with the vital portfolio of minister for the interior, thus making him one of the most powerful figures in the UAE. Two of his younger full brothers have also gained key responsibilities, with Sheikh Ahmad bin Zayed Al-Nahyan, now forty, having recently been made chairman of ADIA. Although Khalifa may still indirectly maintain control of ADIA, the position has nevertheless conferred on Ahmad the daily supervision of the world's largest sovereign wealth fund. Ahmad also serves as chairman of the Zayed Foundation for Charity and Humanitarian Works: although incomparable to Hamdan's UAE Red Crescent Society this is nonetheless another key wealth distribution position. Sheikh Hamad bin Zayed Al-Nahyan—now in his late thirties—became a member of the Abu Dhabi Executive Council and held the chairmanship of the Abu Dhabi Department for Economy and Planning, and although he lost the latter of these positions in 2006 he was effectively promoted, as he soon became the director of the crown prince's department—an entity which, as will be shown, is now one of the most powerful in the emirate. The most junior of the bani Mouza have yet to find their place within the establishment, but their situation is likely to improve rapidly, with Sheikh Omar bin Zayed Al-Nahyan—now thirty-six— already serving as the president's aide-de-camp, and with Sheikh Khalid bin Zayed Al-Nahyan—now thirty-one—having completed his postgraduate studies at a British university.[24]

The third grouping of full brothers within the bani Zayed are on average a little older than the bani Mouza, but overall are less powerful. They are the four sons of Sheikha Aisha bint Ali Al-Darmaki from the Daramikah section of the Dhawahir[25]—another of the Al-Nahyan's oldest tribal allies. The most senior of the 'bani Aisha' is the forty-four year old Sheikh Said bin Zayed Al-Nahyan. As chairman of the Abu Dhabi Seaports Authority and as a member of the all-important Abu Dhabi Executive Council he is not without influence, even though he may not control bani Fatima or bani Mouza-strength portfolios. His younger full brothers are Sheikhs Nahyan, Falah, and Diab bin Zayed Al-Nahyan. Respectively they are now forty-one, thirty-nine, and thirty-eight. Of the three, only Diab has gained significant responsibilities, having assumed a director level position in his father's court in 1996 and then later becoming both the director of the presidential court, a member of the Abu Dhabi Executive Council, and chairman of the Abu Dhabi Water and Electricity Authority, which now has a controlling stake in the Abu Dhabi National Energy Company.

The fourth and smallest of the bani Zayed blocs consists of the two sons of Sheikha Amna bint Salah Al-Badi from the Badawi section of the Dhawahir.[26] The eldest of the 'bani Amna'—Sheikh Isa bin Zayed Al-Nahyan—is now forty-three and has held a director level position in his father's court in addition to building up a small real estate company, Pearl Properties. The youngest, Sheikh Nasser bin Zayed Al-Nahyan, used to be a commander in the ruler's bodyguard and would now be forty years old, but died tragically in a helicopter accident off the coast of Abu Dhabi in summer 2008.[27]

Sheikh Khalifa's succession and the future of the bani Fatima

Since the late 1990s there had been frequent rumours that Sheikh Zayed bin Sultan Al-Nahyan was seriously ill, often fuelled by the expatriate medical community and exacerbated by the tightly controlled flow of information from those close to the ruler. However, although undoubtedly declining in health, Abu Dhabi was blessed with Zayed's leadership for several more years and it was not until late 2004—aged eighty-six—that he passed away. Understandably many in Abu Dhabi and across the federation were concerned, not least because earlier on in the day that Zayed's death was announced a cabinet reshuffle had taken place, supposedly following Zayed's instructions, although without any of the usual photographic evidence.[28] Moreover, many were anxious given the timing of these events, as the announcement also coincided with the eve of the US presidential elections, thus burying the story in the international media. The announcement also came very shortly before the end of Ramadan, thereby allowing the government to roll their seven day public holiday for Zayed's mourning into the Eid al-Fitr holidays. This provided the Al-Nahyan family with over two weeks of breathing space before Abu Dhabi returned to life.

Although uninformed observers predicted instability and a lack of consensus among the bani Zayed, their father's balance of portfolios and compromise solutions nevertheless held firm. Sheikh Khalifa bin Zayed Al-Nahyan, as crown prince since 1971, was swiftly installed as Abu Dhabi's eighteenth ruler, and Sheikh Muhammad bin Zayed Al-Nahyan, as deputy crown prince since the year before, was upgraded to crown prince. At the federal level, the succession was similarly smooth, with Dubai's ruler and the United Arab Emirates' vice president—Sheikh Maktum bin Rashid Al-Maktum, who been serving as a caretaker president for the week following Zayed's death, quickly handing over the position to Khalifa. This supposedly followed a unanimous decision from the five other members of the Supreme Council of Rulers that Abu Dhabi should remain at the helm of the federation. In addition to becoming crown prince, Muhammad was further accommodated by being elevated from commander-in-chief of the UAE Armed Forces to deputy supreme commander, as Khalifa had assumed his father's old title of supreme commander. Perhaps most significantly, Muhammad also assumed Khalifa's former position as chairman of the Abu Dhabi Executive Council, thereby making him the new de facto prime minister of the emirate.

It is inevitable that new rulers will try to secure the future succession of their own sons. Although in Khalifa's case this would have meant deviating from his father's 2004 compromise, there is some evidence that he set about installing checks on Muhammad's new powerbase and promoting the ambitions of his two sons—both of whom had administrative experience, military backgrounds, and postgraduate education. Sheikh Sultan bin Khalifa Al-Nahyan—who had already been serving on the Abu Dhabi Executive Council—was immediately reappointed and was joined by his brother, Sheikh Muhammad bin Khalifa Al-Nahyan. Furthermore, Khalifa appointed two of his non-bani Fatima brothers,[29] both of whom are believed to be close to him, and slimmed the Council down from 17 members to just 11. Similarly, Khalifa may have aimed to balance Muhammad bin Zayed's new status in the UAE Armed Forces by appointing one of his allies from the Rumaithat section of the Bani Yas—Hamad bin Muhammad Al-Thai Al-Rumaithi, the former director of military intelligence[30]—to the vacant position of commander-in-chief.[31] This was an unusual choice given that the post had most often been occupied by a member of the Al-Nahyan. Since 2004 Khalifa bin Zayed has also consolidated his control over the 'old economy' by retaining his chairmanship of the Supreme Petroleum Council and by appointing another of his non-bani Fatima brothers—Sheikh Ahmad bin Zayed Al-Nahyan—as his successor to the chairmanship of the Abu Dhabi Investments Authority.

Nonetheless, there is now no doubt that Muhammad bin Zayed will succeed when Khalifa's reign ends. Apart from his control of the Sorouh property company, Sultan bin Khalifa has gained no further portfolios while Muhammad bin Khalifa has only acquired the chairmanship of the Abu Dhabi Department for Finance. In contrast, over the last three years Muhammad bin Zayed has enormously increased his powers, has surrounded himself by key allies, and has assumed leadership of Abu Dhabi's 'new economy.' In early 2007 his position as crown prince was strengthened further as more executive powers were transferred to his office. As another indication of his rising status, he has appointed one of his full brothers, Sheikh Tahnun bin Zayed Al-Nahyan, to the Abu Dhabi Executive Council, and has expanded its membership to nineteen members, thereby further diluting the influence of Khalifa's two sons. Most significantly, Muhammad's aforementioned Mubadala Development Corporation and all of its subsidiaries have effectively provided him with a free rein in determining the trajectory of Abu Dhabi's domestic economic development, have brought him close to the majority of the emirate's non-ruling business elite, and have allowed him to forge close bonds with reputable international partners. Although far from the usual remit of the crown prince or the chairman of the Abu Dhabi Executive Council, Muhammad has now begun to lead overseas delegations to meet foreign heads of states, including a visit to Camp David in June 2008. Soon he will also publish a book entitled *Sheikh Muhammad bin Zayed Al-Nahyan: The Era of Prosperity and Excellence*.[32] In a move not dissimilar from Sheikh Muhammad bin Rashid Al-Maktum's book *My Vision: Challenges in the Race for Excellence*—which was published shortly before Muhammad bin Rashid became ruler of Dubai—Muhammad bin Zayeds's volume will outline his vision for Abu Dhabi and include choice quotes and documents detailing his key decisions as chairman of the Abu Dhabi Executive Council.

The real question is, who will become Muhammad's crown prince when he succeeds, and, in the interests of future stability, will a deputy crown prince position be assigned once again? Following on from a great patriarch's first successor also poses problems, as subsequent rulers will rarely have mature or powerful enough sons who can assume hegemony over their many uncles. Thus, with the Khalifa line effectively finished, it really depends on how soon Muhammad will succeed. Neither of his eldest sons—Sheikhs Khalid and Hamdan bin Muhammad Al-Nahyan—are senior enough to be appointed deputy crown prince, although the former has recently enjoyed a high profile marriage that may significantly boost his status.[33] As such, if Muhammad were to become ruler within the next few years, it is likely that a younger member of the bani Fatima would be well placed to become crown prince. Unsurprisingly, in recent years there has been considerable jostling within the bloc. Muhammad's eldest full brother, Hamdan bin Zayed, has effectively lost control over federal foreign policy, having been reassigned to a deputy prime minister position in the Council of Ministers.[34] This is a less influential posting, and it is telling that the position of federal minister for foreign affairs was entrusted instead to the youngest of the bani Fatima: Sheikh Abdullah bin Zayed Al-Nahyan. Alongside Abdullah, another potential crown prince is Sheikh Mansur bin Zayed Al-Nahyan. His former federal minister of state position has been upgraded to full ministerial status, he now sits on the Supreme Petroleum Council, he is chairman of First Gulf Bank,[35] and—as mentioned earlier—he has recently gained control over a number of new sovereign wealth funds in addition to his ongoing chairmanship of IPIC and ADFD.[36] Indeed, in the increasingly lucrative world of Abu Dhabi overseas investments his influence is now perhaps second only to the Ahmad / Khalifa

ADIA alliance. In 2004 he also married a daughter[37] of Muhammad bin Rashid, thus making the ruler of Dubai his father-in-law. However, Mansur's personal involvement in the acquisition of Manchester City and his stake in Barclays Bank[38] may have been steps too far and could eventually count against him. The latter investment reportedly involved his private wealth: previously no senior members of UAE ruling families have revealed the extent of their individual fortunes due to obvious political sensitivities. Nevertheless, should both Abdullah and Mansur emerge as potential candidates, much may depend on the allegiances of the two other bani Fatima. Sheikh Hazza bin Zayed Al-Nahyan became Abu Dhabi's National Security Advisor in 2006 while Tahnun, in addition to his new position on the Abu Dhabi Executive Council, has now been placed in charge of the royal air wing—a vital position of trust—and, courtesy of his aforementioned Tamouh and Al-Reem Investments property companies he has become a major stakeholder in the new economy.

Outside the bani Zayed: what remains of the Al-Nahyan

With the bani Zayed and, more specifically, the constituent bani Fatima, now occupying most of the key decision-making positions at both the emirate-level and in Abu Dhabi's contingent in the federal government, it would seem there is little room left for members of other branches of the Al-Nahyan family. Moreover, as Sheikh Zayed bin Sultan Al-Nahyan's grandsons—of which there could eventually be over 100—reach maturity, the situation will become more marked, with members of distaff lineages only ever able to aspire to second or third tier positions. There are, however, certain family lines that may prove to be exceptions. And due to a combination of historical circumstances, proven loyalties, and—one would hope—bureaucratic competence, there will remain a few non-bani Zayed within the highest ranks of the establishment. Should either of these groups begin to be squeezed out of place as their numbers dwindle, this may become a significant source of tension within the dynasty which—if mismanaged—could spiral into resentment towards the 'ruling faction' from the extended Al-Nahyan family and their tribal allies.

Fortunately for the bani Zayed, they have only a small number of first cousins. Much like the two great patriarchs before him,[39] Sheikh

Zayed bin Sultan Al-Nahyan had very few brothers. The eldest of these—former ruler Sheikh Shakhbut bin Sultan Al-Nahyan—was exiled and his two sons died in their youth, leaving behind only one son each. While the elder of Shakhbut's two grandsons—Sheikh Tahnun bin Said Al-Nahyan—married one of Zayed's daughters,[40] and while the younger—Sheikh Khalifa bin Sultan Al-Nahyan—secured a position in the ministry for foreign affairs, they have never advanced further in the establishment. The second of Zayed's older brothers— Sheikh Hazza bin Sultan Al-Nahyan—had died in 1958 leaving no sons, while the third—Sheikh Khalid bin Sultan Al-Nahyan—had only one son, Sheikh Muhammad bin Khalid Al-Nahyan. Although Zayed initially appointed Muhammad as his deputy finance advisor in the late 1960s, the latter had lost this position by the early 1970s[41] and he and his three eldest sons instead concentrated on building up their various businesses, most of which were based in their district of the city: Khalidya. Muhammad's youngest son—Sheikh Abdullah bin Muhammad Al-Nahyan—would now seem to have become prominent in the western region, having recently awarded prizes at festivals and having cut ribbons at other events.[42]

Many of the other Al-Nahyan lines, most of which date from the upheavals of the 1920s, have been similarly inconsequential. Neither Sheikh Tahnun bin Zayed bin Khalifa Al-Nahyan nor Sheikh Said bin Zayed bin Khalifa Al-Nahyan had any sons, while Sheikh Hamdan bin Zayed bin Khalifa Al-Nahyan's only son[43] in turn had only one son—Sheikh Muhammad bin Hamdan Al-Nahyan—who has never gained a key portfolio. Of Sheikh Saqr bin Zayed bin Khalifa Al-Nahyan's offspring, their aforementioned exile in Saudi Arabia eventually came to an end and they returned to become merchants in Sharjah.[44] Of Saqr's grandchildren today, only Sheikh Abdullah bin Zayed Al-Nahyan—the third son of Saqr's third son—appears to have any serious influence: his appointments as UAE ambassador to the US in 1989 and then to Spain in 1992[45] would seem to have been based on merit.

The bani Muhammad bin Khalifa

The sons and grandsons of Sheikh Muhammad bin Khalifa Al-Nahyan—the only son of the great kingmaker Sheikh Khalifa bin

Zayed Al-Nahyan, who was responsible for switching the ruling line from Sheikh Saqr bin Zayed Al-Nahyan to the sons of Sheikh Sultan bin Zayed Al-Nahyan—have proved to be an exception. They have remained extremely powerful and continue to be the second most influential branch of the Al-Nahyan after the bani Zayed. Given that Sheikh Zayed bin Sultan Al-Nahyan relied on the administrative support of Muhammad and his sons so heavily during the early years of his reign, and given that there have since been numerous marriages—at least ten[46]—between the bani Zayed and the bani Muhammad bin Khalifa, some observers are keen to dismiss the notion that the latter represents a separate faction within the Al-Nahyan. Yet as the bani Zayed have matured the bani Muhammad bin Khalifa have lost most of their original portfolios. The political culture of Abu Dhabi is increasingly such that wives, with few exceptions, tend to become full members of whichever bloc they marry into.

The eldest of Muhammad's sons—Sheikh Hamdan bin Muhammad Al-Nahyan—was a vocal supporter of Zayed's succession in 1966 and served as wali of Das Island for the remainder of the 1960s. This was a key position as Das represented the centre of Abu Dhabi's new offshore oil industry. It is thought that during the first five years of Zayed's reign Hamdan might have been appointed crown prince out of deference to his father and grandfather.[47] Although this never happened, Hamdan was nevertheless brought back to the capital to chair the new Abu Dhabi Department for Public Works,[48] and in 1973 he was appointed federal minister for public works. His most significant position was as federal deputy prime minister during the late 1970s and early 1980s, where he played an instrumental role during the 1979 constitutional crisis, serving as the chairman of Zayed's committee charged with discussing the future of the federation.[49]

The second eldest of the bani Muhammad bin Khalifa—Sheikh Mubarak bin Muhammad Al-Nahyan—was similarly influential. After his initial appointment as Zayed's first chief of police he later went on to be federal minister for the interior. The third, Sheikh Tahnun bin Muhammad Al-Nahyan, took over as wali of Al-Ayn and as the ruler's representative for the entire 'eastern region' in 1970.[50] Throughout the 1970s and 1980s he accumulated several other key positions including the deputy chairmanship of the Abu Dhabi

Executive Council, membership of the Supreme Petroleum Council, board positions at the Abu Dhabi Investments Authority and the Abu Dhabi Fund for Development, and, most notably, chairmanship of the Abu Dhabi National Oil Company. The fourth of the sons, Sheikh Saif bin Muhammad Al-Nahyan served as both the chairman of the Abu Dhabi Department for Planning and as federal minister for health during the 1970s.[51] The fifth and seventh of the bani Muhammad bin Khalifa—Sheikhs Khalifa and Said bin Muhammad Al-Nahyan respectively—never rose to prominence. But the sixth, Sheikh Surur bin Muhammad Al-Nahyan, soon emerged as a major figure in both the emirate-level and federal governments. As described, he was the first chairman of the Abu Dhabi Department for Justice until it was absorbed into a federal ministry in 1972. He then assumed director level positions in both ADNOC and ADIA, became the deputy chairman of the ADFD, and was a member of the Abu Dhabi Executive Council and the Supreme Petroleum Council. In addition he was chamberlain of the presidential court, and at one point was even governor of the UAE Central Bank.[52] In 1988 an independent observer noted that Surur was probably the most energetic and talented of the Al-Nahyan, and that he was a possible future crown prince to Sheikh Khalifa bin Zayed Al-Nahyan.[53]

Alongside their fathers, some of the more mature sons of the bani Muhammad bin Khalifa also rose to prominence. Hamdan's eldest son—Sheikh Khalifa bin Hamdan Al-Nahyan—became chairman of the Abu Dhabi Department for the Economy and was a member of the Abu Dhabi Executive Council. His other sons included Sheikh Sultan bin Hamdan Al-Nahyan—who became chairman of protocol at the presidential guest house; and Sheikh Hamad bin Hamdan Al-Nahyan—who became a successful businessman and has since been nicknamed 'the rainbow sheikh,' given his fleet of multicoloured cars. At an early age Mubarak's second eldest son[54]—Sheikh Nahyan bin Mubarak Al-Nahyan—became minister for higher education and accumulated a number of other education-related positions including the presidency of the UAE's first university: the United Arab Emirates University of Al-Ayn. Mubarak's third son, Sheikh Hamdan bin Mubarak Al-Nahyan was similarly influential, and at one point was chairman of the Abu Dhabi Department for Civil Aviation, chairman of Gulf Air, and a member of the Abu Dhabi Executive Council. Tahnun's eldest son—Sheikh Said bin Tahnun Al-Nahyan—sat on the Abu Dhabi Executive Council in the 1990s and was also chairman of the Abu Dhabi Basic Industries Corporation.

Following the death of their patriarch in 1979, the bani Muhammad bin Khalifa's share of powerful positions has steadily declined. This process was accelerated by a tragic car accident that incapacitated Mubarak, and then the death of their eldest member, Hamdan, in 1989. In the 1990s most of their portfolios were reassigned to either Zayed's older sons, who were entering their 20s and 30s, or to close allies of the bani Zayed from outside of the Al-Nahyan family. Hamdan's federal deputy prime minister position has now been split into two bani Zayed posts,[55] while Tahnun has lost both his membership of the Abu Dhabi Executive Council and his chairmanship of ADNOC.[56] Mubarak's erstwhile control over the ministry for the interior has now also shifted to the bani Zayed,[57] while more recently Khalifa bin Hamdan has lost his Abu Dhabi Executive Council membership, and his chairmanship of the Department for the Economy was ceded to Sheikh Hamad bin Zayed Al-Nahyan. Said bin Tahnun has also lost his Abu Dhabi Executive Council membership. The most notable changes have affected Surur. Although he was to later become the chairman of the Abu Dhabi Water and Electricity Authority,[58] and remains the chamberlain of the presidential court, these are politically less significant postings compared to his former Abu Dhabi Executive Council membership and governorship of the UAE Central Bank. Today he is primarily a businessman, having been responsible for building the Abu Dhabi Mall complex and the current Etihad Towers project near to the palace district.

When Khalifa bin Zayed succeeded in 2004 there was some hope that the bani Muhammad bin Khalifa would be rehabilitated within the establishment, as they could perhaps provide Khalifa with a natural counterweight to the bani Fatima. Indeed, of the bani Zayed he was considered to be their strongest ally, having chosen to marry all six of his daughters and the eldest of his sons into the bani Muhammad bin Khalifa.[59] This optimism has been maintained given that Nahyan bin Mubarak has held onto his position as federal minister for higher education despite widespread criticism of the ministry's performance. Furthermore, Hamdan bin Mubarak has now joined his older brother in the Council of Ministers as the federal minister for public works and housing,[60] and their youngest uncle—Sheikh Said bin Muhammad Al-Nahyan—now holds a senior position in the federal minister for the interior.[61] Other hopeful signs have been the assignment of the chairmanship of Etihad Airways and a position on the Abu Dhabi Executive Council to Saif's eldest son—Sheikh Ahmad bin Saif Al-Nahyan. Tahnun's fourth eldest son, Sheikh Sultan bin Tahnun Al-Nahyan, has benefited from a position on the Abu Dhabi Executive Council and the multiple chairmanships of the Abu Dhabi Tourism Authority, the Tourism Development and Investment Company, and the Abu Dhabi National Exhibitions Company. Sultan bin Tahnun and Ahmad bin Saif are now really the only rising stars within the bani Muhammad bin Khalifa, and the relative weight of their positions does not compare with those of their fathers' generation. Perhaps the strongest indication of their lineage's subordinate role to the bani Zayed is that their members can only carry the title of 'His Excellency—HE,' despite being bona fide members of the ruling Al-Nahyan family. This effectively places the bani Muhammad bin Khalifa on a par with several other non-Nahyan families and tribal sections who are also entitled to carry the HE prefix. Indeed, only the bani Zayed and their offspring are eligible to carry the 'His Highness—HH' title.

Nevertheless, as History turns full circle there may yet be a glimmer of hope for the bani Muhammad bin Khalifa: with the crown prince now needing to strengthen the positions of his own sons *vis-à-vis* his brothers, the distaff branch of the family may become useful allies once more. Certainly, with Sheikh Khalid bin Muhammad Al-Nahyan's December 2008 marriage to one of Surur's daughters, preceded by a massive 2,000–guest banquet at the Emirates Palace,[62] it is likely that Sheikh Muhammad bin Zayed Al-Nahyan will expect long term support from his son's father-in-law and perhaps the extended bani Muhammad bin Khalifa.

Old alliances and tribal capitalism

As the Al-Nahyan family continues to expand, Sheikhs Khalifa and Muhammad bin Zayed Al-Nahyan will continue to have more than enough candidates to fill key decision-making positions in both the emirate-level and federal governments. As with their father and indeed all previous rulers of Abu Dhabi stretching back into the eighteenth century, it remains imperative that positions are also distributed to representatives of those other Bani Yas sections and tribes that have been historically supportive of the Al-Nahyan. As will be discussed in the following chapter, the rulers of Abu Dhabi continue to draw great legitimacy from their roles as tribal leaders rooted in the history and culture of the lower Gulf, and thus many powerful government and military portfolios remain in the hands of the non-ruling tribal elites. The advent of the new multi-sector economy and all of its constituent new parastatals and joint ventures, means that there is a superfluity of fresh opportunities for this elite's inclusion in the establishment. Consequently, centuries-old alliances are being incorporated into a present-day system of 'tribal capitalism' by providing the latest generation of Al-Nahyan sheikhs with the loyal captains of industry and malleable middlemen they need to administer the dozens of entities that are propelling forward Abu Dhabi's ambitious strategic plans.

There is a well defined hierarchy in place and several clearly identifiable circles of power in the emirate. Although there are some notable exceptions in which educated or otherwise talented members of long ago naturalized merchant families have risen to prominence, Abu Dhabi's national population is overwhelmingly tribal, as the sheikhdom never experienced a large influx of foreigners as per Dubai, Sharjah, and other nearby settlements. Today, the most senior of Abu Dhabi's tribal families tend to be those from other Bani Yas sections—especially those that fought alongside the Al-Nahyan's parent Al-Bu Falah section, and less often those that had earlier rebelled or emigrated, such as the Al-Bu Falasah. Alongside these Bani Yas sections are those tribes that historically cohabited the Al-Nahyan's original bases in Liwa and Buraimi. And in particular those—such as the Manasir and the Dhawahir—that are of the same Hinawi faction and Maliki school of Sunni Islam as the Bani Yas. Conversely, those tribes of the rival Ghafiri faction and Hanbali school, or those that earlier embraced Wahhabism, accepted Saudi bribes, or joined alliances against Al-Nahyan rulers are most often underrepresented in the contemporary establishment, even if their respective quarrels were concluded decades or centuries ago.

The Bani Yas are best understood as being a rather loose tribal federation. Some of the thirty or so sections of the tribe even consider themselves to be independent tribes, especially when they are dwelling in other, non-Bani Yas dominated emirates. Perhaps the most influential of these section-cum-tribes in Abu Dhabi is the Suwdan (Al-Suwaidi). With no connection to the eponymous African state, the section traces its lineage to a Yemeni sheikh called Suwad Al-Kindi[63] and has long enjoyed the confidence of the Al-Nahyan. Without doubt, this link strengthened following the succession of Sheikh Zayed bin Khalifa Al-Nahyan, whose mother was from the Suwdan, and his attempts to install the Suwdan chief as his representative in distant outposts in the late nineteenth century.[64] Under Sheikh Zayed bin Sultan Al-Nahyan, Ahmad bin Khalifa Al-Suwaidi enjoyed great status as Abu Dhabi's first advisor on foreign relations, and then went on to become the deputy chairman of the Abu Dhabi Investments Authority and the federal minister for presidential affairs. Similarly, Zayed's other key Suwdan advisor, Muhammad bin Habrush Al-Suwaidi, advanced from his original portfolio as finance advisor to become a member of the Abu Dhabi Executive Council, a member of the Supreme Petroleum Council, and a director within the Abu Dhabi Investments Authority. Throughout the 1980s and 1990s several more of the Suwdan assumed key positions, with Abdullah bin Nasser Al-Suwaidi being appointed chairman of the Abu Dhabi Gas Liquefaction Company; with Rashid bin Saif Al-Suwaidi serving as a director within the Abu Dhabi National Oil Company; with Muhammad bin Musbah Al-Suwaidi being appointed ambassador to Italy; and with Hassan bin Muhammad Al-Suwaidi being appointed ambassador to the Philippines. Today, the Suwdan's influence is equally strong, with two positions on the Abu Dhabi Executive Council—an equal contingent to the bani Muhammad bin Khalifa. The more senior of these, Nasser bin Ahmad Al-Suwaidi, is also the chairman of the Abu Dhabi Department for Planning and the Economy, having taken over the position from Sheikh Hamad bin Zayed Al-Nahyan in 2006. He also serves as the deputy chairman of the Abu Dhabi Investment Company. The other Suwdan Abu Dhabi Executive

Council member is Hamad bin Muhammad Al-Hurr Al-Suwaidi, who is also the undersecretary to Sheikh Muhammad bin Khalifa Al-Nahyan at the Abu Dhabi Department for Finance and is the chair-man of the Abu Dhabi National Energy Company. Other powerful members of the Suwdan include Khalifa bin Muhammad Al-Kindi who is the chairman of ADIC—thereby ensuring that the Suwdan occupy the two top positions in Abu Dhabi's second largest sovereign wealth managing institution—and Muhammad bin Sultan Al-Suwaidi, the UAE's ambassador to Lebanon. Jamal bin Sanad Al-Suwaidi remains the director general of the Emirates Centre for Strategic Studies and Research—a think tank now under the umbrella of the federal ministry for foreign affairs; and Sultan bin Nasser Al-Suwaidi has held onto his governorship of the UAE Central Bank,[65] in addition to director level positions in both ADIA and ADIC.

The Mazari (Al-Mazrui) is the second most influential and probably the most populous of the Bani Yas sections. Although originally thought to be part of a separate Ghafiri faction and Hanbali school tribe, it would seem that the Mazari of Abu Dhabi conform to the Maliki school.[66] They provided many tribesmen to fight for Zayed bin Khalifa against Wahhabi incursions in the nineteenth century and, although some disgruntled members left Abu Dhabi in the 1950s, many remained and continued to play an important role in securing the interior, often employed as guards by the oil exploration companies.[67] Up until 1955 Ahmad bin Fadhil Al-Mazrui was even Shakhbut bin Sultan's wali for Liwa and the entire oil-rich western region.[68] From the 1960s to the 1990s the Mazari, like the Suwdan, occupied many important portfolios in the emirate and in some cases even at the federal level. Most notably, Yousef bin Omar Al-Mazrui was the federal minister for petroleum until 1994, when he moved to the more powerful Supreme Petroleum Council. Similarly powerful, Ghaim bin Faris Al-Mazrui was secretary general of ADIA and held a director level position in the ruler's private department. Other influential Mazari men during this period included Suhail bin Faris Al-Mazrui, the director general of ADNOC and chairman of the Abu Dhabi Marine Areas Company; Rashid bin Muhammad Al-Mazrui and Ahmad bin Khalaf Al-Mazrui[69]—both members of the Federal National Council; and Khalid bin Abdullah Al-Aynayn of the Al-Bu

Aynayn section of the Mazari, who served as the air force advisor to the UAE Armed Forces. At present, the Mazari remain prominent, with even the ruler's wife being of the section. Yousef bin Omar is now the chairman of ADNOC, Ahmad bin Mubarak Al-Mazrui is a member of the Abu Dhabi Executive Council and chairman of the Abu Dhabi Health Authority, Khalifa bin Muhammad Al-Mazrui is chairman of the rapidly expanding Abu Dhabi Airports Company, Muhammad bin Khalaf Al-Mazrui is director general of the new Abu Dhabi Authority for Culture and Heritage, and Muhammad bin Hamad Al-Mazrui is director general of the western region development council. Perhaps most influential—and especially in the emirate's new economy—is Muhammad bin Saif Al-Mazrui, who sits on the boards of both the Mubadala Development Corporation and the Tourism Development Investment Company.

Also in control of a significant number of positions is the Qubaisat (Al-Qubaisi) section of the Bani Yas. Despite their breakaway attempts and Wahhabi overtures during the nineteenth century, the Qubaisat was eventually re-integrated into the sheikhdom and became perhaps the section most heavily involved in the pearling industry, thus making its members amongst the wealthiest of Abu Dhabi's residents. From the late 1920s and onwards they became a key part of the establishment, assisted by Sheikh Sultan bin Zayed Al-Nahyan's influential Qubaisat wife,[70] who was also Zayed bin Sultan's mother. Prominent Qubaisat under Zayed included Musallam bin Said Al-Qubaisi, a member of the Abu Dhabi Executive Council; Said bin Khalfan Al-Ghayth, who was a former federal minister of state for cabinet affairs; Sayah bin Muhammad Al-Qubaisi, who was an undersecretary at the federal ministry for electricity and water; and Buti bin Salim Al-Qubaisi, who was a former director of the department for civil defence. Current high profile Qubaisat are Muhammad bin Buti Al-Hamad, who remains the ruler's representative for Liwa and the western region (and therefore the only non-Nahyan wali in the emirate), and who was also a former member of the Abu Dhabi Executive Council and a former chairman of the Abu Dhabi Municipality. Equally, if not more, influential would be Khadem bin Abdullah Al-Qubaisi, who is currently managing director of the International Petroleum Investment Company and used to be vice chairman of Borealis—the petrochemicals giant.

The Al-Bu Mahair (Al-Muhairi) section of the Bani Yas, although more populous in other emirates, notably Sharjah, has also risen to prominence in Abu Dhabi. Under Zayed they were assigned high status positions in the military, including Muhammad bin Khalfan Al-Muhairi who was appointed commander of the UAE Navy and assigned several positions in military intelligence. On occasion the Al-Bu Mahair also held positions on the Abu Dhabi Executive Council and director level portfolios in the federal ministry for petroleum, in ADNOC, and in Abu Dhabi Commercial Bank. Today the section's most notable members include Waleed bin Ahmad Al-Mokarrab Al-Muhairi, the aforementioned CEO of Mubadala; and Mubarak bin Hamad Al-Muhairi, the director general of the Abu Dhabi Tourism Authority.

The similarly named, but distinctly separate, Mahiribah (Al-Muhairbi) section of the Bani Yas is somewhat comparable in status with the Al-Bu Mahair. Originating from Liwa, the Mahiribah famously provided Zayed bin Khalifa with one of his most trusted army commanders—Suwaidan bin Zaal Al-Muhairbi[71]—and most of the section resides in the western region today. Under Zayed bin Sultan they accumulated many positions including Khalfan bin Ghayth Al-Muhairbi's membership of the Abu Dhabi Executive Council and Hajji bin Abdullah Al-Muhairbi's presidency of the Abu Dhabi Chamber of Commerce and brief tenure as speaker of the Federal National Council. Other Mahiribah positions have included a director level portfolio in the federal ministry for petroleum,[72] membership of the Federal National Council,[73] and various administrative posts in the military.

The Hawamil (Al-Hamili) section of the Bani Yas now makes up the majority of Liwa's population, but has also held key positions in both the capital and in the eastern region. Abdullah bin Ghanim Al-Hamili temporarily served as the wali of Buraimi after the death of the Dhawahir wali in 1936. Under Zayed bin Sultan they continued to prosper, gaining several high-ranking positions in the military, including both commander and deputy commander of the UAE Air Force,[74] and director of battle operations. In government, Saif bin Ahmad Al-Hamili became a member of the Abu Dhabi Executive Council while Shiba bin Said Al-Hamili was undersecretary in the federal ministry for petroleum. Other Hawamil positions have included director level portfolios in Abu Dhabi Television,[75] the department for civil aviation,[76] and the federal ministries for education and information. In 2008 they gained their first ministerial position in the federal government when Muhammad bin Dhayn Al-Hamili was appointed minister for energy.

Despite part of their section having broken away from Abu Dhabi and moved to Dubai in the 1830s, the Rumaithat (Al-Rumaithi) have been similarly influential in the military. During Zayed bin Sultan's reign the section held director level positions in the ruler's bodyguard unit,[77] in military intelligence, and in the office of the commander-in-chief of the UAE Armed Forces.[78] In the early 1990s a Rumaithat was even Abu Dhabi's chief of police.[79] In the federal government, the section has also been quite well represented, with high status portfolios in the president's office[80] and in the ministry for the interior.[81] At present, the Rumaithat's military tradition is stronger than ever, with the aforementioned Hamad bin Muhammad Al-Thai Al-Rumaithi now serving as commander-in-chief and therefore Muhammad bin Zayed's deputy in the UAE Armed Forces.

Smaller sections of the Bani Yas that also have influence include the Marar (Al-Murur). Although originally based in Liwa they were one of the first sections to move to the new town of Abu Dhabi in the early nineteenth century. Many left the sheikhdom under Sheikh Shakhbut bin Sultan Al-Nahyan's rule, but in the mid-1960s most returned, and their leader, Mani bin Otaibah Al-Murur, went on to become one of Zayed's chief advisors during the early years of his reign. Since then many of the Marar have become successful business-men in the emirate with some being heavily involved in the major industrial parastatals.[82] Similarly small but powerful has been the abovementioned Mishaghin (Al-Masghuni), which provided Zayed with one of his wives. Until the mid-1990s a member of the section was Al-Ayn's chief of police, while others have served as UAE ambassadors to Pakistan and Jordan, as directors of the Abu Dhabi Seaports Authority, and in prominent positions in the UAE Air Force.[83]

The Hinawi and Maliki Manasir (Al-Mansuri) is the second most populous tribe in Abu Dhabi after the Bani Yas. And, although there been a few exceptions,[84] they have historically been the most loyal supporters of the Al-Nahyan. As mentioned above, they fought along-side Abu Dhabi's rulers in almost all of the conflicts of the nineteenth century, and were also key allies in the tribal conflicts with Dubai in the 1940s,[85] often providing bodyguards for the Al-Nahyan.[86] Since then they have been entrusted with key positions in both the military and the government. Notably the Manasir have held posts in the UAE Armed Forces' special operations unit and director level positions in the Al-Ayn police force,[87] in ADIA, in the UAE Central Bank,[88] and in the Abu Dhabi Chamber of Commerce.[89] They have also had members sitting in the Federal National Council,[90] undersecretary positions in the ruler's office and in the federal ministries of labour and petroleum, and ambassadorships to France and South America.[91] At present, their most prominent members include Sultan bin Said Al-Mansuri, the new federal minister for the economy; Majid Al-Mansuri, the secretary general of the Environmental Agency of Abu Dhabi; Hamoud bin Hamoud Al-Mansuri, the general manager of the western region municipality; and Abdullah bin Nasser Al-Mansuri, the chairman of the Abu Dhabi Shipbuilding Company. Courtesy of the Manasir's constituent Al-Bu Khail (Al-Khaili) subsection—which provided Zayed with one of his wives, the mother of the bani Mouza[92]—the tribe also has one current member of the Abu Dhabi Executive Council, Mugheer Al-Khaili. He also serves as general manager of the Abu Dhabi Education Council. The CEO of Zones-Corp, Jaber bin Harib Al-Khaili, is also of the Al-Bu Khail.[93]

The similarly Hinawi and Maliki Dhawahir (Al-Dhaheri) tribe historically formed the other major tribal pillar of support for the Al-Nahyan, second only to the Manasir.

Although there were occasional disputes in the late nineteenth century, the Dhawahir's loyalty to the Al-Nahyan and the Bani Yas was most often unswerving, and their cooperation played a critical role in both Zayed bin Khalifa's consolidation of control over Buraimi and then Shakhbut's resistance to Saudi-Wahhabi interference in the 1950s.[94] The aforementioned Ahmad bin Muhammad bin Hilal was the long-serving wali of Buraimi between the 1890s and 1930s and—although this position was eventually transferred to Al-Nahyan family members—the Dhawahir have ever since been rewarded with key portfolios in the emirate's administration, often through two of their most prominent subsections: the Badawi (Al-Badi) and the Darami-kah (Al-Darmiki). Both of these sections provided Zayed bin Sultan with wives: the mother of the bani Amna[95] and the mother of the bani Aisha.[96] Under Zayed the Dhawahir had two members of the Abu Dhabi Executive Council: Ali bin Ahmad Al-Dhaheri and Muhammad bin Sultan Al-Dhaheri. The chairman of ADIC was at one point also from the Dhawahir,[97] as was the commander-in-chief of the Union Defence Force before Muhammad bin Zayed took over.[98] At the federal level the Dhawahir have held equally senior positions, with Ahmad bin Said Al-Dhaheri being the federal minister for health in the early 1990s and then later the minister for petroleum, with Hamudah bin Ali Al-Dhaheri being federal minister for the interior and then a minister of state without portfolio, and with Muhammad bin Nakhira Al-Dhaheri until recently being the federal minister for justice. Elsewhere in government, the Dhawahir have provided chairmen for the Al-Ayn Muncipality,[99] Abu Dhabi Commercial Bank, and the Abu Dhabi Department for Civil Aviation.[100] They have provided undersecretaries for the ruler's representative to the eastern region,[101] for the crown prince's court, and for the federal ministries of the interior, justice, and finance. Other positions have included a director level position in ADNOC,[102] head of protocol at the presidential court,[103] vice president of the UAE University of Al-Ayn, membership of the Federal National Council,[104] and an ambassadorship to Bahrain.[105] In the military, Hazza bin Sultan Al-Darmaki was once commander of the UAE Navy, and the Dhawahir have held a host of army portfolios including the directorship of military medical services and chief of the supplies organization.[106] Influential members of the tribe currently include Jouan bin Salem Al-Dhaheri, who sits on the Abu Dhabi Executive Council and is chairman of the Abu Dhabi Department for Municipalities and Agriculture; Awad Al-Darmaki, who is the general manager of the Al-Ayn Municipality; and Sultan bin Said Al-Badi, who is an undersecretary in the Abu Dhabi Department for Justice. At the federal level they have maintained a presence in the Council of Ministers with Hadef bin Jouan Al-Dhaheri recently being appointed minister for justice.

The third of the Hinawi and Maliki tribes of Abu Dhabi is the Awamir (Al-Amiri). Although less populous and historically more nomadic than either the Manasir or the Dhawahir, their loyalty was nevertheless critical for the Al-Nahyan, especially in ensuring the protection of small towns and distant outposts. Some of the tribe came into conflict with the Manasir in the 1920s, and some sided with Saudi Arabia in the disputes of the 1950s and even left Abu Dhabi. But those who remained were soon rewarded with key portfolios.[107] In particular, Salim bin Hamm Al-Amiri was one of Zayed's most influential advisors, while Rakkad bin Salim Al-Amiri joined the federal government—first as minister for public works and housing, and then as minister for petroleum. The tribe has also held director level positions in the UAE Armed Forces,[108] in the federal ministry for the interior,[109] in the ministry for foreign affairs, and in the ministry for finance and industry.

Of the Ghafiri faction or Hanbali school tribes, there are—broadly speaking—three exceptions to their underrepresentation in Abu Dhabi, seemingly as the result of changing historical circumstances or high profile marriages into the Al-Nahyan. The Naim (Al-Nuami) are perhaps the most significant of these exceptions, being the largest Ghafiri tribe to have residents in the emirate. As discussed, they frequently opposed the Bani Yas during the nineteenth century, often siding with the Qawasim, and at one point even converting to Wahhabism, despite the daughter of their most prominent chief having married Zayed bin Khalifa. As late as the 1950s their Al-Bu Khuraiban (Al-Kharabani) subsection was still disloyal to the Al-Nahyan by openly siding with Saudi Arabia. Nevertheless, one subsection of the Naim—the Al-Bu Shamis (Al-Shamsi), did begin to gain the confidence of the Bani Yas, and by 1970 it had declared itself an independent tribe. The Abu Dhabi-based branch of the section[110] would seem to have resisted Wahhabism more effectively than the rest of the Naim and was duly rewarded. During Zayed bin Sultan's reign they held the secretary generalship of the Federal National Council[111] and undersecretary positions in several of the federal ministries, notably water and electricity. More recently, they have acquired director level positions in the Abu Dhabi Municipality,[112] and, as of 2008, Maitha bint Salem Al-Shamsi is serving as a federal minister of state without portfolio—one of the UAE's four female ministers.

The second exception would be the Bani Qitab (Al-Qitbi) tribe and its constituent Bani Huwaidin section, which have had a mixed history of good and bad relations with the Bani Yas, having fought against their Manasir allies in the 1920s and having sided with Dubai in the conflicts of the 1940s.[113] Since the marriage of Sheikha Fatima bint Mubarak Al-Qitbi to Zayed and the rising influence of her six sons—the bani Fatima—the tribe has undoubtedly become a key voice in the establishment. They have been assigned director level positions in the military,[114] undersecretary portfolios in the federal ministry for health, and at one stage Humaid bin Darwish Al-Qitbi was even general manager of ADIC. At present their most influential member is probably Obaid Al-Hairi Salem Al-Qitbi: a member of the Abu Dhabi Executive Council and the deputy director of the Abu Dhabi police force.

The third and most understandable exception is the Bani Zaab (Al-Zaabi) tribe, given that they are actually of the Hinawi faction despite being of the Hanbali school—an unusual combination. As discussed earlier in this book, they had moved to Abu Dhabi in the late 1960s at the specific behest of Zayed, thus assisting him in his efforts to boost the sheikhdom's national population. With their loyalty to the Al-Nahyan never in question, the Bani Zaab have benefited from a slew of high status positions. They have often dominated the federal ministry for foreign affairs, assuming director level positions[115] and supplying ambassadors to Kuwait, Saudi Arabia, Qatar, Indonesia and other key Muslim countries. Their members have served as directors in the UAE Air Force[116] and in the crown prince's court,[117] and have taken undersecretary portfolios in the Abu Dhabi Department for Planning. Today, their most prominent member is Jassim bin Muhammad Al-Zaabi, who is both the CEO of ADIC and the CEO of Mubadala's new Al-Yah Satellites subsidiary.

Underneath, alongside, and in some cases above these tribes there also exists a small number of merchant families that moved to Abu Dhabi generations before, most notably during the pearling era. By far the most prominent of these is the Otaibah (Al-Otaibi), who are now often considered as something of an honorary section of the Bani Yas. Some claim the Otaibah are distant relatives of the abovementioned Marar section, although it would seem likely that most of the family came to Abu Dhabi at about the same time that the disgruntled merchants of Persian origin—the *ajami*—were fleeing Persia and settling in Dubai and other towns of the lower Gulf. Regardless of their origin, they soon become wealthy, and in the 1920s the daughter of one of their notables married Sheikh Muhammad bin Khalifa Al-Nahyan,[118] thus bringing the Otaibah into the inner circle. Under Zayed their influence grew, most notably through the rise of Mana bin Said Al-Otaibi. He became Zayed's first advisor on oil policies, and then went on to become the federal minister for petroleum. Remarkably, following Abu Dhabi's accession to the Organization of the Petroleum Exporting Counties he served as OPEC's president for a record six terms. Today he remains a key advisor to the current ruler, while his son—Yousef bin Mana Al-Otaibi—was in 2008 appointed to serve as the UAE's ambassador to the United States. Similarly prominent has been Abdullah bin Rashid Al-Otaibi, who now sits on the Abu Dhabi Executive Council and is the chairman of the Abu Dhabi Department for Transport. In recent years the Otaibah have also held the chairmanship of the Abu Dhabi Chamber of Commerce, and the deputy chairmanships of Abu Dhabi National Bank and Etisalat—the UAE's primary telecommunications provider.[119] Other prominent merchant families would include the Al-Mubarak, whose talented and educated members have often staffed key positions. Most notably, Khalifa bin Ahmad Al-Mubarak served as the UAE's ambassador to France until he was tragically assassinated in 1978.[120] And today, his much admired, US-educated, son Khaldun bin Khalifa Al-Mubarak has emerged as one of the key figures in Abu Dhabi's new economy, serving as managing director of Mubadala, as a member of the Abu Dhabi Executive Council, and as the chairman of one of Muhammad bin Zayed's primary advisory bodies—the Executive Affairs Authority.

6

LEGITIMIZING THE MONARCHY

Backed by internal dynastic strength and carefully co-opted tribal allies, the Al-Nahyan family has further reinforced the traditional monarchy by exploiting several additional sources of legitimacy. Invariably these have gained the trust and loyalty of the broader national population, and have reduced the need for potentially troublesome political reform. A formal government has built upon the hybrid foundations of traditional and tribal politics, thus providing a much needed veneer of accountability and transparency. Moreover, for nearly forty years Sheikh Zayed bin Sultan Al-Nahyan's early strategy of oil-financed wealth distributions has been maintained, and under Sheikh Khalifa bin Zayed Al-Nahyan Abu Dhabi remains one of the purest examples of a benevolent allocative state. Similarly, the ruling family's generous acts of public charity and unswerving financial support and patronage for Islamic causes, as well as for the emirate's history, culture, and environment, have further boosted the monarchy's appeal, while simultaneously strengthening the all important sense of national identity. As another extension of its wealth-distributing capacity, Abu Dhabi's massive foreign aid programme has bought the monarchy enormous credibility and respect both domestically and across the Arab and Muslim world.

The expansion of formal government

The abundance of councils, departments, ministries, authorities, and other seemingly formal institutions that have been built up since the

1960s to oversee the massive expansion in Abu Dhabi's government services have also been useful as a means of accommodating and balancing powerful traditional networks. These institutions all help in coating the surviving traditional monarchy and its allies with an important veneer of modernity and legitimacy. Indubitably, if decisions can be taken and policies crafted by recognized bodies that have constitutions, boards of directors, and scheduled meetings, then they are perceived to carry the weight of a legal rational process.[1] This has allowed for at least some circumvention of the old king's dilemma of balancing modernity with tradition,[2] as the emirate's increasingly enriched and educated population—the beneficiaries of rapid socioeconomic development, who have mostly remained politically demobilized—can take heart from the notion that governmental decisions are not merely autocratic dictates. In many ways, Abu Dhabi represents the finest example of such a hybrid political system, simply given the enormous number of institutions that exist relative to its modest population, and given all of the additional institutions that have been required to support the federal government. In the near future this number will increase further, as all of the new economic sectors begin to demand supervisory bodies and are backed by government-sponsored parastatals

Of these dozens of institutions it is most useful to focus on those responsible for the bulk of decision-making and those that seek direct input or at least some form of consultation from a slightly wider circle. At the apex of the emirate-level government there are the private offices and courts of both the ruler and the crown prince. These have their own staff and, being appointed a chamberlain or director to one of these bodies is a high status position that allows an individual to serve as an intermediary between the supreme, traditional power and the regular government and citizenry. Similarly, the eastern and western regions of Abu Dhabi still have their ruler's representatives— Sheikh Tahnun bin Muhammad Al-Nahyan and Muhammad bin Buti Al-Hamad respectively—and each has his own private office and court. Nevertheless, while it remains possible for unilateral decisions to be made by the ruler's office and then issued as 'emiri decrees,' most legislation is now crafted by the Abu Dhabi Executive Council before then being approved by the ruler's office and introduced as law.

Thus, the Abu Dhabi Executive Council is by far the most signifi-cant institution in the emirate, and since its inception in early 1971 it has continued to be the real engine of development. It is more formal than the executive councils in other emirates:[3] it meets regularly, determines all public spending in Abu Dhabi, and has annual policy agendas that publicly list all of its goals for that year. Whoever is its chairman is effectively Abu Dhabi's prime minister, and a family's inclusion or exclusion from the Council's membership is an accurate barometer of prestige and influence. From its original six members chaired by Sheikh Khalifa bin Zayed Al-Nahyan in the 1970s it swelled to seventeen members in the 1990s. During this period its members included two of the bani Zayed in addition to Khalifa and his eldest son; five of the bani Muhammad bin Khalifa, and four other Bani Yas men: one Suwdan, one Hawamil, and two Qubaisat. When it was streamlined to eleven positions in 2004 under the new chair-manship of Sheikh Muhammad bin Zayed Al-Nahyan the balance was somewhat different: with two other bani Zayed members, with both of Khalifa's sons, with only one bani Muhammad bin Khalifa representative, with one Al-Bu Mahair, with one Suwdan, with one Dhawahir, and with Muhammad's close ally Khaldun bin Khalifa Al-Mubarak. Today, with nineteen members, the Council is the largest it has been, reflecting the increasing number of services and responsibili-ties that fall under its umbrella. Including Muhammad, there are now nine of the Al-Nahyan in the council: four other bani Zayed,[4] both of Khalifa's sons, and two bani Muhammad bin Khalifa.[5] These are joined by two Suwdan[6] and one Mazari,[7] and from beyond the Bani Yas there is one Manasir,[8] one Dhawahir,[9] one Bani Qitab,[10] one Otaibah,[11] and a few technocrats including Khaldun bin Khalifa Al-Mubarak. Underneath and reporting to the Abu Dhabi Executive Council are all the regular government departments one would expect, in addition to the influential Supreme Petroleum Council, three municipalities and three police forces (one for the capital and one for each of the two regions), and a score of new bodies including the Abu Dhabi Education Council, the Abu Dhabi Tourism Authority and its Office of the Brand of Abu Dhabi, the Abu Dhabi Authority for Cul-ture and Heritage, the Urban Planning Council, the Environmental Agency of Abu Dhabi, and the Executive Affairs Authority.

Ostensibly providing the Abu Dhabi Executive Council with suggestions and feedback is the National Consultative Council (NCC). Again, compared to those in other emirates[12] Abu Dhabi's body is relatively more formal, perhaps with the exception of Sharjah's, which even has a 'youth parliament.' Having been established by emiri decree in late 1971,[13] the NCC has since been charged with considering draft laws, discussing 'public subjects,' and considering any petitions it receives.[14] Traditionally, there have been six subcommittees that have worked under the NCC and have been responsible for producing recommendations: interior and defence; financial and economic affairs; legislative and legal affairs; health, labour, and social affairs; education, agriculture, and information; and municipalities and public utilities. In addition there also exists a committee to prepare the agenda for NCC meetings, and committees for both the eastern and western regions. Given that it is not a decision-making institution and is supposed to represent the views of the general public, there have never been any Al-Nahyan members, and relatively few members of 'senior' Bani Yas sections. Indeed, the bulk of its membership (which fluctuates between forty and fifty-five[15]) has predominantly been made up of representatives from either smaller Bani Yas sections or well respected non-Bani Yas tribes such as the Manasir, Dhawahir, and Awamir. As a consultative council the NCC's usefulness is somewhat questionable, not least given that the Abu Dhabi Executive Council is not required to consider all of the recommendations it receives. Moreover, after thirty-seven years of operation the NCC remains entirely appointive, with article 3 of its founding law still unchanged: 'the ruler will select, appoint, and accept the resignation of the members of the NCC by emiri decree.' Furthermore, as per article 4 of the law, 'the term of the membership in the NCC will be for two renewable years... those members whose membership has expired can be reselected.'[16] In effect this has meant that some members have been perpetually reappointed. Sultan bin Surur Al-Dhaheri was the NCC's chairman for no less than nineteen years, several of the current members were originally appointed in 1971, and—incredibly—only three of the current members were first appointed in the last eighteen years. None of the members are female, in contrast with the Sharjah council which now has 17 percent female membership.[17]

In some ways the federal government of the UAE mirrors Abu Dhabi's emirate-level administration. There exists an all powerful but essentially traditional body—the Supreme Council of Rulers (SCR)—which is made up of the hereditary rulers of the seven member emirates, as per the original federal agreements of 1971. While the provisional constitution allows for an SCR presidential election to take place every five years,[18] there has only been one such occasion, in late 2004, when Khalifa smoothly succeeded his father. Indeed, for the time being rulership of Abu Dhabi remains synonymous with the presidency of the UAE, not least because of Sheikh Zayed bin Sultan Al-Nahyan's founding vision and Abu Dhabi's almost single-handed financing of those federal development projects that do exist. The SCR also reflects Dubai's elevated status in the UAE by awarding only the rulers of Abu Dhabi and Dubai veto power in its meetings—as per article 49 of the constitution,[19] and by having always appointed the ruler of Dubai as the vice president. For example, upon Sheikh Muhammad bin Rashid Al-Maktum's accession as ruler of Dubai in early 2006 he was automatically installed as vice president of the UAE. In support of the SCR, or more specifically the president, there exists a presidential office and a presidential court with its own staff. However, given the ruler of Abu Dhabi's similar emirate-level institutions it is unclear if the two function independently.

Responsible for the federal government's decision-making is the Council of Ministers (COM). Since its establishment in 1972 its composition has always reflected the relative power and influence of the member emirates, in much the same way that the Abu Dhabi Executive Council reflects the prestige of various tribes and families in Abu Dhabi. As a former minister explains, of the COM's original cabinet, 'there was a belief that wealth and family background alone would guarantee security and stability.'[20] Although originally made up of eleven ministers in addition to the prime minister, Khalifa, the COM was soon expanded to nineteen positions as the other emirates began to supply their contingents of appointees.[21] The premiership transferred to the crown prince of Dubai, Sheikh Maktum bin Rashid Al-Maktum, before the constitutional crisis of 1979 persuaded Sheikh Rashid bin Said Al-Maktum himself to become prime minister as well as vice president. For much of this period Abu Dhabi held the lion's share of COM positions including the deputy premiership, the ministry for the interior, the ministry for higher education, and the ministry for public works. By the time of Khalifa's succession, Abu Dhabi's real control over the federal government was even stronger given that Sheikh Hamdan bin Zayed Al-Nahyan was the minister for foreign affairs in all but name and given that Dubai's control of the ministry for defence had remained hollow compared to the powers invested in the Abu Dhabi-based deputy supreme commander and commander-in-chief of the UAE Armed Forces. Today, the COM's membership has increased to twenty ministers and five ministers of state, but remains equally in favor of Abu Dhabi, with Sheikh Abdullah bin Zayed Al-Nahyan having become minister for foreign affairs, with Sheikh Mansur bin Zayed Al-Nahyan becoming minister for presidential affairs, and with a second deputy premiership having been created for Hamdan. In total, there are now seven members of the Al-Nahyan serving as ministers, in addition to a Dhawahir minister for justice,[22] a Manasir minister of the economy,[23] a Hawamil minister for energy,[24] and at least two further ministers who are believed to be de facto members of the Abu Dhabi contingent.[25]

Fulfilling the same role at the federal level as the NCC in Abu Dhabi, the Federal National Council (FNC) is a consultative body made up of contingents from each emirate. Originally comprised of 40 appointees, including an internally elected speaker and two deputies, this chamber also sits for sessions of two years at a time, and has a number of subcommittees, most of which have identical titles to those of the NCC. Again, much like the COM, the more powerful emirates dominate—as per article 72 of the provisional federal constitution,[26] with Abu Dhabi and Dubai each supplying eight members, while Sharjah and Ra's al-Khaimah supply six, and the other three emirates supply just four.[27] In turn, these contingents are most often made up of senior representatives of non-ruling tribes or sections. In recent years there has been mounting criticism of the FNC, with many of its members and other citizens claiming that it is largely ineffective. While it has been successful in petitioning ministers on some rather banal subjects,[28] it has been incapable of making more substantive interventions,[29] and has often been unable to elicit responses from ministers.[30] As the following chapter will detail, measures have been taken to strengthen the FNC, but unfortunately there has not yet been any significant improvement and it remains perhaps the weakest component in an otherwise impressive blend of formal and traditional political institutions.

The allocative state

Since Sheikh Zayed bin Sultan Al-Nahyan's initially modest distributions of wealth in the late 1960s and early 1970s, much of Abu Dhabi's oil surpluses have been channelled into a massive allocative state that has taken care of almost all the citizenry's needs, literally from the cradle to the grave. This strategy has served multiple aims: it continues to connect all families—even those with no representations in any of the abovementioned formal bodies—to state institutions; it undoubtedly engenders a mood of satisfaction towards such a benevolent, traditional monarchy; and—as a by-product of this satisfaction—it provides yet another means of circumventing or rather reducing pressure for meaningful reforms. Broadly speaking, the allocations have fallen into three categories: direct transfers of wealth and free services, low-cost or even free housing, and significant employment and business advantages. Today, with Abu Dhabi's per capita value of oil reserves per national standing at over $18 million,[31] there are greater opportunities for wealth distributions than ever before.

With regard to the first of these categories, from the 1970s and onwards the government has provided completely free education and healthcare to all nationals. And this remains the case, so long as nationals choose to use public schools and the national health service. Tellingly, in the former all students will receive free textbooks and—at the university level—even laptop computers, while in the latter all patients can expect to receive free prescriptions. More directly, those families whose combined household income falls below a certain threshold—about $2800 per month—are also eligible to receive generous social security benefits. Although it is difficult to arrive at an average figure, given the complication of family size, it is likely that these benefits are equal if not more than those provided to low income families in western European welfare states. In addition, there are also large domestic charities that target the more indigent members of the national population, but significantly these remain closely connected to the state and in almost all cases are publicly patronized and subsidized by specific members of the ruling family. There exists, for example, the Khalifa bin Zayed Al-Nahyan Foundation which donates to a wide range of causes, and the Emirates Foundation which is chaired by Sheikh Muhammad bin Zayed Al-Nahyan and has recently focused on distributing grants for nationals with special needs.[32] Ironically, giving money to the poor directly and thereby bypassing such state-sanctioned charities is difficult, and actually frowned upon. In advance of Ramadan in 2008—the holy month during which all practising Muslims have a duty to be charitable—the ministry for the interior issued a statement that beggars should not be tolerated, and that those caught would be arrested, deported, and blacklisted from returning to the UAE, meeting the cost of the deportation themselves. In 2007 it was reported that over seventy such beggars, mostly of Arab origin, were arrested and deported in this manner, with any nationals caught having been directed to official charities and threatened with punishment if they repeated their behaviour in the future.[33]

Throughout the 1980s and 1990s, with an annual budget of over $170 million[34] the Zayed Housing Programme provided thousands of new homes—often sizeable villas—for those nationals below the monthly threshold. This first led to the construction of ribbon developments along the highways linking Abu Dhabi to Al-Ayn and Dubai, before then spreading further into the hinterland with the construction of entire new towns such as Khalifa City, Muhammad City, and Shahama. In recent years the strategy has remained a central component of the allocative state with over 100 keys to new homes being distributed in 2005 to residents of the new Al-Adla development near to Sweihan;[35] with 800 new homes being gifted in 2008 in the western region—the Dhafra Meadows project;[36] and with impromptu *majaalis* or meetings being held in Liwa during which Sheikh Khalifa bin Zayed Al-Nahyan handed out both house keys and money to nationals.

For those nationals who sought public sector employment from the 1970s to the 1990s it was all but guaranteed that they would find a job in one of the many government departments or ministries. And, providing they achieved the required educational qualification, their promotion was invariably assured. Soon after Khalifa's succession in 2004 it was announced that all nationals working in the public sector would receive a 25 percent pay increase: an understandably popular decision.[37] Although this is perhaps less straightforward today, given heavier competition for public sector positions and a streamlining of government posts,[38] the many new parastatals and other abovementioned bodies are nevertheless providing suitable alternatives. In parallel to such strong salaried employment prospects, the state has also provided self-employed nationals with considerable advantages. Since 1981 the Khalifa Committee of the Abu Dhabi Department for Social Services and Commercial Buildings has ensured that all nationals have access to soft loans for setting up new businesses.[39] Since its launch it is thought that nearly $10 billion has been dispensed in this way. Similarly, the original strategy of providing nationals with free plots of land for commercial buildings and agricultural enterprises has been continued, and it remains possible for nationals to walk into ready-made farms complete with all of the necessary farming equipment. Since the mid-1980s business-minded nationals have also profited greatly from legislation that has required all foreign companies to seek an indigenous partner. Specifically, as per the Federal Commercial Companies Law of 1984, this national sponsor or *kafil* has had to be the controlling partner in the joint venture. As per article 22 of the law: 'the sponsor's share shall not be less than 51% of the company's capital. Therefore, any company's contract that does not incorporate such a provision shall be considered to be null and void.'[40]

The Emirati identity

The generosity of such wealth distributions can only be sustained should the national population remain relatively small and as distinct as possible from the expatriate population. Crucially, although enjoying one of the highest fertility rates in the world,[41] the indigenous population of Abu Dhabi is still less than 250,000,[42] with the remainder of the emirate's 1.5 million or so other residents[43] originating from other parts of the Arab world, south Asia, east Africa, or even Europe. Only the nationals or 'locals' matter in terms of politics, given that expatriates are for the most part willing immigrants, seeking a higher standard of living and are most often satisfied with simply a tax-free salary. Thus, in many ways the entire national population forms a natural upper class, as they are the only members of society entitled to explicit government transfers. As such, the Abu Dhabi or—in the case of the federation—the Emirati national identity has to be fiercely preserved, as it carries with it a guarantee of financial prosperity. This has made naturalization a difficult process and largely impossible, with only the 'original' families of the lower Gulf having been entitled to the state's full largesse.

Indeed, in Abu Dhabi and elsewhere in the UAE, simply having a UAE passport is insufficient to be classed as a 'national,' as one must also have the vital 'family card' or *khulsat al-qaid*, which in most cases confirms one's lineage. Without this card one is considered *bidoon*—a stateless person. In the summer of 2008, for the first time since the UAE's inception in 1971, a small number of new family cards were issued to those who could somehow prove their pre-1971 ancestry.[44] Of the 1700 or so that queued to receive them, many were in a highly emotional state, being conscious of the decades-long wait their families had suffered, and being fully aware that they were on the cusp of enormous material benefits. As one new national described of the process: 'this will change everything for us and for our children… becoming Emirati will be like being born again.'[45] Another stated that 'I will carry the country's emblem on my head and my love for it in my heart.' Shortly after the distribution of these new cards the federal minister for the interior, Sheikh Saif bin Zayed Al-Nahyan, warned that 'loyalty is a condition of citizenship and new citizens are expected to embrace the values that have ensured social stability and security for all. The constitution allows for revoking citizenship from anyone who does not deserve it.' When a newly naturalized citizen was asked for his thoughts on this message, he stated simply that 'those who drink from a well would never throw dirt in it.'[46]

Significantly, in parallel to these family cards the dress code for nationals has become far more rigid, with almost all men wearing a pure white *dishdasha* while women will almost always wear a black *abaya* to cover their clothes and a *shaila* to cover their hair. The uniformity of these garments is a modern creation of the allocative state, as prior to the 1970s the clothing worn by the indigenous population of the lower Gulf was far more varied and individualistic, often with several different kinds of headwear in popular use.[47] As such, the present outfits are worn with pride and constitute a national uniform: some special editions of *abaya* even depict the faces of rulers or the UAE flag. Moreover, they also constitute a uniform of privilege, as such clothes immediately distinguish an Emirati (or other Gulf state national) from other, expatriate, Arabs. Often this results in preferential public treatment.

Also reinforcing Emirati identity and reducing any dilution of the national population has been an informal yet effective public policy on marriage partners. While men have always been free to choose partners of any nationality, or indeed any religion, national women have been largely restricted to choosing national males. Several unpublished emiri decrees in the late 1990s forbade women from marrying non Gulf-state nationals,[48] and if they did then their husbands and children would not be able to claim citizenship. Today, this policy remains in place, with a transgressing woman likely to be banished from her family, even if her betrothed is also Arab and Muslim. Again, as with the current dress codes, these marriage restrictions are a product of the allocative state, as in the past many women married into non-Emirati Arab Muslim families.

Tying together this emphasis on national purity with basic wealth transfers have been the strong state-sponsored financial support mechanisms for those men who marry national females. In the late 1990s Sheikh Zayed bin Sultan Al-Nahyan began the practice of paying for mass weddings for pure, national couples. With escalating dowry costs—on average $80,000—many men began to take this option.[49] More formally, in 1992 a 'Sheikh Zayed Marriage Fund' was announced: as a department within the federal ministry for labour and social affairs it provided a payment of about $13,000 to help men offset the costs of their marriage. Importantly, the fund could only be accessed if the bride were Emirati.[50] Within its first decade over 60,000 youths benefited from a total of about $630 million in fund distributions.[51] Unsurprisingly, with even higher costs of living today, the fund remains popular and the allowances have been considerably increased. Moreover, sponsored mass weddings are becoming increasingly attractive. In summer 2008 Sheikh Muhammad bin Zayed Al-

Nahyan provided over $1 million for a wedding involving 175 couples in Liwa.[52] The deadline for applications was left open until the day before the event in an effort to encourage as many as possible to participate.

History, culture, and imagery

In recent years there has been considerable spending on museums, the staging of heritage events, and the sponsorship of traditional literary and cultural productions. These activities all serve to reinforce the national identity and reinvigorate tribal histories, thereby reminding the population of the historical roots of the traditional monarchy's legitimacy. In addition to the much discussed ruling family-backed camel races that take place across the emirate,[53] and the annual Dhafra camel festival in the western region complete with its own camel beauty contest,[54] a number of new festivals have been launched, all of which are generously sponsored and provide a venue for members of the ruling family to meet their citizens in a traditional, tribal context. Notably, since 2003 there has been an annual hunting and equestrian exhibition in the emirate that has hosted falcon hunting demonstrations, horse beauty contests, and traditional dancing workshops.[55] Similarly, since 2004 there has been a large annual date festival organized in Liwa, complete with poetry recitals and other activities. In 2008 there were over $1 million in prizes to be won, seemingly provided by Sheikh Muhammad bin Zayed Al-Nahyan. Indeed, upon touring the festival the crown prince remarked 'date palms were the main source of food for our ancestors… the success of this festival is yet another testimony to the correctness of the vision of the late Sheikh Zayed…'[56] Furthermore, many of the described house key-distributing *majaalis* that are staged in the hinterland are often accompanied by traditional activities and poetry, the content of which invariably praises the ruler.

Poetry readings are ubiquitous in Abu Dhabi's heritage revival. Most often it is Bedouin *nabati* poetry that relates great feats of heroism and adventure and thereby helps to evoke memories of the pre-oil era. While perhaps not as central to the Al-Nahyan's legitimacy formula as it is in Dubai, where Sheikh Muhammad bin Rashid Al-

Maktum's official website declares that 'poetry has allowed [him] to express the creative, sensitive side of his nature that he has little chance to display in the political arena,'[57] these recitals have nevertheless been embraced by the monarchy and transformed into prime time entertainment for the national population. In particular, much like the US reality television show 'American Idol,' there exists Abu Dhabi Television's 'Millions Poet.' This event is sponsored by Muhammad bin Zayed, who sometimes sits at the front of the auditorium watching contestants compete for a prize of about $360,000. Many of the poems honour members of the ruling family, and in one case a poet compared his rival contestants to a sheikh's racing camels.[58] During the show's intermissions high profile Lebanese and Egyptian singers perform, often singing in *khaleeji* Arabic—the dialect of the Gulf. Indeed, the show's promotion of khaleeji would now seem to have gone very far with the Middle East's best selling artist—Angham—having promised that her forthcoming album will be sung entirely in khaleeji. And Amal Maher and Nancy Ajram have already included several khaleeji tracks on their recent releases.[59]

Other culturally related state sponsored prizes include the annual Sheikh Zayed book award, which since its launch in 2005 has been dispensing prizes of over $2 million to authors contributing to the artistic or literary development of the Arab world. Most recently, in summer 2008 a massive photography competition was launched by the Office of the Brand of Abu Dhabi. The theme was the History and culture of Abu Dhabi, and over 2000 entries were received. Unsurprisingly, substantial cash prizes—described in the media as being funded by Muhammad—were awarded.[60] Significantly, many of the entries featured Sheikh Zayed bin Sultan Al-Nahyan, or at least pictures of him. This continues a trend begun in the late 1960s when Zayed instructed the postal service to produce new stamps bearing his image.[61] Earlier stamps had never featured rulers' faces, but ever since their production there have been large scale posters and placards featuring Zayed on street corners in Abu Dhabi and Al-Ayn. Many continue to feature the former ruler engaged in traditional pursuits: either on horseback or holding a hunting falcon.

Commendably—and also connected to this strategy—there have been entire open air heritage villages constructed in Abu Dhabi, where one can witness traditional bread baking, glass blowing, and pottery taking place. Although undoubtedly attractive to tourists, many of the visitors are actually nationals. Moreover, those few old buildings that remain in the emirate are now being venerated and preserved. A law is in the planning stages that will ensure that all 'listed buildings' will fall under the control of the new Abu Dhabi Authority for Culture and Heritage. This list will include buildings where key events have taken place, including the birthplaces of various members of the ruling family.[62] Where old buildings do not exist, there would also seem to be a healthy industry in constructing fake towers, crenellations, barasti palm frond houses, and in some cases even entire forts.[63]

Religious resources

Further legitimizing the Abu Dhabi ruling family has been its members' strong support for Islamic activities and causes, and—importantly—also their support for other tolerated religions. The Al-Nahyan may not be guardians of holy shrines, as the Al-Saud are able to claim, but their tribal history is nevertheless intertwined with Islam. Thus, if they can at least be seen to openly promote Islam then they will be held in high esteem. Since the first oil booms the simplest way to carry out such promotion has been to build mosques and pay the salaries of all *ulema* or preachers.[64] With several mosques on each street and—in theory—with mosques at walking distance from all national males in the emirate, Abu Dhabi has eclipsed even Saudi Arabia in this regard. While there may be high rise skyscrapers in the capital, the multitude of minarets nevertheless still makes it look Islamic and prevents confusion with a modern, secular city elsewhere in the world. Symbolically, the enormous Sheikh Zayed Mosque was finally completed in 2007 at a reported cost of over $540 million. With 82 domes and minarets of over 100 metres in height, and capable of holding over 40,000 worshippers it is now recognized as the third largest mosque in the world.[65] Giant mosques have also been built by Abu Dhabi elsewhere in the region, and in most cases these carry the name of their sponsoring sheikh, thereby extending the piety of the ruling family beyond the UAE's borders. Most notably, the Sheikh Khalifa bin Zayed Mosque is currently under construction in Bethany, on the

West Bank. At a cost of nearly $5 million, the mosque will have the tallest minarets in Palestine.[66]

During Sheikh Zayed bin Sultan Al-Nahyan's reign, Abu Dhabi began to invite esteemed ulema from other countries to give lectures, often during Ramadan. Such visits have since increased in their frequency and scale. In 2004 a conference was held under Sheikh Khalifa bin Zayed Al-Nahyan's patronage on the subject of the Prophet's guidance. Hundreds of scholars were invited, many of whom were personal guests of the ruling family.[67] In Ramadan 2008 over 30 religious leaders were invited to Abu Dhabi at Khalifa's expense to 'expose the UAE to the latest learned debates on Islam.' The delegates included Egypt's minister for Islamic affairs[68] and the grand mufti of Syria,[69] in addition to several prominent academics from Azhar University in Egypt.[70] In parallel Sheikh Muhammad bin Zayed Al-Nahyan's office also sponsored lectures during Ramadan, including esteemed Saudi scholars[71] and a number of non-Muslim lecturers and dignitaries.[72] Delivered in Arabic and English, they were held in the crown prince's majlis twice a week.[73]

There has been a strong emphasis on promoting religious tolerance, especially between Islam and Christianity. For many years the rulers of Abu Dhabi have donated land for the construction of Christian churches of all denominations, and these continue to be embraced by the whole community. Certainly Christian festivals and holy days are respected and newspaper reports will often focus on Christian gatherings in Abu Dhabi or elsewhere in the UAE. At Christmas time, decorations and Christmas trees abound in the many hotels and shopping malls. When an ancient pre-Islamic Christian church was discovered on one of the emirate's outlying islands, its restoration was immediately ordered.[74] Since the 1970s there has also been support for inter-faith dialogue and institutions working to project the moderate face of Islam. Abu Dhabi has historically been one of the largest donors to the Islamic Solidarity Fund, and has supplied its chairman since 1988. More recently, in 2005 the Tabah Foundation was established in Abu Dhabi.[75] Chaired by a respected Yemeni scholar,[76] the foundation was instrumental in pacifying reactions following the 2005 Danish cartoons scandal and the 2006 comments made by Pope Benedict XVI that were deemed defamatory to Islam.[77] The foundation even invited a group of Danish students to visit Abu Dhabi and meet with local students.[78] In 2008, it was announced that for the first time non-Muslims would be allowed to enter an Abu Dhabi mosque, and the Abu Dhabi Tourism Authority has since begun to advertise 90 minute guided tours of the Sheikh Zayed Mosque for all interested parties, regardless of their religion.[79]

Championing the environment

Yet another legitimacy resource for the traditional monarchy has been support for nature and the environment. Abu Dhabi's rulers have always been at the forefront of any environmental work taking place in the UAE, and today—with future energy and green industries being established—such a strong environmental stance dovetails perfectly with the emirate's diversifying economy. As early as 1967 Sheikh Zayed bin Sultan Al-Nahyan began to sponsor major environmental projects, with his first budget earmarking nearly 6 million Bahraini dinars—a comparable sum to that spent on healthcare[80]—for a zoo to protect endangered species.[81] Since then Zayed also famously embarked on a massive afforestation programme of Abu Dhabi in an effort to green vast expanses of the hinterland and improve the soil quality for agricultural activities. In 1973 he invited a delegation of the United Nations Food and Agricultural Organisation (UNFAO)[82] and following their recommendations ordered the planting of over 4 million trees by 1981. With three gallons of water required daily to irrigate each tree the cost was enormous—about $15 per day[83]—nevertheless over time forests did develop and some parts of the emirate are now rather verdant, with thousands of new trees currently growing.[84]

In 1994 Zayed set up the Environmental Research and Wildlife Development Agency (ERWDA) to oversee a network of protected areas in Abu Dhabi, and in 1998 he launched the UAE's first Environment Day as part of a campaign to increase environmental awareness throughout the federation. Towards the end of his reign, he also founded the Abu Dhabi Global Environmental Data Initiative (AGEDI) so that the emirate would become a repository for data used by international researchers.[85] The original zoo that had been established has since expanded into a large nature reserve and in 1997

Zayed bin Sultan won the World Wildlife Fund Golden Panda award in recognition for his commitment to the project.[86] Furthermore, in 2005 he was also to receive posthumously the United Nations Environment Programme's Champion of the Earth Award.

The new generation of Al-Nahyan rulers have maintained all these policies and continue to expand the state's role in environmental projects, notwithstanding all of the developments taking place at Masdar. ERWDA has been restructured into the Environmental Agency Abu Dhabi (EAD), and in cooperation with the Urban Planning Council this new entity has begun to set up national parks, including in the mangrove swamps. Worryingly, however, development will still be permitted in the parks as long as it is deemed to be 'environmentally sensitive construction.'[87] EAD has also reintroduced previously extinct mangrove flowers from seeds obtained in Pakistan[88] and the Tourism Development Investment Company is ensuring that at least one of the beaches on Saadiyat island will be reserved for turtles. The TDIC is also developing 'discovery islands' in the western region that will become wildlife sanctuaries.[89] The future would also seem bright, with the Abu Dhabi Executive Council having commissioned the Stockholm Environmental Institute in Sweden to formulate a rigorous climate policy for the emirate. This policy is expected to impact on government policies by 2010[90] and will be underpinned by the new Zayed Future Energy Prize which—from 2009 onwards—will see Sheikh Muhammad bin Zayed Al-Nahyan award the winning companies or government departments with prizes of over $2.2 million.

Overseas aid

Linking the allocative state with a support for Islam and the Arab world, and in some cases even environmentalism has been Abu Dhabi's enormous overseas aid programme. The majority of this largesse receives extensive and detailed domestic newspaper coverage, which invariably stresses the historically strong relations between the recipient country and Abu Dhabi or the UAE. Indeed, a day will rarely go by without a major UAE overseas aid-related headline appearing in domestic newspapers, often rather crudely stating the dollar figure of the aid involved. Also mentioned will be the member of the ruling family presiding over the charitable body and perhaps a specific story of a stricken family or village in the country in question. The first of the major aid organizations to be founded was the Abu Dhabi Fund for Arab Development in 1971—later renamed the Abu Dhabi Fund for Development. This had an initial capitalization of 50 million Bahraini dinars[91] and by 1974 it was estimated that overseas aid accounted for over 20 percent of Abu Dhabi's GDP.[92] Notably, surplus oil revenues were being channelled into war torn Palestine and a $200 million gift was given to Egypt and Syria to help them recover from their war effort.[93] Throughout the 1980s the ADFD's work gathered pace, with funds being channelled into Iraq and with over $3 million of flood relief being supplied to the Yemen. The ADFD helped to rebuild the giant Marib Dam in the Yemen at great cost in 1986 and continued to contribute to its maintenance costs up until 2002.[94] The 1990s saw the circle being widened even further, with aid being dispensed to Somalia and the dispossessed Muslim communities of Kosovo. Moreover, following Iraq's annexation of Kuwait, over 60,000 Kuwaiti nationals fled to the UAE, the majority arriving in Abu Dhabi. All were provided with accommodation and free medical care.[95]

In 2008 a federal minister of state without portfolio[96] in the Council of Ministers controversially stated that the UAE gave 3.6 percent of its GDP in overseas aid. A British United Nations representative for humanitarian affairs[97] countered that such a percentage was highly dubious given that the average aid contributions for first world donor countries was about 0.7 percent. This view was backed up by the head of the UN's Office for Coordination of Humanitarian Affairs[98] who agreed that 3.6 percent was extremely high and called for 'more visibility and transparency' from Abu Dhabi. Since this debacle Abu Dhabi has set up an External Aid Liaison Bureau—headed by Sheikh Hamdan bin Zayed Al-Nahyan—in an effort to provide a better interface between the various UAE aid donors and foreign bodies.[99] However, given Abu Dhabi's long history of generous overseas aid and its ongoing commitment to such programmes, the original figure may have been accurate after all.

In recent years it is thought that the ADFD alone has dispensed over $6 billion in aid to fifty-two different countries.[100] Assistance to Palestine over the last decade is believed to have been in excess of $4 billion, including a $62 million Sheikh Zayed Residential City having been built in Gaza in 2004[101] and the $70 million rebuilding of the Jenin Camp after its destruction in 2002.[102] When the current Israeli bombardments of Gaza cease, and the dust settles, it is more than likely that Abu Dhabi will be the first to offer material assistance. After the resolution of the Lebanese civil war Abu Dhabi injected between $500 and $700 million into the stricken country, and funding was provided for the Lebanese Army to purchase high-tech mine-clearing equipment.[103] Following the 2006 conflict, the UAE Red Crescent Society provided the Lebanon with a further $300 million as part of the Emirates Solidarity Project. Most of the money has been spent on rebuilding physical infrastructure damaged by Israeli bombings and constructing new hospitals and schools.[104]

Other major projects have included the supply of 40 tons of medicines and foodstuffs to the Sudan[105] and the Khalifa bin Zayed Al-Nahyan Foundation's building of over 100 new water wells in Sierra Leone.[106] Since the Anglo-American invasion in 2001 UAE Red Crescent Society aid to Afghanistan has amounted to $41 million, with a further $30 million having been supplied by other Abu Dhabi-based groups.[107] This has been used to construct a large hospital, six clinics, a public library, eleven schools and even a 6,000 student capacity Zayed University of Afghanistan. Soon there will also be a Zayed City, to house over 2000 displaced persons, and 150 water wells.[108] Khalifa's foundation also announced that it would pay for the construction of a $100 million Khalifa bin Zayed City on the outskirts of Cairo to help house poor Egyptian city-dwellers. In some ways the project can be interpreted as a double act of charity, as Abu Dhabi has awarded the lucrative contract to the beleaguered Dubai developer, Emaar Properties.[109]

The greatest recent recipient of Abu Dhabi aid has, however, been Iraq. Over the past five years several large donations have been made, including a gift of $215 million in 2005 for the reconstruction effort,[110] and the UAE Armed Forces' supplying of helicopters and other equipment for the new Iraqi military.[111] In summer 2008 Sheikh Khalifa bin Zayed Al-Nahyan even announced that he would scrap all of Iraq's outstanding debts to the UAE—amounting to some $7 billion. He explained that this would 'help alleviate the economic burdens endured by the brotherly Iraqi people,' and then invited the Iraqi prime minister[112] to Abu Dhabi to confirm the deal. Remarkably, in the near future there may be an even greater beneficiary of Abu Dhabi largesse than Iraq, as it has been reported that the Arab League is so short of funds that its secretary general has begun to press a number of member states for increased donations in order to keep the league alive. The secretary general has already stated that the UAE has been one of the most accommodating donors thus far.[113]

7

UNRESOLVED PROBLEMS
EXTERNAL AND STRUCTURAL

While Abu Dhabi's political stability and sound economic policies are causes for much optimism, there are several outstanding problems that have not been sufficiently addressed, some of which are already hampering the emirate's development, while others may become obstacles in the future. These difficulties fall into two categories: complex external threats and internal structural failings that are the byproduct of monarchical survival strategies. With regards to the former, a well equipped military and a surfeit of peacekeeping initiatives have done much to preserve Abu Dhabi and the United Arab Emirates' neutrality in an otherwise volatile region. Nevertheless, there remain unresolved disputes with potentially antagonistic neighbours. And although terrorism is unlikely to be an immediate concern for Abu Dhabi, given the careful and sensitive nature of its development thus far, it cannot be ruled out. Of the latter category there exists the dilemma of labour nationalization and motivating a national population long accustomed to very generous state patronage. The only solution would appear to be improved education, but this sector is failing abysmally. Other structural concerns include the absence of a proper roadmap towards political reform. The current hybrid government, buttressed by well funded and ingenious attempts to embed its wider legitimacy, has protected the traditional monarchy thus far, but strategies for future political participation ought to be considered, especially when close neighbours are opening up their polities. There is also much consternation over media censorship, boycotting practices, and human rights' issues. The bodies responsible for such matters appear anachronistic and are undoubtedly liabilities in a new era that requires Abu Dhabi to gain international recognition and credibility. Finally, dating back to the disagreements of the 1970s, there still remains the issue of federation-building. A persisting lack of coherence, an increasing wealth gap, and uncertainties regarding the union's future have yet to be adequately addressed.

The UAE Armed Forces and Abu Dhabi's active neutrality

Since the amalgamation of the various emirate-level militaries in 1996, the Abu Dhabi-led UAE Armed Forces has evolved into one of the most advanced militaries in the developing world. In the near future its technological sophistication will increase even further given the array of military-related joint ventures, including the Abu Dhabi Shipbuilding Company, Abu Dhabi Aircraft Technologies, Abu Dhabi Systems Integration, Emirates Advanced Investments, and Al-Yah Satellites.[1] Annual spending amounts to several billion dollars,[2] and the UAE Armed Forces is now one of the few non-NATO customers eligible to purchase the latest western armaments.[3] Most often, Abu Dhabi has purchased French equipment. This is perhaps owing to Sheikh Zayed bin Sultan Al-Nahyan's initially poor experiences with British manufacturers in the 1960s and 1970s compared to more straightforward transactions with French companies.[4] For years the UAE Air Force has relied upon French Mirage jets, and has now taken delivery of another large order of Mirage 2000s, complete with laser-targeting pods.[5] An even bigger French purchase has been $3 billion worth of Leclerc main battle tanks—in preference to British Challengers.[6] In the near future French manufacturers will be supplying the UAE Armed Forces with modular infrared units that will allow, among other capabilities, night vision and live communication between soldiers and field commanders. Other major army acquistions have included Turkish armoured personnel carriers and South African and Dutch howitzers. The UAE Air Force has also taken receipt of British Aerospace Hawk 128s, Sikorsky Black Hawk helicopters, Apache AH64 gunships,[7] and a large number of F16E Desert Falcons from Lockheed Martin.[8]

143

Most recently Abu Dhabi has placed a special emphasis on missiles and integrated defence systems. After all, even the latest aircraft and tanks can only ever serve as a tripwire against a determined foe. Moreover, the UAE Armed Forces lacks manpower: although it may claim to have about 60,000 personnel, it is an open secret that several thousand—and most likely the majority of the lower ranks—are Arab expatriates.[9] It is certainly difficult to recruit nationals to serve as anything less than commissioned officers given the benefits the state offers. Thus, the UAE has one of the world's largest mercenary armies. Among the missile acquisitions have been British-manufactured precision guided missiles specially customized for desert conditions,[10] and similarly customized cruise missiles—the Black Shaheen—supplied by a European manufacturer.[11] In summer 2008 it was announced that Abu Dhabi was poised to procure a further $9 billion worth of missiles—one of the largest missile orders in history. Russia's Almaz Central Design Bureau was at one stage believed to be the preferred contractor, and would have supplied S-400 Triumphs as part of a lorry-based missile system capable of intercepting aircraft, cruise missiles, and ballistic missiles at a range of up to 400km. However, at least $7bn of the missile budget has now been spent on the Terminal High Altitude Area Defense system (THAAD) manufactured by Lockheed Martin and capable of destroying enemy missiles in the stratosphere. The remainder may be spent on a mixture of other defensive US missiles including Patriots and Slamraams.[12] Backing up these missile launchers will be a number of early warning systems including a US-manufactured radar facility,[13] Boeing early warning and control aircraft, and a German submarine surveillance system.[14]

For the final line of its defence the UAE Armed Forces has also been promised immediate support from superpower militaries, some of which have committed to dispatching rapid reaction forces in the event of conflict. Unsurprisingly, given its history of lucrative arms deals, France has made the firmest guarantees to Abu Dhabi. For the past nine years there has been some form of agreement in place[15] and recently it was discreetly announced that in 2009 a French base housing between 400 and 500 soldiers would be established somewhere in Abu Dhabi. Interestingly, the option of hosting of permanent foreign bases on United Arab Emirates' soil was repeatedly rejected during

Zayed's reign.[16] The US has been less forthcoming with promises, but it is well known that several US military and intelligence personnel have been stationed temporarily at Abu Dhabi's Dhafrah airbase.[17] Embarrassingly, after the 2005 crash of a US spy drone embarking on a mission over Afghanistan it was revealed that its take-off base at Dhafrah had been used by the US Army Air Force since 2002.[18] Furthermore, while much has been written about Dubai's Jebel Ali Port and International Airport being heavily used by the US Navy and other US military contractors,[19] it is less well known that Abu Dhabi's Mina Zayed is the US Navy's second most used port in the Persian Gulf.[20]

Abu Dhabi has continuously positioned itself as a wealthy active neutral. Historically, it has tried to intervene in almost every regional dispute, with the Union Defence Force and then later the UAE Armed Forces having regularly dispatched gift-bearing peacekeeping forces to troubled neighbours and with the ruler having frequently sought to broker peace deals. This strategy has allowed Abu Dhabi to build upon its overseas aid programmes by strengthening its reputation as a concerned Arab intermediary, which has undoubtedly helped to deflect public Arab opinion away from the UAE military's heavy dependency on a western superpower umbrella. The first example of such diplomacy was in 1974 when Zayed mediated a territorial dispute between Egypt and Libya.[21] In 1977 the UDF was deployed for the first time, when a contingent was sent to join the Joint Arab Deterrent Force in Lebanon.[22] In 1991 Zayed attempted to save Iraq from full scale invasion by meeting with King Fahd bin Abdul-Aziz Al-Saud and Muhammad Hosni Mubarak in an effort to forge an agreement between Saddam Hussein and the displaced ruler of Kuwait, Sheikh Jaber Al-Ahmad Al-Sabah.[23] The following year the UAE Armed Forces made its maiden intervention outside the Middle East by sending a peacekeeping force to assist US operations in Somalia.[24] During the mid-1990s more UAE troops arrived in Somalia in addition to Rwanda and Mozambique.[25] Significantly, in 1995 the UAE Armed Forces became the first Arab military to intervene in a modern European conflict when it began to airlift wounded Muslims out of Bosnia. By 1999 Abu Dhabi was again proactive in the Balkans, sending a force to help protect the embattled Kosovars.[26]

In an uncanny echo of his 1991 negotiations, in early 2003 Zayed proposed an emergency summit with the aim of diverting the US from attacking Iraq. A meeting was held in Sharm el-Sheikh and presided over by the Arab League secretary-general.[27] Zayed was reported to have offered Saddam Hussein and his family sanctuary in Abu Dhabi if he complied with US demands to leave Iraq.[28] Since Sheikh Khalifa bin Zayed Al-Nahyan's succession, Abu Dhabi's actively neutral foreign policy has remained unchanged. In early 2007 the federal minister for foreign affairs, Sheikh Abdullah bin Zayed Al-Nahyan, flew to Iran to meet with that country's leaders,[29] and later in the year (and within the space of just one week) Khalifa separately hosted both Mahmoud Ahmadinejad and Vice-President Dick Cheney, presumably with the intention of defusing the Iran-US nuclear standoff.[30]

In 2008 Abu Dhabi was if anything a more energetic peacekeeper and middleman than ever before. Early in the year it was revealed by the BBC that several hundred UAE Armed Forces' troops and armoured cars had been deployed to Afghanistan to maintain supply line security and deliver humanitarian aid. On occasion this contingent has had to fend off Taleban attacks thus making it the only Arab force in Afghanistan that is actually engaging the enemy.[31] The commanding officer stated 'if we have any types of personal attacks we react with fire. And after that we go to the elders in this area and say: "Why are you shooting us? We came here to help you." And we try to convince the people about the US, about British. They came to give peace.'[32] Later in the year Condoleeza Rice, who was enroute to East Asia, was invited to Abu Dhabi to debrief US envoy William Burns on his Iran negotiations and also to meet with Abdullah. Just one week before, Sheikh Muhammad bin Zayed Al-Nahyan had received Ali Rida Sheikh Attar—an envoy of Mahmoud Ahmadinejad and undersecretary to the Iranian minister for foreign affairs.[33] Shortly afterwards Khalifa followed up his debt relief for Iraq by sending Abdullah to Baghdad: the first high-ranking Gulf Cooperation Council ministerial visit since the outbreak of war, and then appointed a UAE ambassador to Iraq for the first time in five years.[34] Combined, these actions earned Khalifa praise during United Nations Security Council meetings in August 2008.[35]

Nevertheless despite the military buildup, the superpower support, and the skilful diplomacy, Abu Dhabi is still vulnerable to conventional attack, or more likely collateral damage from a proximate conventional war—especially one that results in the blocking of key oil export arteries such as the Straits of Hormuz, or that endangers the waters close to the emirate's offshore operations or the hinterland of its onshore operations. Of these threats the greatest is undoubtedly that of Iranian aggression, perhaps if Iran is the subject of an Israeli or US interdiction and Tehran retaliates by hitting a pro-US Gulf state. This risk is considerably elevated by the ongoing dispute over the three islands occupied by Iran in 1971. An accommodation had been reached shortly after the invasion between Muhammad Reza Shah Pahlavi and the ruler of Sharjah, Sheikh Khalid bin Muhammad Al-Qasimi. This was supposed to ensure that the only inhabited island—Abu Musa—would technically remain a municipality of Sharjah. However, in the early 1990s Iran reneged on the deal as Revolutionary Guards began to demand that all Sharjah national residents of Abu Musa obtained Iranian entry visas.[36] Since then, Iran has opened an airport and a town hall on Abu Musa[37] and in 2008 Tehran announced it would build a coastguard station and a registration office for ships and sailors. Most worryingly, in addition to conducting naval exercises close to the islands, it has been reported that Iran intends to deploy 200km range anti-ship missiles on Abu Musa: these would be capable of closing the Straits of Hormuz indefinitely.[38]

Terrorism in Abu Dhabi

There has been much discussion of the possibility of terrorist attacks in the United Arab Emirates, and there is already a history—albeit rather guarded—of incidents, foiled attempts, and arrests.[39] But one can only surmise that Dubai is the most vulnerable target in the UAE given its palpable relaxations of local customs and its enthusiastic accommodation of non-Muslim, non-Arab, expatriates. By contrast Abu Dhabi seems to be regarded as a relatively more innocent party, with most observers ostensibly content with the emirate's more careful and respectful development plans. Most UAE-related terror threats posted on radical websites specify Dubai as their primary target.[40]

With a few exceptions,[41] most of Abu Dhabi's projects seem reasonably compatible with the region's religion, culture, and traditions. Should an incident occur in Dubai, as it well might given the flurry of credible warnings that have been intercepted by international intelligence agencies,[42] Abu Dhabi would not be unscathed, but the damage could probably be contained. Undoubtedly Dubai's flimsy development model—which relies heavily on an unstained international reputation and rather elastic foreign direct investment and tourism—would suffer greatly, and perhaps unravel even further. But Abu Dhabi's oil-backed economy, complemented by its new economy made up of far more resilient sectors, should remain unaffected.[43]

Nevertheless the danger to Abu Dhabi remains real, and has long been apparent. In 1977 the federal minister of state for foreign affairs[44] was assassinated at Abu Dhabi International Airport,[45] and the following year the UAE's ambassador to France[46] was gunned down upon arrival in Paris. In the mid-1980s bombs exploded at the airport,[47] and in 1994 Omani intelligence agents uncovered a large cell of revolutionaries based in Abu Dhabi who were plotting the overthrow of Sultan Qabus bin Said Al-Said.[48] Most notably, in late 2002 the Saudi-born Abd Al-Rahim Al-Nashiri—mastermind of the attacks in 2000 on *USS Cole* and *USS The Sullivans*, and the attack in 2002 on France's *SS Limberg*—was arrested in the emirate.[49] Alarmingly, he was picked up while in the final planning stages of a terrorist attack on 'vital economic targets' in the UAE.[50] More recently, in June 2008 the Joint Terrorism Analysis Centre of the British government advised that terrorists were planning to carry out attacks in the UAE, thus prompting the British Foreign and Commonwealth Office to raise their terror threat warning for the UAE to the highest possible level.[51] The following month the Commander of the UAE Navy—Muhammad Al-Tanaji—stated at a conference of Gulf naval commanders that 'the UAE and its neighbours faced a growing threat from terrorism, piracy and smuggling.'[52]

Fortunately, Abu Dhabi shares none of the complacency of its neighbours and has invested heavily in anti-terrorism measures. Since 2001 the emirate has maintained a biometric database of iris prints to prevent unwanted individuals from returning. After becoming fully operational in 2003 it is thought that several dozen suspects were intercepted and denied entry within the first six months.[53] Soon, the database will benefit from biometric face scans, courtesy of the aforementioned Biodentity joint venture.[54] More obviously, Abu Dhabi has gone to great efforts to plug its long and porous border with Oman. For many years it was suspected that Al-Qaeda operatives were travelling from the subcontinent to the Omani coastline and then transferring across land—through Abu Dhabi—to reach the Gulf coast.[55] In 2003 construction on a wall was begun, and in summer 2008 the border was finally sealed, with the previously open border between Abu Dhabi-controlled Al-Ayn and the adjoining Oman-controlled Buraimi cities being restricted to just a handful of new checkpoints.[56]

Labour nationalization and the education sector

The state has been a cornerstone of Abu Dhabi's political stability, yet many of the structures it has created have limited the indigenous population's potential to participate fully in the emirate's extraordinary economic development. Notably, a citizenry has been cultivated over thirty-five years that is now wholly accustomed to material benefits and to no forms of extraction. Moreover, with all the various *kafil* sponsorship systems, soft loans, and public sector employment opportunities, nationals have lacked the motivation to enter into competitive job markets. In the mid-1990s even Sheikh Zayed bin Sultan Al-Nahyan warned of the phenomenon that was partly his creation, criticizing the inactivity of young national men who should be gainfully employed.[57] Unfortunately, since then the problem has been compounded by strategies that aimed to encourage nationals to participate, but in effect priced them out of the market and made them even less attractive employees. In particular, labour laws that guaranteed access to special pension funds and limited their working hours greatly increased the cost of hiring nationals.[58] Even more heavy handed have been the quota systems introduced in certain industries.[59] These have made expatriate colleagues resentful of their Emirati counterparts and have made employers increasingly wary.

With the new economy beginning to take shape, this problem will become increasingly acute as many of the new sectors are being spearheaded by semi-governmental bodies or in some cases even genuine private sector companies. As such there is a real danger that the current generation of Abu Dhabi nationals will fail to integrate with the new economy. After all, *ceteris paribus* a private sector employer will prefer to hire foreign nationals with a proven work ethnic and lower salary expectations. Today, it is difficult to ascertain the true extent of the problem, partly due to the lack of authoritative statistical surveys. Conservative estimates for the whole of the UAE, according to the the federal National Human Resource Development and Employment Authority (Tanmia), are that nationals make up only nine percent of the workforce[60] and there are currently 17,000 unemployed Emirati adults.[61] Other estimates have put the figure as high as 35,000,[62] with many of these being degree holders.[63] The majority of these are likely to be in Abu Dhabi. More broadly, it is thought that well over 50 percent of those nationals in receipt of the generous social security benefits are able-bodied and capable of work.[64]

The only long-term solution is improved education at all levels. Nationals must acquire the qualifications demanded by employers and thereby meet directly the needs of the new economy. Moreover, they must have an educational experience that not only equips them to compete on level terms with expatriates but also encourages them to accept authority and think critically—essential skills that have rarely been transferred in the UAE's schools and were never a requirement of the old system of distributed public sector jobs. Unfortunately the education system in Abu Dhabi and the UAE is still failing badly, with the Education Development Index having ranked the UAE 90th out of 125 surveyed countries for the quality of its education provision.[65] Moreover, in 2007 the World Bank indicated that the UAE's knowledge economy—that is the sectors of the economy relating to the production of knowledge and requiring educated professionals—has actually shrunk since 2005, with the blame being placed on a deterioration of the domestic education sector.[66] Perhaps most disgracefully, given Abu Dhabi's vast riches, the illiteracy rate in the UAE was over 22 percent in 2003,[67] and currently still stands at between 10 and 16 percent.[68] This compares unfavourably with many other Arab states, including those such as Jordan, which has never had access to great wealth.[69] Gross enrollment is also thought to be very poor,[70] only

11 percent of nationals hold degrees,[71] and there is a huge gender imbalance at the tertiary level with only 28 percent of university students being male.[72] A counter claim is often made that many Emirati males have the opportunity to study overseas, but the number that do cannot account for this shortfall.

Incredibly, part of the problem has been a lack of funding. Although the federal budget allocation for education now exceeds $2 billion, this is only a third of the allocation for military expenditure and, in relative terms, is about a quarter of the educational expenditure of some other Arab states.[73] This has led to per student financial support declining by over 20 percent since 2000,[74] which has meant that some institutions have had to turn students away in order to maintain the quality of their programs.[75] Understandably, the national population has responded by sending their children to private sector institutions for all stages of their education, and it is now thought that over 40 percent of national students are in the private sector.[76] The federal ministries for education and higher education, in addition to the education-related emirate-level government departments have complained that they have little authority to regulate outside of the public sector. Although the situation in Abu Dhabi is less grave than in Dubai, where many of the private sector institutions effectively exist in free zones, it is nonetheless proving difficult to maintain standards and form a coherent strategy. There is also a chronic shortage of Emirati staff in the education sector, thus denying young nationals indigenous role models. Education has traditionally been viewed as a low status profession, and this has resulted in very small numbers of nationals—especially males—training as teachers or lecturers.[77] Even high quality expatriate staff are becoming difficult to recruit, as salaries have remained stagnant for many years, prompting many veteran educators to move to Qatar, Kuwait and other parts of the Gulf that are offering far more competitive remuneration.

Nonetheless there is some hope, with every indication being that the government is now seriously committed to reforming the sector. New initiatives are in place, and these may soon have a significant impact. At the secondary level Mugheer Al-Khaili's Abu Dhabi Education Council has established a public-private partnership agreement for the management of public schools. With cooperation from the

Singapore National Institute for Education this should lead to firmer controls over the qualifications of educators, especially college principals—who must now possess a degree in education—and struggling teachers, who will now have access to a mentor.[78] An accreditation system will also soon be applied in an effort to bring public schools up to international standards. New curricula will be introduced with an emphasis on critical thinking rather than rote learning, and with more weight being placed on English language instruction. Combined, it is hoped these curricular developments will prepare students better for the expectations of the tertiary sector.[79] By 2012 all schools will have to comply with the new requirements, and private schools will face closure unless they have independently sought accreditation from a reputable international body.[80]

The tertiary sector is set for a similarly comprehensive overhaul, with several major projects involving esteemed regional and international partners already in the pipeline. These do not aim simply to build lavish new campuses and physical infrastructure for higher education in Abu Dhabi, but also to improve standards and expectations. The new Khalifa University of Science, Technology, and Research will enter into an industrial partnership with Abu Dhabi National Bank. The latter will advise on employer demands and provide nearly $7 million of research funding.[81] Abu Dhabi University, which was founded in 2003, will soon benefit from a memorandum of understanding with the London Stock Exchange. The latter will help ADU to set up internationally accredited degrees and certificates in finance studies,[82] thereby dramatically boosting the institution's reputation. Other high profile linkages have included the opening of a branch of the Sorbonne University in 2006,[83] and soon Abu Dhabi will host a branch of New York University[84] in addition to the aforementioned multitude of research centres involved in the Masdar project. As part of a reciprocal agreement the new Sheikh Muhammad bin Zayed University Scholars Programme will select students competitively from Abu Dhabi's two public sector universities (Zayed University and the United Arab Emirates University of Al-Ayn) and then send them to New York University or other international partner institutions.[85]

Equally important is the coordination of these many projects, as Abu Dhabi seeks to connect together all of the new universities, research centres, and think tanks. As a spokesperson for the Abu Dhabi Education Council has admitted: 'many of the universities haven't got a specific research focus as institutions… they're concentrating on the business side of higher education rather than focusing on research, and they probably won't collaborate on research very easily. Their focus has not been on it and they're in competition.'[86] It is hoped that a new National Authority for Scientific Research will provide the solution: backed by the federal ministry for higher education and supplied with an annual budget of nearly $30 million it will host committees of leading academics that will apply quality control to national research output and help determine future research trajectories.[87]

A roadmap for political reform

As discussed earlier in this book, Abu Dhabi and the federal government have developed a hybrid polity of informal and formal institutions, which fortunately seems to be working.[88] However, there are pressures building that will soon require revisions to the system, especially as the indigenous population continues to grow[89] and as increasing urbanisation[90] and female economic participation[91] reduce large, extended families to more nuclear units, and old informal structures are placed under strain. Quite simply, nationals will find it more difficult to access directly sheikhs in their courts or to find suitable traditional intermediaries. Secondly, a wave of reform is spreading through the United Arab Emirates' neighbours: although little more than window-dressing in most cases, the subject is at least debated across the Gulf and legislation is slowly being enacted.[92] Thirdly, in Abu Dhabi and Dubai's keenness to integrate their new economies into the international system, the UAE has duly joined several international organisations. Some of these, including the World Trade Organisation—which admitted the UAE in 1996—require all member states to have a roadmap towards good governance.[93] Thus, Abu Dhabi has to have some kind of plan in place. Given the mixed experiences with western style democratic implants in Iraq and elsewhere in the Gulf, it is likely that the ruling family will try carefully to readjust the existing polity in such as way that it remains connected to the country's anthropological reality.[94]

There is already some evidence of fairly safe measures being taken to reinvigorate or at least extend the lifespan of the old system. Informal 'agents' or chamberlains are being appointed by members of the ruling family to serve as conduits between themselves and regular citizens, but invariably these are still viewed by Emiratis as being part of the 'old guard.' There has also been a keen interest in various forms of 'e-government' with the reasoning that websites and Internet fora provide opportunities for government officials and even sheikhs to maintain at least some semblance of direct connection with the citizenry. Dubai has pioneered such services in the Gulf, with a plethora of government electronic portals—all of which allow grievances to be filed online—and with even the ruler himself having an interactive website and a Facebook profile. Dubai has even launched a public service that allows members of the public to telephone or email municipality officials at designated times of the week.[95] Nonetheless, Abu Dhabi is catching up, with a spokesperson for its current e-government project explaining that they 'sought to adopt the best standards and practices to meet the target of ranking Abu Dhabi among the best five governments worldwide.'[96] The emirate is also being highly innovative, with its municipality launching online videos on the YouTube website and on Ikbis—an Arabic video website for children. Both sites are very popular among web-savvy young Emiratis. These videos showcase the achievements of the municipality and, according to one of its directors: 'we took this step so as to spread our views about our activities and get comments to build a stronger social structure and to make sure to be in contact with the public.'[97] In total, there are now about 500 Abu Dhabi government services accessible online.[98]

No matter how effective such services are they can still never amount to much more than a partial definition of what a government should be. This too has been recognised and a number of experiments have now begun to reform the consultative councils, namely the Federal National Council that has already attracted much criticism due to its perceived ineffectiveness. Unfortunately the steps that have been taken thus far have backfired and have if anything made the ruling establishment more wary of future adjustments. In early 2006 a new Council of Ministers portfolio entitled federal minister of state for

Federal National Council Affairs was created and the incumbent was made responsible for strengthening the FNC.[99] The plan was to stage elections for half of the forty positions, but instead of allowing universal suffrage for the entire UAE national population, only those approved to join an 'electoral college' were permitted to vote. By the time the elections were held in late 2006 it had transpired that less than 6700 nationals had been admitted to this electoral college—of which fewer than 1200 were women.[100] The whole process was therefore delegitimised in many people's minds. Only 60 percent of voters actually cast their ballots and most observers considered the process to have been a sham.[101] One prominent Abu Dhabi national[102] described the elections as 'a setback that showed clear tendencies towards tribalism.'[103] Since then, the position of minister of state portfolio for Federal National Council affairs has been removed from the Council of Ministers.[104]

It is unclear what the next step will be; Abu Dhabi and the UAE have been in a transitional political state since these elections, with different proposals being forwarded. Municipal councils have been introduced in the western region of the emirate, and elections to positions in the Abu Dhabi Chamber of Commerce have now been occurring for some years.[105] But in both cases these involve only a limited number of people, and the entities involved are far from the emirate's centre of gravity. In 2007 it was suggested that the FNC would undergo a second round of elections in 2010, in which all forty of the positions would be contested and the electoral college greatly expanded.[106] This proposal met with only a lukewarm response and has received no further press coverage. Instead it appears that the FNC is being given a little more power. Sheikh Khalifa bin Zayed Al-Nahyan has publicly stated his commitment to making it a stronger bridge between the government and the citizenry,[107] explaining that it will have a 'bigger role… by empowering it to be an authority that will provide great support and guidance of the executive… the FNC will become more capable, more effective and more sensitive to the issues affecting the nation and the people.'[108] Since mid-2007 the FNC has begun to host a number of debates, many of which have criticized ministries and—most significantly—some of which have allowed non-FNC members to attend and participate. Current members of the FNC have claimed that they are more active than ever before, and that they feel they are 'pushing at an open door' and are likely to soon have an even more expanded role.[109] Examples of such debates have included a lively session on federal education policies,[110] a session in which five ministers were collectively quizzed on their performance, and a session on how to best control the increase in personal loans. Perhaps the FNC's most notable success has been its debate on a new commercial fraud law: this involved the participation of the federal minister for finance[111] and duly led to the creation of a new credit database.[112]

Secrecy and transparency

Many parts of the Abu Dhabi establishment remain opaque and secretive. Often the private nature of Bedouin culture is used as a convenient explanatory device by establishment figures or long-serving expatriate advisors. However when most male members of the ruling family occupy key positions in government and when government-backed authorities are effectively in control of the country's natural resources, its overseas assets, and therefore its future prosperity, there is a growing feeling that these individuals and institutions must submit to more domestic scrutiny. With so much ostensibly public wealth at stake it would seem fair that the broader citizenry should at least have access to basic information, and should especially be assured of the ethicality of any sovereign wealth investments or other foreign linkages. It is likely, for example, that in late 2007 many nationals would have objected to the Mubadala Development Corporation's setting up of a joint venture with Las Vegas' MGM Mirage[113] had they been aware that the latter is the world's second largest gaming company.[114] Moreover, as Abu Dhabi's massive funds extend deeper into other countries' institutions and companies, the emirate will also have to be prepared to submit to more thorough external investigations.

Thus far, the Abu Dhabi Investments Authority has borne the brunt of international criticism: despite its enormous influence and power it still does not have an effective communications department. Moreover, when the majority of the world's sovereign wealth managers attended the World Economic Forum in Switzerland in early 2008 ADIA did not see fit to send a delegation.[115] In March 2008, the US began to place pressure on Abu Dhabi by obliging ADIA to sign an undertaking in which it had to agree that its investments would be purely commercial and that it had to have more disclosure.[116] Nonetheless, such commitments to improving transparency have not yet had much impact, with Sheikh Khalifa bin Zayed Al-Nahyan stating in a rare interview with a Lebanese newspaper that 'the estimations of ADIA's wealth are exaggerated and they do not reflect the truth and size of Abu Dhabi's investments abroad.'[117] Such comments are nothing new, with Abu Dhabi having often tried to downplay the true extent of its wealth. As one commentator has explained, these appeals for modesty can probably be best understood by domestic political and transparency concerns: '...the Al-Nahyan are the stewards of the money, not the owners. Hence, it could be awkward for the ruling family if the country was overly informed of the amounts, investments, and procedures of the funds under their fiduciary responsibility.'[118]

Should these attitudes persist, they will frustrate the ambitions of Abu Dhabi's infant new economic sectors. All of the high technology heavy industries, the future energy sector, the real estate developers, and the tourism developers are reliant on a sound international reputation for Abu Dhabi. In addition, the abovementioned efforts to promote a new knowledge-based economy involving top international university brands cannot succeed if perforce they must operate within a closed system. Most of the parastatals and companies pioneering these developments need to be respected by their global partners as credible corporations with boards of directors and transparent codes of practice. Tellingly, the Mubdala Development Corporation and all of its subsidiaries supply the public domain with an immense amount of information and have relatively accessible spokesmen. Fully fledged websites feature biographies of all senior decision-makers in addition to strategic plans and statistics relating to the size and direction of their investments. Moreover, those sections of the government focusing on these new sectors and thereby 'allied' to Mubadala are similarly transparent.

The Abu Dhabi Executive Council, the Abu Dhabi Tourism Authority, and all of the other departments either chaired by Sheikh

Muhammad bin Zayed Al-Nahyan or falling under his umbrella would come into this category, thus underscoring the divide between the new and old in the emirate's political economy. By the beginning of 2009 Muhammad's power to enforce transparency may increase a little further with the creation of a new Abu Dhabi Accountability Authority, likely to be supervised by anther Al-Mubarak veteran of Dolphin and Mubadala—Riyad bin Abdulrahman Al-Mubarak. Established by Law 14 of 2008, the authority will have the power to investigate the financial reports of any government-backed entity that the crown prince wishes to place under greater scrutiny. Unfortunately, an article of this legislation states that the new authority can only examine entities in which the government share is less than 50 percent,[119] thus effectively keeping ADIA and the other major sovereign wealth funds above inspection.

Media and Internet censorship

Despite the occasional glimmer of hope, for the most part the atmosphere of secrecy prevails, as attempts for transparency remain thwarted by a number of conservative, anachronistic bodies that seek to control tightly the flow of information. For years the most maligned of these was the federal ministry for information and culture which, in addition to acceptable duties such as the censorship of culturally offensive material, also effectively controlled all domestic newspaper and television output and the importation and distribution of all books and films across the United Arab Emirates. Although the ministry was finally disbanded in 2006, with many of its employees being rehoused in the new ministry for culture, youth, and the community; a number of its employees were assigned to the new National Media Council (NMC). This council's responsibilities include the supply of official press releases through its Emirates News Agency (WAM), the blacking out of nudity in media output (still by using black felt tip on newspaper and magazine articles), and the provision of funding for local filmmakers. In many ways this latter activity can be interpreted as another form of censorship, as only projects deemed suitable will receive funding. Indeed, when interviewed, successful recipients have admitted they self-censor in order to get the money.[120]

The NMC's other duties include running a department for external information. When there is bad publicity concerning Abu Dhabi or the UAE in foreign newspapers the department contacts the publication in question and seeks to limit the damage. The department also seeks to limit the output of certain academics: a policy which undermines any commitment the UAE may have to freedom of speech and is undoubtedly offputting for future academics wishing to develop an interest in the region. Moreover, despite claims that it has become more tolerant and predominantly censors books that offend Islam or are pornographic in content,[121] there is little doubt that the NMC still actively bans a wide range of books, or—more accurately perhaps—simply avoids providing the necessary approval to willing distributors. The US Bureau of Democracy, Human Rights, and Labor annual reports on the UAE confirm this view, regularly detailing banned publications in the UAE.[122] Ironically, Abu Dhabi now hosts an annual book fair which aims to 'revitalise the censorship-strangled Arab publishing industry,' and whose director has stated that 'if we encourage freedom of speech and protect writers and publishers, other countries will follow us.'[123]

The NMC is also responsible for enforcing the federal press and publications law. Although this legislation is currently being amended, and the NMC can no longer lightly impose jail terms on offending journalists,[124] very large fines remain an option,[125] and journalistic misconduct is still considered to be a criminal offence rather than a civil matter. If anything, the new version of the law may be more restrictive than before, with fines for journalists who 'damage the UAE's reputation' or 'harm the economy.'[126] More importantly, the NMC can effectively rely on a national body of journalists who have been weaned on decades of self-censorship:[127] the majority of reporters are expatriates and few are willing to jeopardize their tax free salaries and livelihood in Abu Dhabi or elsewhere in the UAE. This is exacerbated by an atmosphere of ambiguity, with few journalists or editors quite able to establish what is permissible. Despite some noises being made about greater openness, as recently as early 2008 the director general of the NMC admitted during a US radio interview that it was still a punishable offence for journalists to criticize directly members of the UAE's seven ruling families.[128] This attitude serves as a brake on freedom of speech, especially given that so many positions in the federal and emirate level governments are staffed by members of these families, who are therefore voluntary public figures.

In the most awkward position has been Abu Dhabi's nascent English language press. With a new broadsheet owned by a subsidiary of the Mubadala Development Corporation having been conceived as a vehicle for improving transparency and promoting Abu Dhabi's credibility to both domestic and international audiences (with copies of the newspaper being made available in major UK and US cities), its predominantly western-trained editorial team has faced a difficult task since its launch in mid 2008. Although the newspaper has managed to go one step further than the UAE's other daily English newspapers by adding much need inhouse analysis to WAM's press releases, and by indulging in a some healthy schadenfreude when discussing developments in Dubai and other emirates, the mood of freedom surrounding its inception has nonetheless waned as the usual self-censorship has taken root and the reality of operating under the umbrella of the NMC has set in. Commissioned and quality approved pieces on key topics in the national interest have been killed,[129] column space has been used by government officials to discredit private individuals and civil society actors without seeking comments from the injured parties,[130] and major US newspapers have reported on claims made by its editorial team that they are not there to champion freedom of speech.[131]

Equally at odds with Abu Dhabi's new economy is the persisting censorship of electronic and telecommunications. It is widely believed that website usage, emails, and telephone calls are monitored.[132] Moreover, the bulk of households and commercial buildings still have their Internet access fed through proxy servers controlled by either Emirates Internet and Multimedia (EIM)—an arm of Etisalat, or through the aptly named Du—the newer, second half of the UAE's telecommunications duopoly. These in turn are supervised by the Telecommunications Regulatory Authority (TRA). As per official memoranda, the TRA is only supposed to block websites falling into specific 'prohibited content categories.' These categories include websites that allow users to circumvent the proxy, websites that promote criminal or terrorist activities, social networking websites that may facilitate premarital or homosexual relations, websites relating to narcotics, pornographic websites, Internet gambling services; hacking and spyware websites, websites with content offensive to religion, and Internet services such as Skype that allow person-to-person telecommunications (thereby bypassing the duopoly's telephone tariffs).[133]

However, a large number of other websites are either permanently or periodically blocked. Notably, sites containing information about political prisoners, human trafficking, or other human rights abuses that either directly or indirectly mention the UAE are sometimes blocked.[134] Uaeprison.com and Arabtimes.com remain permanently blocked with no explanation given for their blocking.[135] The former details abuses of the justice system in the UAE, often involving South Asian expatriates. Inoffensive websites containing information on the Bahai Faith, Judaism, and testimonies of former Muslims who have converted to Christianity are also often blocked.[136] International news websites that contain critical stories relating to members of the ruling families are also sometimes censored, including, on occasion even British horseracing newspapers that have discussed the shortcomings of various horse owning sheikhs. Perhaps least forgivably, personal blogs have also been blocked, and only reopened following international petitions from the blogging community. In summer 2005 a blog was blocked on the grounds that it contained nudity: the blog in fact contained no images, but was openly critical of the establishment.[137] In summer 2008 it was announced by the TRA that the duopoly would soon unblock thousands of censored websites. Unfortunately these newly accessible sites were simply those whose content had been modified specifically in line with the TRA's requirements, thus self-censoring.

As with the banning of books (which can always be ordered online), Internet censorship is becoming even more of an anachronism, as many of the new free zones and universities—especially those in Dubai—already have 'direct' Internet connections and are therefore above the proxy servers. Also, many of the UAE's new real estate developments, or at least those in Dubai, often have their own Internet connections, many of which offer unobstructed access.[138] A new generation of Internet technologies will further undermine these controls as 'bit torrent' services allow downloads of content directly from other computers, including websites that may be blocked by the proxy server. Social networking sites have also evolved, and have become an every day feature of people's lives: the UAE's proxy will never be able to censor Facebook or MySpace on the grounds that they facilitate premarital relations—which they can—as the uproar from millions of residents would be immeasurable. Including perhaps both the ruler of Dubai and Muhammad bin Zayed, whose respective Facebook fansites have 18,000 and 2,500 members.

The Israeli boycott

Similarly problematic for Abu Dhabi's international reputation is its maintenance of a government-run Israel boycott office. The origins of this office are understandable given the described monarchical legitimacy resources derived from Islam and the pouring of aid into Palestine and Arab states of the 'refusal front'[139] that have actively confronted Israel. Much like Saudi Arabia and other Gulf monarchies, the United Arab Emirates has felt duty bound to take an anti-Zionist stance from time to time.[140] Not much is known about the office itself, but it is likely to be squirrelled away in the federal government ministries and staffed by members of different ministries or Abu Dhabi emirate-level government departments. Since 1971 its duties have been enshrined in a federal law,[141] articles of which state that '… any natural or legal person shall be prohibited from directly or indirectly concluding an agreement with organisations or persons either resident in Israel, connected therewith by virtue of their nationality or working on its behalf.'[142]

However, the office's work extends far beyond a straightforward embargo on trade between UAE-based companies and Israel: telephone calls to Israel are barred, websites with an Israeli suffix are blocked in conjunction with the Internet proxy,[143] and Israeli nationals are not permitted to enter the UAE, nor—in theory—are any visitors allowed to the UAE that possess Israeli visa stamps.[144] Moreover, government-backed think tanks such as the shortlived Zayed Centre for Coordination and Follow-Up have published anti-Semitic material and hosted renowned anti-Semitic speakers.[145] According to the US Bureau for Democracy, Human Rights, and Labour, the National

Media Council also fails to prevent anti-semitic cartoons from being published in the two bestselling government-owned Arabic newspapers: *Al-Ittihad* and *Al-Bayan*.[146] The cartoons often depict Israeli leaders being compared to Hitler and Jews being portrayed as demons. In January 2009, at the height of the Gaza conflict, the UAE's bestselling English language newspaper, *Gulf News*, not only featured such a cartoon (featuring an Israeli solider with a forked red tongue),[147] but also published a Holocaust denial piece which claimed '…it is evident that the Holocaust was a conspiracy hatched by the Zionists and the Nazis, and many innocent people gave their lives as a result of this inhuman plot… the Holocaust was a major crime in history and the Israeli culprit is at it again today.'[148]

As with the NMC's extended responsibilities, the boycott office is becoming increasingly anachronistic, especially as Abu Dhabi and Dubai strive to position themselves as global economic hubs. Israel represents a natural economic partner in the Middle East for the UAE and there are frequent reports of Israeli businessmen being invited to Dubai, often in connection with that emirate's gold and diamond trade. Thus, at least one emirate is already actively breaking the boycott. In 2005 Bahrain chose to shut down its equivalent boycott office without any apparent backlash.[149] The UAE should perhaps now do the same, as the office's existence has brought many problems over the last few years. In the penultimate year of his reign Sheikh Zayed bin Sultan Al-Nahyan was vilified in the US press for his well intentioned attempt to establish a chair in Islamic Studies at Harvard University. The student and faculty body had made a connection between Zayed, the ZCCF, and the UAE's Israeli boycott. The Abu Dhabi donation was duly blocked, and in the process Zayed was branded 'a donor who funds hatred' and held responsible for the UAE's 'shameful human rights record, corporal punishment of dissidents, and dictatorial governance.'[150] Joining the World Trade Organisation has also placed pressure on the UAE to drop or at least relax the boycott. When Dubai agreed to host the 2003 annual general meeting of the WTO, delegations from all member states had to be invited, and there was no way to prevent the arrival of an Israeli delegation.[151] The maintenance of the boycott is also jeopardising future trade links between the US and the UAE, with the US Department of Commerce's Office of Antiboycott Compliance dutifully recording all examples of the UAE's boycott requests. These are normally clauses inserted into contracts issued by UAE companies, most often with the following wording: 'the seller shall not supply goods or materials which have been manufactured or processed in Israel nor shall the services of any Israeli organisation be used in handling or transporting the goods or materials.'[152]

Human rights' violations

Abu Dhabi and the UAE's human rights' record is very much under the international spotlight. For many years there have been concerns over the plight of domestic workers in the emirate. These were considerably elevated following the high profile trial of Saraha Balagan in the late 1990s. As a Filipina maid in Al-Ayn, she had killed her Emirati employer following an alleged rape. Although granted $27,000 compensation for the rape she was ordered to pay $40,000 in blood money to the man's relatives. The prosecution appealed the case and had her sentenced to death. Following a presidential appeal her sentence was finally reduced, but she still had to pay the blood money, serve a year in prison, and face 100 lashes.[153] The region also has a long and much discussed history of slavery,[154] and in recent years there has been considerable pressure placed on the federal government to take action on the use of Pakistani child camel jockeys. The UAE has also been criticized for its ambivalence towards human trafficking organizations, most of which airlift in prostitutes from former Soviet states and East Asia—many of whom are separated from their passports upon arrival.[155]

Although prostitution remains rife, especially in Abu Dhabi and Dubai, thankfully some action is now being taken on most of the other forms of modern slavery. In early 2005 a new law was introduced to ban child camel jockeys,[156] in 2006 a law concerning the combating of human trafficking was passed,[157] and in 2007 the UAE produced its first annual report on combating human trafficking and finally ratified the UN Protocol to Prevent, Suppress, and Punish Trafficking in Persons.[158] A seventy strong anti-trafficking department has now also been set up in the federal ministry for the interior.[159] This has been enough for the Annual Trafficking in Persons Report to downgrade the UAE from its previous ranking on the highest tier of offences to the second tier, stating that it is now a country that is merely 'vulnerable to losing ground on its human rights record.'[160]

In 2008 other shortcomings were exposed when a peer review of the UAE's record was undertaken under the auspices of the United Nations Human Rights Council in Geneva. Although the UAE agreed to work on several of the Council's most straightforward recommendations—introducing a law to protect children's rights, reforming the press and publications law, and signing up to the UN Convention Against Torture (of which the UAE is not yet a signatory)—over twenty further suggestions on how to improve the UAE's human rights record were rejected. According to WAM's press release the rejections were made on the grounds of 'legal, social, and cultural contradictions.'[161] Similarly, a spokesperson for the ministry for foreign affairs stated that the UN's suggestions were 'less helpful in being outside our framework, norms, and religious values.'[162] The suggestions included calls for legal trade unions to represent the hundreds of thousands of migrant construction workers, the abolition of the death penalty, the legalizing of political parties, and an end to discrimination based on gender and sexual orientation.[163] The UAE has also still not signed up to the International Covenant on Civil and Political Rights, the International Covenant on Social and Cultural Rights, and the Convention on the Protection of the Rights of all Migrant Workers and Members of their Families. Most often, the explanation is given that the UAE is still a young country and therefore needs time to 'catch up' in these matters, but in an increasingly globalised world this excuse is unlikely to hold up any longer.

Interestingly, the federal minister of state for foreign affairs, Anwar bin Muhammad Gargash, partly responded to these criticisms and recommendations by pledging to consider setting up a national human rights body.[164] But in mid-2006 such a body had already been established: the Emirates Human Rights Association, which was supposed to have been committed to the Universal Declaration of Human Rights. Unfortunately it has always remained semi-governmental, as is the case with many civil society organizations in the UAE.[165] It was set up by the federal ministry for social affairs[166] and a whistleblower has since claimed that its formation involved illegal practices.[167] An informed observer[168] even questioned 'where is the human rights society? It has done nothing since its creation. It is just a name, just a banner.'[169] Furthermore, the UAE's two most notable human rights activists—Muhammad bin Abdullah Al-Roken and Muhammad Al-Mansuri—are effectively barred from writing articles or giving interviews. The former has on at least one occasion been arrested and separated from his passport, while arrest warrants have been issued for the latter. Both have frequently given interviews to international newspapers.[170]

Those human rights organizations and activists that operate in the UAE appear unable to intervene in more substantive matters and several human rights INGOs, including Amnesty International, continue to file regular reports on detained individuals in the UAE, many of whom claim to have been tortured while in custody and to have received an unfair trial. An internal Abu Dhabi police study in 2005, perhaps leaked, revealed there to be rampant bribery, nepotism, embezzlement, and abuse of power throughout the organization.[171] Most political prisoners are initially arrested by the *Amn al-Dawla* security services and then interrogated in undisclosed locations. Sometimes they will appear before a closed court that does not permit family members to attend, before then being transferred to Abu Dhabi's Al-Wathba prison. In theory dissidents can now be jailed for up to six months before even being brought to trial.[172]

Particularly unpleasant current examples in Abu Dhabi and elsewhere in the UAE include the detainment of an Emirati agricultural engineer who was supposedly charged with 'obtaining secret information' and has complained of being beaten with a hosepipe, suffering sleep deprivation, forced to carry a chair on his back, and being threatened with sexual assault.[173] In May 2008 a Pakistani national was arrested and reportedly tortured. The authorities deny holding him in custody, prompting fears of an 'enforced disappearance.'[174] In November 2007 a Sudanese national was also believed to have undergone an enforced disappearance, and is believed to be held by the Amn al-Dawla.[175] In August 2007 attempts were made to bring criminal charges against the founder of the City of Hope women's shelter in Dubai.[176] And in June 2007 an Emirati teenage girl was arrested for having 'illicit sex' and was ordered to receive 60 lashes.[177] Also that month a Bangladeshi national was sentenced to death by stoning for illicit sex while a migrant domestic worker received 100 lashes and a year's imprisonment.[178] In early 2006 a high ranking officer in the UAE Air Force was detained incommunicado and afterwards had to receive mental treatment following his solitary confinement, while the year before two other Emiratis were arrested, their homes ransacked, and access to lawyers or to their families was denied.[179] In 2008–9 real estate developers caught up in an anti-corruption dragnet have been held in custody for over nine months and some have not even been charged.[180] Other recent examples include a national who was held in solitary confinement for six years before eventually being released without charge,[181] and a domestic worker who received 150 lashes for becoming pregnant outside of wedlock.[182] Female genital mutation is not illegal, and it is believed to be practised amongst East African expatriate populations with no substantive interference from the authorities.[183]

Less dramatic but also worrisome practices have included the intro-duction of mandatory identity cards for all UAE nationals. These cards carry extensive biometric data, and there is thought to have been great opposition to their implementation. Nevertheless federal law number 9 of 2006 made it a requirement to possess one, and any UAE national not in possession of one by January 2009 has been classed as an illegal resident. In summer 2008 300,000 Emiratis still did not have one. Although optional for children under the age of fifteen, a child cannot register with a school unless they possess one.[184] Also of concern is the current policy on HIV: all expatriate UAE residents are required to take HIV tests as part of a health check when they first receive their visa. If they test positive they are promptly deported. In summer 2008 the International Labour Organisation (ILO) increased its pres-sure on the UAE to change this practice and stated that 'there is clear discrimination against HIV-positive workers… if they can function in their job, then they should not be sent back [to their countries of origin] because it is a clear violation of their rights according to all the international standards and conventions.' A spokesperson for the ILO also stated that the UAE retained personal details of these individuals and shared a 'black list' of named HIV/AIDS deportees that ensured infected persons were never recruited again in any of the Gulf Cooperation Council states.[185] HIV positive Emirati convicts are reported to be discriminated against in courts, and unable to receive commuted sentences.[186]

Among the UAE national population it is thought that there are now over 1000 people that have tested positive, but this remains a taboo subject.[187] In late 2007 a young French national male was raped by three Emirati men: the authorities withheld as long as possible from the Frenchman's family information that one of the assailants was HIV positive. The Frenchman was then warned that he himself could face charges of accepting 'forced homosexuality' and a year of imprisonment.[188] Other controversial practices include mandatory pre-marital screening for UAE nationals in order to identify hereditary diseases or HIV.[189] In 2007 this was extended to all expatriates who sought to marry in the UAE. Again, it is unclear what measures are in place to accommodate those who are identified as having such diseases. It is believed that if one or both partners tests positive for HIV then the marriage cannot take place, and if other diseases are identified then the couple are left to decide whether they want to proceed with the marriage.[190] The highest profile controversy in recent years involved an alleged requirement for apprehended transsexuals to receive compulsory hormone treatment, in addition to imprisonment. In late 2005 eleven homosexual couples, including eleven transsexuals were arrested at a hotel on Abu Dhabi's border with Dubai as they were performing a mass wedding ceremony.[191] According to the international media the latter were all prescribed this treatment.[192]

Federal unrest and the increasing wealth gap

With the aforementioned amalgamation of the militaries and with the improvement of physical infrastructure connecting the various emirates, the federation was seemingly strengthening by the late 1990s. Since then some of the old autonomies have resurfaced, especially in Dubai. Despite the formalizing of a permanent federal constitution, the words of a former federal minister are still pertinent for the United Arab Emirates: 'the features of independence for the individual emirates are predominant in all executive, legislative and judicial spheres over the features of unity and the merging of powers.'[193] Undeniably the relationship between the federal government and emirate-level governments has remained strained. There is an obvious lack of real federal ministries for energy, defence, and foreign affairs given Abu Dhabi's overwhelming control of these matters.[194] There are also still no federal ministries for tourism, aviation, and ports: three key areas for the rapidly diversifying economies of all seven emirates. Moreover, with Abu Dhabi's Education Council and with Dubai's new Knowledge and Human Development Authority (KHDA), the federal ministries for education and higher education have been undermined. And in many other cases emirate-level entities are able still to operate independently of federal control, or at the very least have overlapping responsibilities.

Although there is now a federal law that permits real estate ownership across the UAE, the federal ministry for the interior nevertheless appears unable to guarantee residency visas to property owners across the federation. As one spokesperson explained, 'since there is no federal law guaranteeing residence visas to property owners, we are facilitating these through companies—property developers and offshore companies. These companies sponsor the investors' residence visas.' In summer 2008, Ra's al-Khaimah—which is perhaps now the most desperate of the emirates to attract foreign residents—even began to propose issuing visas that were longer than the usual three years.[195] Similarly, there is much discussion in Dubai of introducing even longer visas so as to allow postgraduate students to study in Dubai without needing proof of employment.[196] Federal financial regulation has also advanced little further, with the Central Bank having repeatedly been unable to intervene in emirate-level affairs. A scandal that erupted in 1999 and afflicted seventeen banks across the UAE was blamed on the Central Bank's powerlessness,[197] and more recently the discussions over the UAE's plans to depeg the dirham from the US dollar appear to be taking place in emirate-level departments of economy rather than in the Central Bank. Specifically, the Abu Dhabi Department for Planning and the Economy is believed to be promoting depegging, arguing that it will give the Central Bank more control over interest rates and inflation, while Dubai is thought to be more reluctant.[198] Moreover, these departments might even be able to determine what rate of value added tax will be introduced in their respective emirates: thus the UAE may not even have federal tax bands.[199] The Central Bank has also been unable to preside over the various international financial centres that have been set up, including the Abu Dhabi-based Securities Market and the Dubai International Financial Centre. The latter is technically a free zone, and has adopted English common law in an attempt to boost credibility and woo investors.[200]

The federal ministry for justice appears similarly ineffectual. Although there is a federal supreme court, of which all sharia courts across the UAE have been answerable to since 1994, certain emirates have retained much of their judicial independence. Many of the abovementioned corporal punishments for illicit sex took place in Ra's al-Khaimah, where the courts still seem to act with considerable autonomy,[201] and there have even been instances of sentences passed that stipulated mutilations for convicts, most often in Ra's al-Khaimah or Fujairah.[202] In all cases the ruler's office of an emirate still has to approve the eventual release of any of its convicted nationals—and this often leads to considerable delays.[203] There is also the question of divergent foreign policy: although membership of the Organization of the Petroleum Exporting Counties and relations with Iraq are now no longer issues of contention, relations with Iran are once again on a knife edge. Dubai has undoubtedly been resisting US calls for sanctions on Iran, preferring to maintain its role as Iran's primary conduit to the outside world. Dubai's total annual trade with Iran was over $14 billion in the most recent statistics—several times greater than its trade with the US—and, at its peak, the Dubai real estate market was thought to have benefited greatly from Iranian investment.[204] This has placed Abu Dhabi and the federal ministry for foreign affairs in an awkward position. Incredibly, only a few weeks after Sheikh Muhammad bin Zayed Al-Nahyan's visit to Camp David in June 2008, Sheikh Muhammad bin Rashid Al-Maktum also visited George Bush,[205] thus confirming the hydra-headed nature of UAE foreign policy.

Although less conspicuous, perhaps the greatest threat to the federation is the increasing wealth gap between the two richest emirates and the five poorest. Abu Dhabi has a long history of assisting its more indigent neighbours and Sheikh Zayed bin Sultan Al-Nahyan was instrumental in inserting an article[206] into the federal constitution that called for the federal ministries to ensure a commitment to uniform health, education, and welfare across the UAE.[207] In relative terms the wealth has never been spread sufficiently and this has hampered the poorer emirates from developing their own economies. Some have Emirati populations living in poverty-stricken circumstances, and opponents have claimed that unemployment for nationals in Fujairah and Ra's al-Khaimah could be as high as 60 percent. The earliest federal development initiatives earmarked several million Bahraini dinars for projects across the UAE, but this was little compared to the hundreds of millions of dinars being spent over the course of Abu Dhabi's first five-year domestic plan.[208] Recently, it was announced that the federal budget had been raised to $7.7 billion[209] and that a 'rescue package' of $4.3 billion had been allocated to oversee physical infrastructure projects in the northern emirates. But again this remains a comparatively small sum compared to the enormous amounts being spent on developments in Abu Dhabi and Dubai. Unsurprisingly, the announcement of the package was greeted with skepticism by some of the recipient municipalities, with one anonymous spokesperson stating: 'we often hear about these projects from Abu Dhabi, but we haven't seen them come into action.'[210]

There have been three major consequences of this growing divide between the rich and the poor. Most obviously, the share of the federation's total GDP accounted for by Abu Dhabi and Dubai has continued to increase.[211] Secondly, given that the bulk of job opportunities for aspiring UAE nationals are in Abu Dhabi and Dubai, many nationals of the poorer emirates have had little choice but to commute to the two wealthiest emirates, or perhaps even relocate. Very often such commuters have to share rented apartments close to their workplace and can only return home to their family residences at the weekends, thus making them labour migrants within their own country.

Equally alarming has been the gradual squeeze on federal ministerial positions for the northern emirates. The February 2008 reshuffle of the Council of Ministers won the UAE positive international headlines given that it doubled the number of female ministers from two to four. However, the incoming females were both ministers of state without portfolio, and the reshuffle's real outcome was that very few positions—and certainly no significant ones—were allocated to representatives of the four poorest emirates. No less than eleven positions in the cabinet are now controlled by members of hereditary ruling families and ten of these are shared out among the Abu Dhabi and Dubai ruling families—the highest number there has been since the first federal cabinet of 1971. Even Sheikha Lubna bint Khalid Al-Qasimi—a niece of the ruler of Sharjah who is now federal minister for foreign trade—can also be considered a member of Dubai's ministerial contingent given that her previous professional experience was with the Dubai Ports Authority and the Dubai Chamber of Commerce and Industry.

This painfully obvious federal disequilibrium is now fomenting opposition. The most notable example being the 'return' of the former crown prince and deputy ruler of Ra's al-Khaimah—Sheikh Khalid bin Saqr Al-Qasimi. Sidelined and then exiled by his younger brother, Sheikh Saud bin Saqr Al-Qasimi—who was supposedly appointed crown prince by their ailing father[212] in the summer of 2003—Khalid moved to Oman[213] and then the United States. In November 2008 he employed a Californian public affairs strategy company, launched a website, and posted several YouTube videos explaining the legitimacy of his claim. It is no coincidence that Khalid has chosen the moment of maximum economic pessimism in Ra's al-Khaimah for his comeback. With a 'pledge for progress' he is highlighting the inappropriateness of his younger brother's Dubai-style economic model, the extent of poverty, and the need for stronger federal cooperation and political reform. One of his video speeches, entitled *The Truth about Ra's al-Khaimah* begins with him saying 'Dear brave and loyal citizens of Ra's al-Khaimah who offer resistance in this difficult time, we are harmed severely and for that we are all paying a high price for many years.' He also states that he holds an Emiri decree signed by his father in 2004 that reconfirms his position as crown prince.[214] His website and blog feature many posts from disgruntled nationals, most of which are complaints about poor economic circumstances.

Dubai's crash and the future of the federation

In the short term, what is missing is a comprehensive federal strategic plan that recognizes which parts of the union have specific, comparative advantages. If such a plan were put in place then Ra's al-Khaimah would receive the bulk of federal funds for tourist projects owing to its natural beauty, while Fujairah would become the United Arab Emirates' principal port given its direct access to the Indian Ocean. At present, most tourists head for Dubai, and over 75 percent of the federation's total non-oil trade passes through Dubai's two ports.[215] In the long term, the future of the federation is unpredictable, and much depends on the Abu Dhabi-Dubai relationship. Many observers contend that since Sheikh Muhammad bin Rashid Al-Maktum's succession as ruler of Dubai in early 2006 and his simultaneous appointments as federal vice president and prime minister, he has been the most active premier since the UAE was founded. Without fear of contradiction it can be said that he has been more energetic than his father and brother were, having made regular 'grand tours' of the northern emirates and having monitored federal developments very closely. Moreover, he was quick to appoint his chief emirate-level lieutenants to the Council of Ministers, with Muhammad bin Abdullah Al-Gergawi now serving as federal minister for cabinet affairs and with the aforementioned Anwar bin Muhammad Gargash now installed as minister of state for foreign affairs.[216] However, as a prime minister he has made little headway in reducing federal imbalances, and his ministerial appointments are perhaps best interpreted as having been an insurance policy for Dubai. The presidency will always remain in Al-Nahyan hands and Abu Dhabi is the only emirate capable of financing federal development projects and subsidizing the poorer emirates. Thus, by having a stronger voice in the Council of Ministers Muhammad has perhaps hoped to exercise more effectively Dubai's veto powers and keep at least some semblance of parity with Abu Dhabi.

Since late 2008, however, Muhammad's position and Dubai's relative autonomy within the federation have been severely compromised by the rapid unravelling of the emirate's 'post-oil' economy in the wake of the global credit crunch. Unrealistically perhaps, Dubai's planners had been relying on an uninterrupted stream of foreign direct investment and a perpetually favourable international credit climate. Long predicted by industry analysts,[217] the real estate bubble began to burst in October 2008 and the value of most properties fell between 20 and

40 percent over the following months as investors found it difficult to get financing for their payments.[218] Troublingly, even when the UAE Central Bank injected $19 billion into the banking system in November 2008[219] liquidity did not improve and prices remained in freefall. By mid-2009, when pre-paid package holidays have been taken, it is likely that Dubai's tourism industry will also be in crisis as overseas visitors decline sharply in number due to unfavourable conditions in their domestic economies. Indeed, even in September 2008 Emirates airlines reported that its half-yearly profits were down by 88 percent— most likely due to high oil prices,[220] but its reports in late 2009 will make much more grim reading. By early December 2008, following several weeks of strenuous denials by government spokesmen, there were further perilous indicators, with two of Dubai's flagship real estate and tourism projects (Dubailand and Jumeirah Gardens) being 'reassessed,'[221] and with Emaar Properties—whose share price plummeted 80 percent between July 2008 and December 2008[222]— finally admitting that it will make redundancies to its 5000 strong workforce.[223]

While certainly a humiliating episode for Dubai, and one that has created much bad publicity for the UAE, the emirate's crash may nevertheless prove to be beneficial for the future integrity of the federation. With its massive sovereign wealth funds and sizeable oil revenues, Abu Dhabi is well placed to intervene and shore up the most struggling components of the Dubai economy. As yet there is little firm evidence that Abu Dhabi is coming to the rescue, apart from the assisted merger of two Dubai mortgage lenders (Tamweel and Amlak) under the umbrella of a new federal entity,[224] and the contract for Emaar to build Sheikh Khalifa bin Zayed Al-Nahyan's new city in Cairo.[225] But then there probably never will be much direct evidence, as Abu Dhabi will be keen to allow Dubai to save face: any deal that is struck will be as private as possible. It is far more likely that in 2009 Abu Dhabi will deploy a number of intermediaries to channel the necessary funds into its beleaguered partner. These may include the UAE Central Bank or the US Bank Citigroup. The former may try to find a way of providing cheap credit for at least some of Dubai's total of $75 billion in debts that it would not otherwise be able to access in international markets. In 2008 the latter is thought to have ploughed over $8 billion into Dubai entities, and in December 2008 it was indicated that Citigroup was securing loans for Dubai Holdings. In the near future it may also help finance the Dubai Electricity and Water Authority's $2 billion debt and Borse Dubai's $3.8 billion debt.[226] It may seem irresponsible for Citigroup to be exposing itself to such potentially toxic Dubai debt, especially given its experiences with the US mortgage market and its own near collapse in November 2008,[227] but the Abu Dhabi Investments Authority's aforementioned $7.5 billion investment in Citigroup in 2007[228] may have been a sufficient sweetener, especially if there is an implicit guarantee from ADIA to cover all Dubai deals.

As to the price Abu Dhabi will exact for its discreet assistance, rumours have abounded that it hopes to take stakes in Emirates airline[229] and other major Dubai parastatals such as Emaar and Nakheel. But it is more probable—and far more in tune with Abu Dhabi's political culture—that it will be satisfied with Dubai's de facto full integration into the federation. Indeed, when Muhammad Ali Al-Abbar, chairman of Emaar, chairman of a legion of Dubai government departments, and the principal architect of Dubai's real estate sector, finally addressed the media in late November 2008, it was telling that he bookended his speech with strong federal undertones. He began with 'Today I am here to talk of Dubai and our shared and proud identity as part of the UAE' and finished by stating that 'We recognize the challenges before us. But this city, as part of one strong nation, will continue to grow and thrive.'[230] Should this newfound spirit of federalism prevail in Dubai, this will have brought to a successful conclusion the long struggle for centralization waged for so many years by the late Sheikh Zayed bin Sultan Al-Nahyan.

NOTES

INTRODUCTION

1. The UAE has 7.9 percent of global oil reserves, of which Abu Dhabi accounts for about 94 percent. US Energy Information Administration. *The United Arab Emirates: Country Analysis Brief* (Washington DC. EIA, 2007).

2. In 2007 Deutsche Bank estimated that the largest of Abu Dhabi's sovereign wealth funds—those controlled by ADIA—to be in excess of $875 billion. Seznec, Jean-François. 'The Gulf Sovereign Wealth Funds: Myths and Reality' in *Middle East Policy* (vol. 15, no. 2, 2008), p. 97. As will be demonstrated in chapter 4, there are several other smaller sovereign wealth funds operating out of Abu Dhabi.

3. UAE Central Bank estimates, 2008.

4. See for example Huntington, Samuel P. *Political Order in Changing Societies* (New Haven: Yale University Press, 1968); Hudson, Michael. *Arab Politics: The Search for Legitimacy* (New Haven: Yale University Press, 1977).

5. For an overview of a generic bargain in the UAE see Davidson, Christopher M. *The United Arab Emirates: A Study in Survival* (Boulder: Lynne Rienner, 2005). pp. 70–97. For a Dubai-specific version of the bargain see Davidson, Christopher M. *Dubai: The Vulnerability of Success* (London: Hurst, 2008). pp. 137–176.

6. For a full discussion of 'rentier' petrodollar states see Beblawi, Hazem, and Luciani, Giacomo (eds). *The Rentier State* (New York: Croom Helm, 1987).

7. In contrast, Dubai has tried to position itself as a post-modern city state. See Davidson 2008. p. 219.

8. Abdullah, Muhammad Morsy. *The United Arab Emirates: A Modern History* (London: Croom Helm, 1978); Davidson 2005; Heard-Bey, Frauke. *From Trucial States to United Arab Emirates* (London: Longman, 1996);

Rugh, Andrea B. *The Political Culture of Leadership in the United Arab Emirates* (New York: Palgrave Macmillan, 2007); Taryam, Abdullah. *The Establishment of the United Arab Emirates, 1950–1985* (London: Croom Helm, 1987); Zahlan, Rosemarie Said. *The Origins of the United Arab Emirates* (New York: St. Martin's, 1978).
 9. Davidson 2008; Wilson, Graeme. *Rashid's Legacy: The Genesis of the Maktoum Family and the History of Dubai* (Dubai: Media Prima, 2006).
10. Wheatcroft, Andrew. *With United Strength: Sheikh Zayed bin Sultan Al-Nahyan, the Leader and the Nation* (Abu Dhabi: Emirates Centre for Strategic Studies and Research, 2005); Tammam, Hamdi. *Zayed bin Sultan Al-Nahyan: The Leader on the March* (Tokyo: Dai Nippon, 1983).
11. Maitra, Jayanti, and Al-Hajji, Afra. *Qasr Al-Hosn: The History and Rulers of Abu Dhabi, 1793–1966* (Abu Dhabi: Centre for Documentation and Research, 2001).
12. Al-Fahim, Muhammad. *From Rags to Riches: A Story of Abu Dhabi* (London: Centre for Arab Studies, 1995); Henderson, Edward. *This Strange Eventful History: Memoirs of Earlier Days in the United Arab Emirates* (London: Quartet, 1988).
13. Mann, Clarence. *Abu Dhabi: Birth of an Oil Sheikhdom* (Beirut: Al-Khayats, 1969); Davidson, Christopher M. 'After Sheikh Zayed: The Politics of Succession in Abu Dhabi and the United Arab Emirates' in *Middle East Policy* (vol. 13, no. 1, 2006).

1. THE EMERGENCE OF ABU DHABI

1. The chronicles were Kashf al-Ghummah written by Sahran bin Saidin in about 1633. The Portuguese forts mentioned in the chronicles were most probably at Julfar, near present day Ra's al-Khaimah. Tammam, Hamdi. *Zayed bin Sultan Al-Nahyan: The Leader on the March (Tokyo: Dai Nippon, 1983).* pp. 22–24; Maitra, Jayanti, and Al-Hajji, Afra. *Qasr Al-Hosn: The History and Rulers of Abu Dhabi, 1793–1966* (Abu Dhabi: Centre for Documentation and Research, 2001). p. 15.
2. Rush, Alan (ed). *Ruling Families of Arabia: The United Arab Emirates* (Slough: Archive Editions 1991). pp. 29–30.
3. Lorimer, John G. *Gazetteer of the Persian Gulf, Oman, and Central Arabia* (London: Gregg International Publishers, 1970). p. 1932.
4. Van der Meulen recorded 27 such Bani Yas sections in the mid-1990s. Van Der Meulen, Hendrik. 'The Role of Tribal and Kinship Ties in the Politics of the United Arab Emirates' (PhD thesis. The Fletcher School of Law and Diplomacy, 1997). pp. 371–376. Today, members of some Bani Yas sections, including the Suwdan and the Mazari, often consider themselves to be separate tribes, especially when they are dwelling outside of Abu Dhabi.

5. The wadi Nahyan is near to Sana in the Yemen.
6. Buraimi's original name was Tuam. Al-Shamsi, Said Muhammad. 'The Buraimi Dispute: A Case Study in Inter-Arab Politics' (PhD thesis. American University, 1986). p. 1.
7. Zayed bin Muhammad being Diab bin Isa's uncle.
8. Maitra and Al-Hajji. p. 17.
9. Rugh, Andrea B., *The Political Culture of Leadership in the United Arab Emirates* (New York: Palgrave Macmillan, 2007). p. 35.
10. Tammam. p. 32.
11. Maitra and Al-Hajji. p. 3.
12. Source of quote lost. Apologies to readers.
13. As late as 1801 the island was still being referred to as Buzubbeh, even by the British Political Resident in Oman. See Sultan bin Muhammad Al-Qasimi (ed). *The Journals of David Seton in the Gulf, 1800–1809* (Exeter: Exeter University Press, 1995). p. 28.
14. Maitra and Al-Hajji. p. 4.
15. From the Farsi word for a beehive-shaped hut made out of wattle and daub.
16. Ibid. p. 9. The circular tower in the present day restoration of the Abu Dhabi fort is perhaps all that remains of Diab bin Isa's original fort.
17. Ibid. p. 10.
18. Ibid. p. 17; Rush. p. 19.
19. Rugh. p. 36; Wheatcroft, Andrew. *With United Strength: Sheikh Zayed bin Sultan Al-Nahyan, the Leader and the Nation* (Abu Dhabi: Emirates Centre for Strategic Studies and Research, 2005). p. 41.
20. Maitra and Al-Hajji. pp. 9, 17.
21. Ibid. p. 18; Tammam. p. 32.
22. Davidson, Christopher M. *The United Arab Emirates: A Study in Survival* (Boulder: Lynne Rienner, 2005). pp. 11–12.
23. Heard-Bey, Frauke. *From Trucial States to United Arab Emirates* (London: Longman, 1996). pp. 25–26.
24. Ibid. p. 11; Maitra and Al-Hajji. p. 18; Tammam. p. 32.
25. Fenelon, Kevin. The *United Arab Emirates: An Economic and Social Survey* (London: Longman, 1973). p. 56.
26. Heard-Bey. p. 114.
27. The taraz tax was estimated to be some five talas per pearl diver during this period. See Maitra and Al-Hajjji. p. 91. The qalta was normally a diver-hauler partnership.
28. The pearling season being the *ghaus al-kabir.*
29. Lorimer. pp. 2284–2287; Heard-Bey. p. 113.
30. Heard-Bey. pp. 118–119.
31. If a farmer produced more than the nisab threshold quantity of dates, then he would have to pay a tax. Ibid. pp. 115–117.

32. The aflaaj system comprised of subterranean stone tunnels that were designed to bring water down to the level of the towns from the high water tables of the nearby mountains. When the tunnels reached the agricultural gardens they would become surface channels allowing the water to be regulated and re-directed to wherever it was most needed. Lorimer. p. 2296.

33. The aflaaj taxes were levied by officials called *arifs*. It would seem that the Al-Nahyan never levied taxes on animal husbandry, perhaps given the nomadic origins of many of the Bani Yas sections. Maitra and Al-Hajji. p. 22

34. Heard-Bey. p. 111.

35. Ibid. pp. 115–117.

36. Maitra and Al-Hajji. pp. 24–25.

37. The fort was built at Al-Miraijib. Wheatcroft. p. 43.

38. Rush. p. 30; Lorimer. p. 764.

39. Rush. p. 30.

40. Maitra and Al-Hajji. p. 43.

41. The Wahhabis preached a more purified brand of Islam: a doctrine of pure monotheism and a return to the fundamental tenets of Islam as laid down by the Koran. As such, they were unitarians, emphasising the centrality of God's unqualified oneness in Sunni Islam. They sought to renew the Prophet's golden era of Islam, and all who stood in their way were to be swept aside, including other Islamic rulers who lived 'impure' lives. In many ways, by the nineteenth century the movement had become something of a 'religio-military confederacy under which the desert people, stirred by a great idea, embarked on a common action.' Peck, Malcolm. *The United Arab Emirates: A Venture in Unity* (Boulder: Westview, 1986). pp. 29–30; Hawley, Donald. *The Trucial States* (London: George Allen and Unwin, 1970). pp. 96–97.

42. Peck. pp. 29–30. The first Wahhabi imam after Muhammad bin Abdul Al-Wahhab's death was a sheikh of the Al-Saud family.

43. Maitra and Al-Hajji. p. 36.

44. Rugh. p. 36; Kelly, John B. *Britain and the Persian Gulf* (Oxford: Oxford University Press, 1968). p. 22.

45. Rush. p. 31.

46. These attacks took place in 1813 and 1814, at the height of Wahhabi incursions into Abu Dhabi territory. Lorimer. p. 651; Maitra and Al-Hajji. pp. 40–41.

47. Al-Gurg, Easa Saleh. *The Wells of Memory* (London: John Murray, 1998), p. 3.

48. Hawley 1970. p. 81.

49. Named after Bin Hanbal.

50. Named after the scholar Malik.

51. Maitra and Al-Hajji. p. 49.
52. Ibid. p. 51.
53. While the original name of the settlement has now become something of a mystery, it seems likely that it was either named after a type of locust, the *daba*, which frequently infested the area; after a snake-eating mastigure lizard referred to locally as a *dhub*; or after a combination of the Hindi word *doh* (two) and the Arabic word *bayt* (house) in reference to two white houses which supposedly stood side by side close to the estuary's mouth. These two houses may also have been referred to as 'the two brides' which at that time may have translated into Farsi as something similar to the word 'Dubai.' Al-Gurg. p. 35; Hawley, Donald. *The Emirates: Witness to a Metamorphosis* (Norwich: Michael Russell, 2007). p. 186.
54. Maitra and Al-Hajji. p. 51
55. Rush. pp. 33–35.
56. Buxani, Ram. *Taking the High Road* (Dubai: Motivate, 2003). p. 70.
57. In many ways the interests of the Company and Persia were compatible, as both sought to exclude the Ottoman Empire and other European powers from the region. Al-Sagri, Saleh Hamad. 'Britain and the Arab Emirates, 1820–1956' (PhD thesis. University of Kent at Canterbury, 1988). pp. 2–3.
58. Heard-Bey. p. 280.
59. Hundreds of letters were dispatched from Bombay to London, most of which held the Qawasim responsible for almost every incidence of damaged or missing British Indian trade vessels. So successful was the campaign that by the turn of the nineteenth century the lower Gulf was referred to throughout the Empire as the 'Pirate Coast,' regardless of the validity of the Company's claims. See Belgrave, Charles. *The Pirate Coast* (London: G.Bell and Sons, 1966). p. 29. It is worth noting that revisionist histories including those of Charles Davies and Sheikh Sultan bin Muhammad Al-Qasimi—the present day ruler of Sharjah—have presented strong cases arguing that the Company's piracy claims were part of a 'big lie' intended to remove a trading rival. See Davies, Charles E. *The Blood Red Arab Flag: An Investigation into Qasimi Piracy, 1797–1820* (Exeter: Exeter University Press, 1997); Al-Qasimi, Sultan bin Muhammad. *The Myth of Arab Piracy in the Gulf* (London: Croom Helm, 1986).
60. Belgrave. p. 36.
61. The task force was led by William Grant Keir and comprised of three battleships and nine cruisers. Ibid. pp. 135–143; Wilson, Graeme. *Rashid's Legacy: The Genesis of the Maktoum Family and the History of Dubai* (Dubai: Media Prima, 2006). p. 26.
62. Buxani. p. 71; Al-Gurg. p. 15.

63. Buxani. p. 71.
64. Gallagher, John, and Robinson, Ronald. 'The Imperialism of Free Trade' in *Economic History Review* (vol. 6, no. 1, 1953). p. 13.
65. Kelly. p. 368.
66. India Office L/P/85/7/195; Rush. p. 31.
67. Maitra and Al-Hajji. p. 47.
68. The British Political Resident in the Gulf was stationed in Bahrain during this period.
69. Kelly. p. 59.
70. Maitra and Al-Hajji. p. 47.
71. Ibid. p. 55.
72. Lorimer. p. 765.
73. Rush. p. 38.
74. Maria Theresa talas were still in heavy circulation during this period.
75. Maitra and Al-Hajji. p. 60.
76. Ibid. p. 60.
77. Ibid. p. 61.
78. Ibid. p. 44.
79. Rugh. p. 39.
80. Ibid. p. 39.
81. Lorimer. p. 765; Maitra and Al-Hajji. p. 62.
82. Maktum was the grandson of Suhail: a prominent eighteenth-century Bani Yas man. Personal interviews, Abu Dhabi, January 2005; Maitra and Al-Hajji. p. 79.
83. The Al-Bu Falasah clan originated from the Al-Sarah oasis in Buraimi and from the islands of Bateen and Tarut. Maitra and Al-Hajji. p. 62; Hopwood, Derek. *The Arabian Peninsula* (London: 1972). p. 225.
84. Lorimer. p. 765. Based on a total population figure of 18,000.
85. Maitra and Al-Hajji. p. 64.
86. Rush. p. 39.
87. Khalifa even moved his primary residence to Buraimi for this supply cutting purpose. Ibid. p. 40.
88. Maitra and Al-Hajji. p. 36. By this stage the Wahhabis may have fallen temporarily under the influence of Muhammad Ali Pasha's Egyptian agents. Ibid. p. 87.
89. Rush. p. 40.
90. Kelly. p. 247.
91. Britain's fear being that inter-sheikhdom disputes over pearling rights might escalate into a regional war. India Office 1596/64625.
92. India Office 1596/64625; Maitra and Al-Hajji. pp. 72–74.
93. Maitra and Al-Hajji. p. 70.
94. Ibid. p. 70. The HMS Elphinstone.
95. Records of the Emirates, British Library, 1990. Volume 2. p. 34.

96. Ibid. pp. 36–40.
97. Maitra and Al-Hajji. p. 75.
98. Lorimer. p. 766; Rush. pp. 42–43.
99. Rush. p. 45.
100. Maitra and Al-Hajji. pp. 74–77; Van der Meulen. pp. 135, 422–423; Lorimer. p. 766. Remarkably, the Political Resident even stated that if the Al-Nahyan family was unable to regain control over the area by itself, then the British would step in and assist. Hawley 1970. p. 145.
101. Maitra and Al-Hajji. p. 76.
102. Lorimer. p. 766.
103. Maitra and Al-Hajji. pp. 76, 80.
104. Van der Meulen. p. 336; Maitra and Al-Hajji. p. 81; Rush. p. 47. Saqr being the third eldest son of Sultan.
105. Maitra and Al-Hajji. p. 81.
106. Ibid. p. 89; Rush. p. 51.
107. Rush. p. 52; Heard-Bey. p. 49.
108. Heard-Bey. p. 49.
109. Rugh. p. 42.
110. Maitra and Al-Hajji. p. 56.
111. Ibid. p. 56.
112. Ibid. p. 56.
113. Rush. p. 54.
114. Ibid. p. 165; Maitra and Al-Hajji. p. 11.
115. Maitra and Al-Hajji. p. 93.
116. Ibid. p. 48.
117. Less powerful local rulers received only a three gun salute, and other non-ruling sheikhs received just one gun. Personal interviews with Sir Donald Hawley, Durham, November, 2006.
118. Maitra and Al-Hajji. p. 92.
119. Rugh. pp. 33–35.
120. Notably Muhammad bin Humaid of the Bani Yas and Rashid bin Fadhil of the Naim's Al-Bu Shamis section. Maitra and Al-Hajji. pp. 93–94.
121. Isa held power for only a few months.
122. Maitra and Al-Hajji. p. 94.
123. Rugh. p. 43.
124. Lorimer. p. 767.
125. Maitra and Al-Hajji. p. 94.
126. Lorimer. p. 710.
127. Maitra and Al-Hajji. pp. 94–95.
128. Ibid. p. 100; Rush. p. 56.
129. Kelly. pp. 392–393; Maitra and Al-Hajji. pp. 103–104.
130. Rush. pp. 56–57.

131. Maitra and Al-Hajji. p. 109.
132. Rush. p. 59.
133. Maitra and Al-Hajji. pp. 121–122.
134. Rush. p. 63.
135. Lorimer. p. 719; Heard-Bey. p. 182.
136. Rush. p. 61.
137. Maitra and Al-Hajji. p. 117.
138. Ibid. p. 115.
139. Ibid. p. 116; Rush. p. 59.
140. Maitra and Al-Hajji. p. 116.
141. Rush. p. 6.
142. Maitra and Al-Hajji. p. 129.
143. Wheatcroft. p. 45.
144. Rush. p. 81; Maitra and Al-Hajji. p. 129.
145. Maitra and Al-Hajji. p. 129.
146. Ibid. p. 130.
147. Rush. pp. 67–68.
148. Rush. p. 81.
149. Rugh. p. 52.
150. Maitra and Al-Hajji. pp. 44, 133; Lorimer. p. 768.
151. Rugh. p. 52.
152. Maitra and Al-Hajji. p. 152.
153. Lorimer. p. 768.
154. Maitra and Al-Hajji. pp. 133–134.
155. Sheikha Latifa bint Said Al-Nahyan. Lienhardt, Peter. *Sheikhdoms of Eastern Arabia* (Oxford: Palgrave, 2001). p. 178.
156. Lorimer. p. 768.
157. Maitra and Al-Hajji. p. 195.
158. Rugh. p. 61.
159. Maitra and Al-Hajji. p. 179.
160. Ibid. pp. 141–142.
161. Lorimer. p. 822; Maitra and Al-Hajji. p. 174; Kelly, John B. *Eastern Arabia Frontier* (New York: Praeger, 1964). p. 106; Heard-Bey. pp. 39–40. The incursions were fought off with the assistance of the Awamir (Al-Amiri) tribe. The Qatari ruler at this time being Sheikh Muhammad bin Thani, the first patriarch of the Al-Thani dynasty.
162. Rugh. p. 54.
163. Heard-Bey. p. 33.
164. Zura was dismantled in 1897.
165. Maitra and Al-Hajji. p. 187.
166. Ibid. p. 166.
167. Ibid. p. 166.
168. Lorimer. p. 769.

169. Hawley 1970. p. 145.
170. Maitra and Al-Hajji. p. 168. The Murrah of the Arabian interior not being related to the Marar (Al-Murur) section of the Bani Yas.
171. Ibid. p. 168.
172. Ibid. p. 167.
173. The HMS Teazer.
174. Hawley 1970. p. 145.
175. Maitra and Al-Hajji. p. 168.
176. Lorimer. p. 770; Rugh. p. 53; Wheatcroft. p. 51.
177. Maitra and Al-Hajji. p. 195.
178. Hawley 2007. p. 96.
179. Sheikhs Abdullah and Saud bin Faisal Al-Saud.
180. Maitra and Al-Hajji. p. 165; Lorimer. p. 485.
181. Rush. p. 84.
182. He married her in 1891. Maitra and Al-Hajji. p. 181.
183. Lorimer. p. 770.
184. Rugh. p. 54.
185. Personal interviews, Abu Dhabi, April 2008.
186. There was a month-long conflict in 1887. Some Dhawahir tribesmen were imprisoned and sought revenge upon their release in 1891. Lorimer. p. 771; Kéchichian, Joseph A. *Power and Succession in Arab Monarchies: A Reference Guide* (Boulder: Lynne Rienner, 2008). p. 292.
187. Maitra and Al-Hajji. p. 182.
188. Heard-Bey. p. 38.
189. Maitra and Al-Hajji. p. 181.
190. He died in single combat with Zayed, who had been leading a force up to Sharjah. Hawley 1970. p. 146; Rugh. p. 143.
191. Rugh. pp. 143–144.
192. Ajman being ruled by a family of the Al-Bu Khuraiban section of the Naim. Umm al-Qawain being ruled by the Al-Mualla family of the Al-Ali tribe. India Office 1596/64625.
193. Despite the presence of Qawasim governors, Fujairah's most populous tribe, the Sharqiyin (Al-Sharqi) had been semi-autonomous since 1888 under the rule of Sheikh Muhammad bin Hamad Al-Sharqi.
194. Lorimer. p. 752.
195. India Office R/15/1/710.
196. Maitra and Al-Hajji. p. 168.
197. Ibid. p. 193.
198. Lorimer. pp. 1450–1451. By signing these documents the trucial sheikhs relinquished external sovereignty and were 'upgraded', at least in British terms, from simply being 'independent Arab sheikhs in special relations with His Majesty's Government' to being full-blown protectorates, albeit without any transfer of territorial sovereignty or application of English law. Al-Sagri. pp. 51, 92.

199. At this time the British Political Agents in Sharjah and other sheikh-doms were often members of pro-British expatriate Arab families. For a full discussion see Onley, James. 'Britain's Native Agents in Arabia and Persia, 1758–1958' in *Comparative Studies of South Asia, Africa, and the Middle East* (no.33, 2003). pp. 129–137; Onley, James. *The Arabian Frontier of the British Raj: Merchants, Rulers, and the British in the Nineteenth Century Gulf* (Oxford: Oxford University Press, 2007). p. 46.

200. Al-Fahim, Muhammad. *From Rags to Riches: A Story of Abu Dhabi* (London: Centre for Arab Studies, 1995). pp. 22–24.

201. Lorimer. p. 2286.

202. Maitra and Al-Hajji. p. 195.

203. Lorimer. p. 2220.

204. Wheatcroft. p. 48.

205. Rugh. p. 62.

206. Maitra and Al-Hajji. p. 197.

2. SHEIKH SHAKHBUT AND THE GREAT DECLINE

1. Although both Sheikh Shakhbut bin Diab Al-Nahyan and Sheikh Zayed bin Khalifa Al-Nahyan had eight known sons, it is likely that the latter had more 'unofficial' sons given his larger number of wives.

2. Sheikha Maitha bint Salman Al-Mansuri.

3. Heard-Bey, Frauke. *From Trucial States to United Arab Emirates* (London: Longman, 1996). p. 50.

4. Lienhardt, Peter. *Sheikhdoms of Eastern Arabia* (Oxford: Palgrave, 2001). p. 178.

5. Rugh, Andrea B. *The Political Culture of Leadership in the United Arab Emirates* (New York: Palgrave Macmillan, 2007). p. 60.

6. The visit to Muscat was probably made in 1904. Kéchichian, Joseph A. *Power and Succession in Arab Monarchies: A Reference Guide* (Boulder: Lynne Rienner, 2008). p. 293.

7. Sheikha Latifa bint Said Al-Nahyan.

8. Although he did have three daughters. Rugh. p. 62; Rush, Alan (ed). *Ruling Families of Arabia: The United Arab Emirates* (Slough: Archive Editions 1991). p. 92.

9. Maitra, Jayanti, and Al-Hajji, Afra. *Qasr Al-Hosn: The History and Rulers of Abu Dhabi, 1793–1966* (Abu Dhabi: Centre for Documentation and Research, 2001), pp. 203–204.

10. Ibid. p. 206; Tammam, Hamdi. *Zayed bin Sultan Al-Nahyan: The Leader on the March* (Tokyo: Dai Nippon, 1983). p. 41.

11. Lienhardt. p. 178.

12. Ahmad bin Khalifa Al-Suwaidi. Rugh. p. 61.

13. Lienhardt. p. 179.

14. Rugh. pp. 60–61.
15. Notably the Awamir.
16. Maitra and Al-Hajji. pp. 208–221.
17. Ibid. p. 223. The cousins were known as the Araifs.
18. Ibid. p. 223.
19. Van der Meulen, Hendrik. 'The Role of Tribal and Kinship Ties in the Politics of the United Arab Emirates' (PhD thesis. The Fletcher School of Law and Diplomacy, 1997). p. 108.
20. Maitra and Al-Hajji. p. 224.
21. Al-Fahim, Muhammad. *From Rags to Riches: A Story of Abu Dhabi* (London: Centre for Arab Studies, 1995). p. 38; Van der Meulen. p. 29.
22. Lienhardt asserts that a strong rivalry existed between the wives of Sheikh Hamdan and Sheikh Sultan. Lienhardt. p. 180.
23. Ibid. p. 180; Rugh. p. 63.
24. Rush. p. 131.
25. These included his daughter Sheika Latifa bint Hamdan Al-Nahyan who was later to marry Dubai's great patriarch, Sheikh Rashid bin Said Al-Maktum.
26. Rush. p. 127; Zahlan, Rosemarie Said. *The Origins of the United Arab Emirates* (New York: St. Martin's, 1978). p. 43.
27. Rugh. p. 61.
28. Maitra and Al-Hajji. p. 227.
29. India Office R/151/14/27; Hopwood, Derek. *The Arabian Peninsula* (London: 1972). p. 198.
30. Rugh. p. 64; Personal interviews, Abu Dhabi, April 2008.
31. Maitra and Al-Hajji. p. 229.
32. Rush. p. 158.
33. Hopwood. p. 228.
34. Lienhardt. p. 181.
35. Ibid. p. 181.
36. Mann, Clarence. *Abu Dhabi: Birth of an Oil Sheikhdom* (Beirut: Al-Khayats, 1969). pp. 87–88; Van der Meulen. p. 110.
37. Lienhardt. p. 181.
38. Rush. p. 96.
39. Sheikha Maryam bint Sultan Al-Nahyan. This marriage may have been to offset an earlier marriage to one of Saqr's daughters. Personal interviews, Abu Dhabi, April 2008.
40. India Office R/151/14/27. Al-Ihsa now being the eastern province of Saudi Arabia.
41. Rush. p. 137.
42. Ibid. p. 139; Zahlan. pp. 132–133; Van der Meulen. p. 380; Maitra and Al-Hajji. p. 180; Records of the Emirates, British Library, 1990. Volume 2. p. 158.

43. Personal interviews, Abu Dhabi, April 2008; some corroboration from Heard-Bey. p. 33.

44. Personal interviews, Abu Dhabi. April 2008.

45. Maitra and Al-Hajji. p. 129.

46. Luce, Margaret. *From Aden to the Gulf: Personal Diaries, 1956–1966* (Salisbury, Michael Russell, 1987). p. 176; Heard-Bey. p. 150.

47. Rush. p. 161.

48. Abdullah, Muhammad Morsy. *The United Arab Emirates: A Modern History* (London: Croom Helm, 1978). p. 104.

49. Al-Fahim. pp. 22–24.

50. Hawley, Donald. *The Trucial States* (London: George Allen and Unwin, 1970). p. 197; Fenelon, Kevin. The *United Arab Emirates: An Economic and Social Survey* (London: Longman, 1973). p. 56.

51. Personal interviews, Abu Dhabi, August 2007; and in the case of Dubai see Wilson, Graeme. *Rashid's Legacy: The Genesis of the Maktoum Family and the History of Dubai* (Dubai: Media Prima, 2006). p. 56.

52. Thought to be over 35 percent. See Al-Gurg, Easa Saleh. *The Wells of Memory* (London: John Murray, 1998). pp. 11, 32.

53. Although estimates for Abu Dhabi are not available the British agent estimated that by 1946 the pearl trade in Dubai was worth a mere £250,000 per annum, compared to over £3 million in the 1920s. Wilson. p. 59.

54. These routes were from Basra to Bombay and from Cairo to Karachi. Imperial Airways needed to have a refuelling base approximately every 200 miles at that time. India Office S/18/B/414.

55. These facilities were at Salalah and on the island of Masirah. Buxani, Ram. *Taking the High Road* (Dubai: Motivate, 2003). p. 84.

56. Abu-Baker, Albadr. 'Political Economy of State Formation: The United Arab Emirates in Comparative Perspective' (PhD thesis. University of Michigan, 1995). p. 43

57. Rush. p. 335.

58. Records of the Emirates. pp. 73–87.

59. And by the 1950s the Sharjah deal was worth £30,000 annually to the ruler. Abdullah. p. 56; India Office R/515/4; Hawley, Donald. *The Emirates: Witness to a Metamorphosis* (Norwich: Michael Russell, 2007). p. 196

60. The flying boats landed on the stretch of the creek near to where Al-Maktum bridge is today. Buxani. pp. 92–93; Fenelon, Kevin. p. 86.

61. Wilson. p. 72.

62. The Iraqi Petroleum Company was 51 percent owned by the British Government. Foreign Office 371/19975.

63. Al-Sagri, Saleh Hamad. 'Britain and the Arab Emirates, 1820–1956' (PhD thesis. University of Kent at Canterbury, 1988). p. 155.

64. Petroleum Concessions Ltd. was dominated by British Petroleum. Hawley 2007. p. 67; Heard-Bey. p. 295; (*in Arabic*) Al-Otaibi, Manna Said. *Petroleum and the Economy of the United Arab Emirates* (Kuwait: Al-Qabas Press, 1977). p. 45.
65. India Office l/P/S/18/B/458; Abdullah 1978. p. 70; Wilson. p. 68.
66. Mann. p. 76.
67. As discussed in the following chapter, there was by this stage a growing consensus that the Trucial sheikhs should be allowed increased contact with the outside world, so as to improve their prospects of future integration and self-sufficiency.
68. Wheatcroft, Andrew. *With United Strength: Sheikh Zayed bin Sultan Al-Nahyan, the Leader and the Nation* (Abu Dhabi: Emirates Centre for Strategic Studies and Research, 2005). pp. 71, 107.
69. A subsidiary of Anglo-Persian Oil Company.
70. Maitra and Al-Hajji. p. 235; Hawley 1970. p. 212.
71. Rush. p. 175.
72. Maitra and Al-Hajji. p. 247.
73. Mann. p. 104.
74. The Trucial Oman Scouts were set up in 1956. They were a small but well-trained army for the Trucial states born out of the earlier Trucial Oman Levies force that had existed to protect British oil company exploration teams from raiders. They were made up of local Bedouin (including Dhofaris) and Jordanians, and were officered by British soldiers and commanded by a British colonel or *qaid*. Al-Gurg. p. 114.
75. Personal interviews, Abu Dhabi, April 2008.
76. Al-Fahim. pp. 86–87; Maitra and Al-Hajji. p. 245. It would seem that Shakhbut had had bad experiences with some Kuwait-based businesses, and this made him more wary of foreign construction firms.
77. Maitra and Al-Hajji. p. 55.
78. Ibid. p. 234; Mann. p. 77.
79. Mann. p. 77.
80. Hawley 2007. p. 90.
81. Davidson, Christopher M. *Dubai: The Vulnerability of Success* (London: Hurst, 2008). p. 79.
82. Maitra and Al-Hajji. pp. 246–247.
83. The merchants he caught were of the Otaibah family. Hopwood. p. 206.
84. The first bank in Sharjah was a branch of Eastern Bank, set up in the mid-1940s while the first real bank to exist in Dubai was the Imperial Bank of Iran, which set up an office in 1948 and which later became known as the British Bank of Iran, before then being renamed the British Bank of the Middle East after the British Government acquired the majority of the bank's shares in 1952.
85. Al-Gurg. p. 65.

86. Darwish bin Karem.
87. Personal interviews, Dubai, December 2005; Al-Gurg. pp. 73–75.
88. Isa bin Saleh Al-Gurg.
89. Al-Gurg. pp. 66–67.
90. Maitra and Al-Hajji. p. 244.
91. Wheatcroft. p. 130.
92. Personal interviews, Abu Dhabi, June 2005.
93. Al-Fahim. p. 95.
94. Wheatcroft. p. 105.
95. Al-Fahim. p. 94.
96. Foreign Office 371/109814.
97. Maitra and Al-Hajji. p. 243.
98. Hawley 1970. p. 236.
99. Foreign Office 371/120553.
100. Al-Fahim. p. 77.
101. Personal interviews, Dubai, June 2006.
102. Mann. p. 95.
103. Wheatcroft. p. 30.
104. Ibid. p. 110.
105. Ibid. p. 135; Foreign Office 371/185531 35590. Shakhbut made this visit in 1966.
106. Hawley 2007. p. 118.
107. Al-Gurg. pp. 134–135. This currency was set up by Qatar and Dubai following the marriage of Sheikh Rashid's daughter, Sheikha Mariam bint Rashid Al-Maktum, to the ruler of Qatar, Sheikh Ahmad bin Ali Al-Thani.
108. Hawley 2007. p. 34.
109. Heard-Bey. pp. 306–307.
110. Hawley 2007. pp. 178–184; Al-Gurg. p. 113; Hawley 2007. p. 177.
111. Maitra and Al-Hajji. p. 242; Heard-Bey. p. 321; Fenelon. pp. 46–47, 49–59.
112. Hawley 2007. p. 114.
113. Al-Gurg. p. 117.
114. Personal interviews, Dubai, January 2007.
115. Van der Meulen. p. 332.
116. Al-Fahim. p. 43.
117. India Office S/18/B/469.
118. Al-Sagri. p. 160. Al-Sagri is quoting the Political Resident's secret political report of 1956.
119. Al-Gurg. p. 115; Van der Meulen. p. 209.
120. Al-Gurg. p. 96.
121. Foreign Office 371/120552. Al-Sayegh, Fatma. 'Merchants' Role in a Changing Society: The Case of Dubai, 1900–1990' in *Middle Eastern Studies* (vol. 34, no. 1, 1998), p. 98; Abu-Baker. pp. 139.

122. Foreign Office 371/120553.
123. Davidson 2008. p. 53.
124. Foreign Office 371/120557; Al-Sagri, p. 190.
125. Foreign Office 371/120557.
126. Heard-Bey. p. 29.
127. Ibid. p. 33.
128. Personal interviews, Abu Dhabi, April 2008.
129. Van der Meulen. p. 400.
130. Maitra and Al-Hajji. p. 248.
131. By the end of Shakhbut's reign in 1966 the figure may have been even less, as these figures are taken from the 1968 census. Kelly, John B. *Britain and the Persian Gulf* (Oxford: Oxford University Press, 1968). pp. 20,51.
132. Rush. p. 152.
133. Rugh. p. 65.
134. Ibid. p. 65.
135. Personal interviews, Abu Dhabi, August 2007; and Zahlan. p. 44 for a partial account.
136. When the party was confronted, they claimed they had lost their way. Henderson, Edward. *This Strange Eventful History: Memoirs of Earlier Days in the United Arab Emirates* (London: Quartet, 1988). pp. 81–82.
137. Al-Sayegh, Fatma. 'The United Arab Emirates and Oman: Opportunities and Challenges in the Twenty-First Century' in *Middle East Policy* (vol. 9. no. 3, 2002).
138. The chief being Rashid bin Hamad Al-Shamsi.
139. Hawley 2007. p. 160.
140. Ibid. p. 160.
141. Ibid. p. 188; Wheatcroft. p. 88
142. Kelly, John B. *Eastern Arabia Frontier* (New York: Praeger, 1964). p. 165.
143. Rush. p. 174; Van der Meulen. p. 154. Some of the Al-Bu Mundir left permanently to live in Saudi Arabia.
144. Kelly 1964. p. 242.
145. Rush. p. 169.
146. Ibid. pp. 211–213.
147. Ibid. p. 231.
148. Personal interviews, Abu Dhabi, August 2007.
149. Rugh. p. 65.
150. Kelly 1964. p. 180. The meeting between Saqr's sons and the Al-Bu Mundir took place in Dubai. The Al-Bu Mundir chief being Muhammad bin Tawfan Al-Mundiri.
151. Rush. p. 211.
152. Ibid. p. 201. Hazza had died of cancer.

153. Ibid. p. 213.
154. Heard-Bey. p. 33.
155. E.g. Tammam, Wheatcroft.
156. Sir William Luce.
157. Foreign Office 371/163025 33829.
158. Foreign Office 371/163025 33829.
159. Wheatcroft. p. 118; Personal interviews, London, May 2008.
160. Foreign Office 371/163025 33829.
161. Foreign Office 371/185578 35760.
162. Personal interviews, London, May 2008.
163. This hotel was close to the British embassy. Personal interviews, Durham, May 2007.
164. Foreign Office 371/185529 35559.
165. Wheatcroft. p. 139.

3. SHEIKH ZAYED THE SECOND: PROSPERITY AND UNITY

1. Hawley, Donald. *The Emirates: Witness to a Metamorphosis* (Norwich: Michael Russell, 2007). p. 221.
2. Al-Gurg, Easa Saleh. *The Wells of Memory* (London: John Murray, 1998). p. 136.
3. Lady Margaret Luce.
4. Al-Gurg. pp. 176–177.
5. Rush, Alan (ed). *Ruling Families of Arabia: The United Arab Emirates* (Slough: Archive Editions 1991). pp. 169–170.
6. Wheatcroft, Andrew. *With United Strength: Sheikh Zayed bin Sultan Al-Nahyan, the Leader and the Nation* (Abu Dhabi: Emirates Centre for Strategic Studies and Research, 2005). p. 80.
7. Between 1945 and 1948 a number of tribes engaged in a series of armed conflicts over Khor Ghanadha, a territory close to the present-day Abu Dhabi-Dubai border. Technically, Sheikh Said bin Maktum Al-Maktum had been the aggressor, as he permitted a Dubai-based tribe to launch a coastal attack on their enemies, thereby violating the maritime peace treaties. Al-Gurg. p. 17; Al-Fahim, Muhammad. *From Rags to Riches: A Story of Abu Dhabi* (London: Centre for Arab Studies, 1995). pp. 44, 49.
8. Wheatcroft. pp. 82–83.
9. Ibid. p. 105.
10. Ibid. p. 104.
11. Davidson, Christopher M. *Dubai: The Vulnerability of Success* (London: Hurst, 2008). pp. 67–69.
12. Wheatcroft. p. 92.

13. Al-Fahim. p. 77.
14. Drs. Pat Burwell and Marian Kennedy of the Reformed Church of America.
15. *Khaleej Times* 6 April 2006.
16. Al-Fahim. p. 77.
17. Personal interviews, Abu Dhabi, August 2007.
18. Foreign Office 371/163025/33829.
19. Wheatcroft. p. 111.
20. This statement was made in 1929. Foreign Office 371/13712.
21. Rugh, Andrea B. *The Political Culture of Leadership in the United Arab Emirates* (New York: Palgrave Macmillan, 2007). p. 78.
22. Glencairn Balfour-Paul.
23. Colonel De Butts.
24. This request was made in Balfour-Paul's best flowery Arabic.
25. *Times (obituary)* 6 July 2008; Wheatcroft. pp. 139–140; Personal interviews, Abu Dhabi, April 2008.
26. Abu-Baker, Albadr. 'Political Economy of State Formation: The United Arab Emirates in Comparative Perspective' (PhD thesis. University of Michigan, 1995). p. 129; Joyce, Miriam. 'On the Road Towards Unity: The Trucial States from a British Perspective, 1960–1966' in *Middle Eastern Studies* (vol. 35, no. 2, 1999). p. 56.
27. Personal interviews, Exeter, July 2007; Hawley 2007. pp. 242,258.
28. Rush. p. 169; Rugh. p. 76.
29. Shakhbut died in 1989. Rugh. p. 78.
30. Van der Meulen, Hendrik. 'The Role of Tribal and Kinship Ties in the Politics of the United Arab Emirates' (PhD thesis. The Fletcher School of Law and Diplomacy, 1997). p. 400.
31. For a full discussion see chapter 5.
32. Van der Meulen. p. 132.
33. Al-Fahim. p. 137.
34. Rugh. p. 88; Van der Meulen. p. 112. The five sons being Hamdan, Mubarak, Tahnun, Saif, and Surur.
35. As discussed in chapter 2, Shakhbut had signed several lucrative concessions between 1939 and 1953, yet there was no evidence of any of this wealth being spent on domestic development in Abu Dhabi during the 1950s and early 1960s.
36. Hawley, Donald. *The Trucial States* (London: George Allen and Unwin, 1970). p. 216.
37. Foreign Office 371/185578/35760.
38. Hawley 1970. p. 204.
39. Wheatcroft. p. 150.
40. Ibid. p. 148.
41. Ibid. p. 148.

42. Ibid. pp. 149, 205.
43. Ibid. p. 149; Personal interviews, Abu Dhabi, August 2007. Rents were also reduced for over 200 shops in the souqs.
44. Wheatcroft. p. 148.
45. Ibid. p. 150.
46. Personal interviews, Abu Dhabi, August 2007.
47. Wheatcroft. p. 150.
48. Ibid. p. 148.
49. Ibid. p. 148.
50. In 1968 Sheikh Khalifa bin Zayed Al-Nahyan handed out over 150 keys to such houses. *Middle East Economic Digest* 2 May 1968.
51. Al-Fahim. p. 140.
52. According to Said bin Rashid Al-Mazrui, 200 dirhams were given for each camel, 100 dirhams for each cow, and 50 dirhams for each goat. *Gulf News* 26 December 2008.
53. Heard-Bey, Frauke. *From Trucial States to United Arab Emirates* (London: Longman, 1996). p. 115; Davidson, Christopher M. *The United Arab Emirates: A Study in Survival* (Boulder: Lynne Rienner, 2005). p. 20. There were six forms of taxes existing on Dalma Island in 1955, all of which were collected by the ruler's representative.
54. Al-Musfir, Muhammad Salih. 'The United Arab Emirates: An Assessment of Federalism in a Developing Polity' (PhD thesis. State University of New York and Binghamton, 1985), p. 76; Van der Meulen. pp. 390–392.
55. Al-Musfir. p. 76.
56. Heard-Bey. pp. 87–88.
57. Van der Meulen. pp. 441, 443.
58. Britain had been running a persistent balance of payments deficit, reflecting both her weakening competitive position industrially and the reduction of her invisible earnings. Reynolds, David. *Britannia Overruled: British Policy and World Power in the Twentieth Century* (Harlow: Longman, 1991). p. 17.
59. By 1967 Britain was spending £317 million on Middle Eastern bases. Wilson, Graeme. *Rashid's Legacy: The Genesis of the Maktoum Family and the History of Dubai* (Dubai: Media Prima, 2006). p. 258.
60. Anthony, John Duke. *The United Arab Emirates: Dynamics of State Formation* (Abu Dhabi: Emirates Centre for Strategic Studies and Research, 2002). p. 25.
61. Said bin Taimur Al-Said.
62. Personal interviews, Beirut, June 2005.
63. Al-Gurg. p. 5.
64. Sheikh Rashid bin Obaid Al-Maktum, whose family had lived there since Sheikh Obaid bin Said Al-Maktum, a cousin of the ruler of Dubai, had left the sheikhdom in the late 1850s. Davidson 2008. p. 272.

65. Personal interviews, Dubai, June 2006; Wilson. p. 64; Rush. pp. 309–310.
66. In 1959 Saudi Arabia vigorously protested against Abu Dhabi's establishment of a police outpost at the disputed Khor al-Udaid.
67. Foreign Office 371/185529/35559.
68. Foreign Office 371/179916.
69. Foreign Office 371/179918/31761.
70. Al-Sagri, Saleh Hamad. 'Britain and the Arab Emirates, 1820–1956' (PhD thesis. University of Kent at Canterbury, 1988). p. 268.
71. Fairhall, D. *Russia looks to the sea* (London: 1971). p. 234.
72. Foreign Office 371/91326.
73. Anthony 2002. p. 19; Al-Gurg. p. 132.
74. Wilson. pp. 196–198, 201.
75. The meeting was held at Zaabeel Palace. Peterson, John E. 'The Nature of Succession in the Gulf' in *Middle East Journal* (vol. 55, no. 4, 2001). p. 581.
76. Foreign Office 371/185531/35590; Wheatcroft. p. 175. A key success was resolving the maritime border between the two sheikhdoms.
77. Wheatcroft. p. 176.
78. A Dubai-Abu Dhabi flag of unity was also created. Personal interviews, Dubai, February 2006; Wilson. p. 265.
79. Wilson. pp. 196–198.
80. Ibid. pp. 128,138; (*in Arabic*) Sharabah, Naji Sadiq. 'The Federal Experiment of the United Arab Emirates, 1971–1977' (PhD thesis. University of Cairo, 1980).
81. Wilson. pp. 196–198.
82. Wheatcroft. p. 116.
83. Foreign Office 371/179916/35465. In 1965 he had been able to persuade Shakhbut to raise his contribution to the Trucial States Development fund from £25,000 to £75,000.
84. Wheatcroft. p. 116.
85. Wilson. p. 234.
86. The province of Fujairah on the Indian Ocean coastline, although nominally falling under Qawasim control, had been identified by American oil companies in 1951 as being effectively outside of the British network. The American and Saudi oil giant, ARAMCO, had already begun to approach prominent members of Fujairah's dominant Sharqiyin tribe. While they were offering to pay rent for oil concessions, it is likely that ARAMCO never really expected to prospect for oil in the area, but instead sought to gain a foothold in the lower Gulf. Given that the IPC was only able to deal with official Trucial rulers, it was unable to compete, prompting Britain to act fast: in 1952 Sheikh Muhammad bin Hamad Al-Sharqi was upgraded to the status of the other 1835 peace treaty

holders, and Fujairah was declared to be a distinct Trucial sheikhdom. Davidson 2008. pp. 27–28.

87. Heard-Bey. pp. 343–344.
88. The representatives were Sheikh Zayed, Sheikh Maktum bin Rashid Al-Maktum (the eldest son of Sheikh Rashid bin Said Al-Maktum), Sheikh Khalifa bin Hamad Al-Thani (the Crown Prince of Qatar), Sheikh Isa bin Salman Al-Khalifa of Bahrain, Sheikh Khalid bin Muhammad Al-Qasimi of Sharjah, Sheikh Saqr bin Muhammad Al-Qasimi of Ra's al-Khaimah, Sheikh Rashid bin Humaid Al-Nuami of Ajman, Sheikh Ahmad bin Rashid Al-Mualla of Umm al-Qawain, and Sheikh Hamad bin Muhammad Al-Sharqi of Fujairah.
89. Wilson. pp. 296–298.
90. Personal interviews, Dubai, February 2006.
91. Wilson. p. 300.
92. The plan was to build eventually a permanent capital on the border between Abu Dhabi and Dubai. Rather ominously the site for the proposed new capital was in the *Wadi al-Mawt* or Valley of Death. Peck, Malcolm. *The United Arab Emirates: A Venture in Unity* (Boulder: Westview, 1986), p. 50; Al-Musfir. p. 74.
93. It is thought that this British intervention prompted Qatar and Bahrain to walk out of the meetings. Personal interviews, Dubai, June 2006; Wilson. p. 316.
94. Tehran claimed that Bahrain was Iran's 14th province. Hawley 2007. pp. 12–13.
95. The Iranian Foreign Ministry even claimed that 'Iran has always been opposed to colonialism in all forms, and the so-called federation of the Gulf emirates, by annexing the island of Bahrain to it, is considered a matter which cannot be acceptable to the Iranian government.' Wilson. p. 295.
96. Hawley 2007. pp. 12–13.
97. Wheatcroft. p. 184.
98. Personal interviews, Dubai, July 2007; Wilson. p. 322.
99. Kelly, John B. *Arabia, the Gulf, and the West: A Critical View of the Arabs and their Oil Policy* (New York: Basic Books, 1986). p. 49. This quote is from Goronwy Roberts' report to the British Cabinet in 1968. Such pleas fell on deaf ears, especially following a House of Commons debate that cautioned against British involvement along such lines for fear of British soldiers being branded as 'mercenaries.' Personal interviews with Lord Richard Luce, London, February 2007.
100. Alec Douglas-Hume.
101. This warning was delivered in March 1971. Wheatcroft. p. 181.
102. The first draft of this federal constitution was drawn up by an Egyptian expert who had also worked on the Kuwaiti constitution, but was re-

jected by Dubai. Personal interviews, Abu Dhabi, March 2007; Al-Gurg. p. 140.

103. Heard-Bey. pp. 369–370; Anthony 2002. pp. 66, 74; Davidson 2008. p. 259. Ra's al-Khaimah still had strong expectations for oil strikes of its own, and it felt that if the oil companies prospecting in its territories were able to announce major discoveries then the emirate's bargaining position in future federal negotiations would be considerably strengthened. Failing such strikes, its rulers had developed an alternative plan in which Ra's al-Khaimah's port facilities would be offered on an exclusive basis to the United States Navy in exchange for international recognition as an independent sovereign state. Tellingly, at the very end of 1971, just twelve days after the oil companies declared that no commercial quantities of oil existed in the emirate, and just one week after their special envoy to the United States returned to the Gulf with no firm support, Ra's al-Khaimah accepted the reality of its situation and sought to join the UAE.

104. Heard-Bey 1996. pp. 369–370.

105. Hawley 2007. pp. 13–14.

106. When Britain withdrew from south-western Arabia in 1967 they had formed the 'Federation of Yemeni Emirates of the Arab South.' This comprised of five sheikhdoms and one sultanate. Over-centralization soon led to tensions emerging and eventually exposed the Yemen to external influences and an unstable Arab nationalist movement. Davidson 2008. p. 59.

107. Kéchichian, Joseph A. *Power and Succession in Arab Monarchies: A Reference Guide* (Boulder: Lynne Rienner, 2008). p. 284; Wheatcroft. p. 173. These were to become articles 2 and 3 of the 1971 provisional constitution.

108. Heard-Bey, Frauke. 'The UAE: A Quarter Century of Federation' in Hudson, Michael (ed). *Middle East Dilemma: The Politics and Economics of Arab Integration* (London: IB Tauris, 1999). p. 135.

109. Rizvi, S. N. Asad. 'From Tents to High Rise: Economic Development of the United Arab Emirates' in *Middle Eastern Studies* (vol. 29, no. 4, 1993). p. 665.

110. Overton, J. L. 'Stability and Change: Inter-Arab Politics in the Arabian Peninsula and the Gulf' (PhD thesis. University of Maryland, 1983). p. 186.

111. Anthony, John Duke. p. 115.

112. Heard-Bey in Hudson. pp. 137–138.

113. Wilson. pp. 386–387; Overton. p. 186.

114. Heard-Bey. pp. 387–393.

115. Al-Musfir. p. 137.

116. Wilson. pp. 386–387.

117. Al-Nabeh, Najat Abdullah. 'United Arab Emirates: Regional and Global Dimensions' (PhD thesis. Claremont Graduate School, 1984). p. 62.
118. Wheatcroft. p. 221.
119. Sheikh Sultan bin Muhammad Al-Qasimi had relied heavily on support from Sheikh Zayed when he was installed in 1972. Sultan also offered to replace the Sharjah flag with the federal flag. Wheatcroft. p. 224.
120. *Middle East Economic Digest* 1 July 1978.
121. Heard-Bey. p. 380.
122. Wheatcroft. p. 208.
123. Al-Nabeh. p. 62.
124. Perhaps in a show of defiance Sheikh Rashid actually tripled the Dubai government's expenditure on the DDF over the following decade. Al-Musfir. p. 161.
125. Davidson 2005. p. 203.
126. Peck. p. 131; Heard-Bey. pp. 397–401.
127. Wilson. p. 390.
128. Personal interviews, Abu Dhabi, September 2003.
129. Heard-Bey. pp. 397–401.
130. Ibid. pp. 396–401.
131. Personal interviews, Dubai, August 2007. Previously the prime minister was Sheikh Rashid's eldest son, Maktum. But given Maktum's young age, it was seen as symbolic position.
132. Wilson. p. 390.
133. Peck. p. 51.
134. Fenelon, Kevin. The *United Arab Emirates: An Economic and Social Survey* (London: Longman, 1973). p. 18.
135. Brown, Gavin. *OPEC and the World Energy Market* (London: Longman, 1998). p. 360; Overton. p. 184.
136. *Oxford Business Group* 'United Arab Emirates: The Report 2000.' p. 111.
137. Rizvi. p. 669.
138. Personal interviews, Dubai, June 2006; Rizvi. p. 669.
139. *Oxford Business Group* 'United Arab Emirates: The Report 2000.' pp. 71–72.
140. Sheikh Zayed's initial contribution seems to have been $500 million. With regard to Zayed's initial share see *Middle East Economic Digest* 1 February 1982. With regard to the BCCI's founding and majority shareholders, see the Report to the Committee on Foreign Relations in the United States Senate by Senators John Kerry and Senator Hank Brown. pp. 102–104.
141. Led respectively by Price Waterhouse and a team of US senators that included John Kerry and Hank Brown. For the latter's report see the 'Report to the Committee on Foreign Relations in the United States

Senate by Senators John Kerry and Senator Hank Brown', 102nd Congress 2nd Session Senate Print, December 1992.

142. Personal interviews, Ra's al-Khaimah, September 2002.

143. The Soviet port was built at Umm Qasr in Iraq.

144. Personal interviews, Ra's al-Khaimah, September 2002

145. Saddam Hussein had requested that the UAE and the other GCC states sever all ties with Ayatollah Khomeini. Al-Gurg. p. 143; Peck. p. 133.

146. Wilson. p. 437. Sheikh Rashid was also insisting that radio stations in Dubai broadcast both the Baghdad and Tehran versions of the news.

147. Davidson 2008. pp. 227–228.

148. Brown. p. 361.

149. Saudi Arabia and Kuwait were founding members of OPEC in 1960, while Qatar joined in 1961. Ibid. p. 361.

150. Dr Roberto Subroto

151. Subroto visited Sheikh Zayed in 1987. Ibid. p. 724.

152. Yousef bin Omar Al-Mazrui.

153. Sheikh Muhammad bin Zayed Al-Nahyan.

154. Personal interviews, Dubai, December 2004; Foley, Sean. 'The United Arab Emirates: Political Issues and Security Dilemmas' in *Middle East Review of International Affairs* (vol. 3, no. 1, 1998).

4. OIL AND BEYOND: ABU DHABI'S NEW ECONOMY

1. Dubai's share is now only 4 percent, with the remainder being made up of minimal exports from Sharjah, Ra's al-Khaimah, and Fujairah. Ajman and Umm al-Qawain do not have commercially exploitable oil reserves. US Energy Information Administration. *The United Arab Emirates: Country Analysis Brief* (Washington DC: EIA, 2007).

2. *Oxford Business Group* 'Abu Dhabi: The Report 2007.'

3. UAE Central Bank estimates, 2008.

4. The ZADCO concession will last until 2026. The ADMA concession will last until 2018. The ADCO concession will last until 2014.

5. Davidson, Christopher M. *The United Arab Emirates: A Study in Survival* (Boulder: Lynne Rienner, 2005). pp. 94–95.

6. *Oxford Business Group* 'Abu Dhabi: The Report 2007.'

7. In 1999 ADNOC revenues were estimated at $13 billion, increasing to $56 billion in 1006. Seznec, Jean-François. 'The Gulf Sovereign Wealth Funds: Myths and Reality' in *Middle East Policy* (vol. 15, no. 2, 2008). p. 99.

8. *Financial Times* 17 December 2008. Quoting National Bank of Abu Dhabi reports.

9. *The National* 24 July 2008; ADGAS statistics 2007.

10. *Oxford Business Group* 'Abu Dhabi: The Report 2007.' p. 151; Davidson 2005. pp. 94–95.
11. *Oxford Business Group* 'Abu Dhabi: The Report 2007.' p. 151.
12. *The National* 24 July 2008; Personal interviews, Abu Dhabi, April 2008.
13. *Financial Times* 8 July 2008.
14. ADGAS statistics 2007.
15. *Oxford Business Group* 'Abu Dhabi: The Report 2007.' p. 152.
16. The remainder being oil and liquid fuelled. *Gulf News* 31 July 2008.
17. *The National* 24 July 2008.
18. Economist Intelligence Unit 2000; *Oxford Business Group* 'United Arab Emirates: The Report 2000.' pp. 54–55. The second phase of the project will involve an underwater pipeline from Oman to Pakistan.
19. *Oxford Business Group* 'Abu Dhabi: The Report 2007.'
20. The Kish and Henjam offshore fields will soon be exploited. *Tehran Times* 2 January 2008.
21. *AME Info* 21 May 2008.
22. '*Taqa*' translates as 'energy' in English.
23. *The National* 5 April 2008.
24. Personal interviews, Abu Dhabi, April 2008.
25. *Oxford Business Group* 'Abu Dhabi: The Report 2007.' p. 202.
26. Ibid. p. 202; *Oxford Business Group* 'United Arab Emirates: The Report 2000.' pp. 94–95.
27. *Oxford Business Group* 'Abu Dhabi: The Report 2007.' p. 212.
28. The latter being built at Ruwais in cooperation with Rio Tinto. *The National* 24 July 2008; Seznec. p. 101.
29. Borealis press release 19 March 2008.
30. *Arabian Business* 29 August 2008.
31. *Oxford Business Group* 'Abu Dhabi: The Report 2007.' p. 203.
32. Ibid. p. 204.
33. *Gulf Today* 18 July 2007; Personal interviews, Abu Dhabi, August 2007.
34. *Oxford Business Group* 'Abu Dhabi: The Report 2007.' p. 214.
35. Personal interviews, London, May 2007; *Euromoney* 1 April 2006.
36. The Government of Singapore Investment Corporation being the largest. *Economist* 17 January 2008.
37. Norges Bank press release May 2008. The largest Norwegian fund being the Government Pension Fund of Norway.
38. Notably the Kuwait Investment Authority. *Reuters* 20 June 2008.
39. Dubai World is thought to control between $90 to $100 billion in funds. Personal interviews, Dubai, August 2008.
40. Notably the Qatar Investment Authority. *New York Times* 11 December 2007.

41. Van der Meulen, Hendrik. 'The Role of Tribal and Kinship Ties in the Politics of the United Arab Emirates' (PhD thesis. The Fletcher School of Law and Diplomacy, 1997). p. 93.

42. Personal interviews, Dubai, January 2007.

43. ADIA is based in the new Samsung building on the Corniche, which was completed in 2006 and has now eclipsed the Hilton hotel's Baynunah Tower to become the tallest building in Abu Dhabi.

44. *Economist* 17 January 2008; Seznec. p. 97, 101. ADIA believed to have $875 billion according to Deutsche Bank. However, Seznec believes the figure to be much lower. But he may have placed insufficient weight on ADIA's history of investments in emerging markets.

45. It was reported in January 2009 that ADIA had lost about $125 billion. *Bloomberg* 15 January 2009.

46. The Abu Dhabi Investment Council was set up according to Abu Dhabi Law 16 of 2006.

47. Jean-Paul Villain joined ADIA in the early 1980s from Paribas. *New York Times* 28 February 2008.

48. Personal interviews, London, May 2008; *New York Times* 27 November 2007.

49. Personal correspondence, August 2008.

50. Said bin Mubarak Rashid Al-Hajiri.

51. *New York Times* 28 February 2008; Personal interviews, London, May 2008; *Oxford Business Group* 'Abu Dhabi: The Report 2007.' p. 43.

52. Seznec. p. 100; Personal correspondence, August 2008. Seznec puts ADIC at $7 billion.

53. Khalifa bin Muhammad Al-Kindi is the chair of ADIC while Nasser bin Hamad Al-Suwaidi is the deputy chair.

54. *Al-Bawaba* 13 July 2008.

55. *AFP* 9 July 2008.

56. *The National* 21 July 2008.

57. Personal interviews, London, May 2008.

58. Seznec. p. 101.

59. Ibid. p. 101; *The National* 5 August 2008.

60. *Zawya Dow Jones* 18 September 2007.

61. *The National* 21 July 2008.

62. *The National* 11 September 2008.

63. Mubadala holds 51 percent of Dolphin. Total and Occidental each hold 24.5 percent. *Oxford Business Group* 'Abu Dhabi: The Report 2007.' p. 128.

64. Seznec. p. 100.

65. Ibid. p. 100.

66. Ibid. pp. 100–101; Mubadala press release December 2007; AMD press release 16 November 2007.

67. *The National* 22 July 2008.
68. *AMEInfo* 23 September 2008. The purchase of this stake was reported as being carried out by Masdar, a subsidiary of Mubadala discussed later in this chapter.
69. *The National* 4 December 2008.
70. *The National* 9 December 2008.
71. *Gulf News* 15 June 2008. The subsidiary is the *Campagnie Eolienne du Detroit* (CED).
72. Seznec p. 101; Personal interviews, Abu Dhabi, April 2008.
73. In summer 2008 Gulf News reported its assets at $23 billion. *Gulf News* 15 June 2008.
74. ADWEA information department 2008.
75. Personal interviews, London, June 2008.
76. *The National* 20 May 2008.
77. *International Herald Tribune* 2 September 2008.
78. *Reuters* 31 October 2008.
79. By 1995 production had dropped to around 300,000 barrels per day. Davidson, Christopher M. *Dubai: The Vulnerability of Success* (London: Hurst, 2008). p. 101.
80. *The National* 26 July 2008.
81. *The National* 18 July 2008; Personal interviews, Abu Dhabi, April 2008.
82. *Oxford Business Group* 'Abu Dhabi: The Report 2007.' p. 38.
83. *Gulf News* 13 July 2008.
84. Ahmad bin Muhammad Al-Samerai.
85. *Oxford Business Group* 'Abu Dhabi: The Report 2007.' p. 54.
86. *Oxford Business Group* 'Dubai: The Report 2007'; Authors' estimates.
87. An exception being Oman's 'Oman Vision 2020.'
88. *Middle East Economic Digest* 6 June 2008.
89. *Financial Times* 17 December 2008 quoting Hussein Nowais, chairman of Abu Dhabi Basic Industries.
90. Mubadala Development Corporation press release July 2008, with reference to the aerospace industry.
91. *The National* 26 July 2008. Quoting the Abu Dhabi Department for Planning and the Economy.
92. *Khaleej Times* 11 May 2008.
93. *Middle East Economic Digest* 6 June 2008.
94. *The National* 12 July 2008.
95. Ibid.; Personal interviews, Abu Dhabi, April 2008.
96. *The National* 22 July 2008.
97. Ibid.
98. *The National* 12 July 2008; Personal interviews, Abu Dhabi, April 2008.
99. *The National* 31 July 2008.

100. *The National* 9 December 2008.
101. *Gulf News* 3 August 2008; *Trade Arabia* 4 August 2008.
102. *Oxford Business Group* 'Abu Dhabi: The Report 2007.' p. 203. The Baynunah Class corvettes are 70m 'multi-mission' naval corvettes. *AMEInfo* 8 January 2007.
103. *The National* 20 July 2008; *Gulf News* 2 August 2008.
104. CMN press release 21 December 2008.
105. *AMEInfo* 8 January 2007.
106. Personal interviews, London, May 2008.
107. *The National* 20 July 2008.
108. *The National* 30 July 2008; Personal interviews, Abu Dhabi, April 2008.
109. It is thought that the light aircraft will be called Mako, and the jeeps are some sort of stealth jeep. Davidson 2008. p. 266.
110. *Gulf News* 20 July 2008; *The National* 14 July 2008; *The National* 20 July 2008.
111. Personal interviews, London, May 2008; to some extent corroborated by *The National* 6 August 2008.
112. Sultan bin Ahmad Al-Jaber, the CEO of ADFEC.
113. *Arabian Business* 8 December 2007.
114. Personal correspondence with Mari Luomi, September 2008.
115. Although there are plans to set up a centre to treat hazardous garbage by the Environmental Agency Abu Dhabi, and a new $200m recycling plant is being built at Al-Mafraq by Abu Dhabi Municipality.
116. *The National* 22 July 2008.
117. See www.masdaruae.com
118. Personal correspondence with Mari Luomi, September 2008.
119. *The National* 23 July 2008.
120. *The National* 10 December 2008.
121. *The National* 22 July 2008.
122. *AMEInfo* 23 September 2008.
123. Masdar City press release July 2008.
124. *Arabian Business* 8 December 2007.
125. *Gulf News* 31 July 2008.
126. *Gulf News* 7 August 2008.
127. Emirates News Agency (WAM) 14 August 2005.
128. At present there only appears to be a non-Muslim specific prayer room above the Marina's main supermarket.
129. In summer 2008 Al-Madina Finance, a Kuwaiti investment vehicle, invested nearly $1 billion in a multi-tower Reem Island project. *The National* 20 July 2008.
130. There has been a very high uptake with Aldar having issued a 3.75 billion dirham bond and with Sorouh having issued a four billion dirham bond. *The National* 14 July 2008.

131. *Financial Times* 9 July 2008. Quoting Fitch ratings agency.
132. See chapter 7. Also see *Bloomberg* 4 December 2008; *Daily Telegraph* 21 November 2008; *Guardian* 5 December 2008; *Financial Times* 14 November 2008.
133. *Financial Times* 15 July 2008.
134. *The National* 18 July 2008; Author's estimates.
135. In summer 2008 it was reported that Abu Dhabi property price increases had begun to outstrip Dubai. A real estate report conducted by HSBC revealed that between late 2007 and mid 2008 Abu Dhabi property rose by 61 percent in price compared to 37 percent for Dubai. *Zawya Dow Jones* 15 July 2008.
136. *The National* 4 December 2008.
137. Khaldun bin Khalifa Al-Mubarak and Khadem bin Abdullah Al-Qubaisi respectively.
138. *The National* 29 July 2008.
139. *The National* 23 July 2008.
140. Personal interviews with Tamouh spokespersons, Abu Dhabi, April 2008.
141. *The National* 18 July 2008.
142. *AME Info* 7 March 2006.
143. *The National* 4 December 2008.
144. *AME Info* 7 March 2006.
145. *Gulf Construction* (vol. 29, no. 8, 2008).
146. *Gulf News* 5 August 2008.
147. *The National* 12 May 2008.
148. *The National* 12 July 2008.
149. *Daily Mail* 19 July 2008.
150. *The National* 12 July 2008.
151. The relationship between Mubadala and the TDIC is unclear. But it is widely understood that the TDIC is under Mubadala's umbrella, with ADTA being its sole shareholder. There is some overlap in board membership with Muhammad bin Saif Al-Mazrui serving on both the Mubadala and TDIC boards.
152. *New York Times* 7 March 2008; *Financial Times* 17 December 2008.
153. *Guardian* 10 August 2006.
154. *AME Info* 11 June 2007.
155. *BBC News* 22 January 2007.
156. *Bloomberg* 26 November 2006.
157. *Al-Bawaba* 16 March 2008.
158. Personal interviews, Abu Dhabi, April 2008.
159. Today, Gulf Air is effectively Bahrain's national carrier and has predicted losses of over $1 billion over the next few years. *The National* 4 August 2008.

160. *Daily Telegraph* 21 July 2004
161. *The National* 14 July 2008.
162. ADAC press release July 2008; *Gulf News* 15 November 2008.

5. THE TRADITIONAL MONARCHY: AN EVOLVING
   DYNASTY

1. Sharjah in 1972 and 1987. Ra's al-Khaimah in 2003 (the switching of crown princes).
2. For a full discussion see Herb, Michael. *All in the Family: Absolutism, Revolution, and Democracy in the Middle Eastern Monarchies* (New York: State University of New York Press, 1999). p. 47.
3. Sheikha Hussa bint Muhammad Al-Nahyan.
4. It is thought that Zayed may have had two wives before Hussa.
5. The first being Ahmad bin Muhammad Al-Dhaheri; the second being Abdullah bin Ghanim Al-Hamili; the third being Ibrahim bin Uthman; the fourth being Zayed.
6. Rugh, Andrea B. *The Political Culture of Leadership in the United Arab Emirates* (New York: Palgrave Macmillan, 2007). p. 89.
7. Van der Meulen, Hendrik. 'The Role of Tribal and Kinship Ties in the Politics of the United Arab Emirates' (PhD thesis. The Fletcher School of Law and Diplomacy, 1997). p. 97.
8. Personal interviews, Abu Dhabi, May 2005.
9. *Economist Intelligence Unit* January 2000.
10. Heard-Bey, Frauke. *From Trucial States to United Arab Emirates* (London: Longman, 1996). p. 397.
11. Sheikha Maazid Al-Masghuni.
12. Rugh. p. 83; Kelly, John B. *Eastern Arabia Frontier* (New York: Prager, 1964). p. 64.
13. Personal interviews, Abu Dhabi, August 2007.
14. Some texts attribute this power loss to Sultan's personality and tumultuous youth, but given that he took a few of his supporters along with him during his temporary exile, it would seem suggestive that a serious argument may have taken place. Peterson, John E. 'The Arab Gulf States: Steps Towards Political Participation' in *Washington Papers* (no.131, 1988). p. 204; Rugh. p. 91.
15. Pope, M. T. G. *Businessman's Guide to the United Arab Emirates* (Sharjah: Dar al-Fatah, 1996). p. 295.
16. Kéchichian, Joseph A. *Power and Succession in Arab Monarchies: A Reference Guide* (Boulder: Lynne Rienner, 2008). p. 302.
17. Zahlan, Rosemarie Said. *The Origins of the United Arab Emirates* (New York: St. Martin's, 1978). p. 145. The Bani Qitab had great influence in many areas of the hinterland where oil exploration was taking place.

18. A good example being the 'Mother of the Nation' festival held in early 2007 at the Emirates Palace Hotel.
19. *Economist Intelligence Unit* January 2000.
20. Davidson, Christopher M. *The United Arab Emirates: A Study in Survival* (Boulder: Lynne Rienner, 2005). pp. 127–128.
21. *Economist Intelligence Unit* November 1999.
22. Davidson 2005. p. 102.
23. Van der Meulen. p. 123.
24. Institute for Middle Eastern and Islamic Studies, Durham University.
25. This marriage took place at a time when Zayed had invited a group of Daramikah that had been exiled by Shakhbut to return to Abu Dhabi and settle in Al-Ayn.
26. Amna came from a Badawi family based in Dubai's Hatta enclave, rather than the main Dhawahir bastion in Buraimi.
27. Emirates News Agency (WAM) 3 June 2008.
28. These events took place between 1 November and 2 November 2004. Rumours had begun two weeks earlier that Zayed had died or was receiving life support. Davidson, Christopher M. 'After Sheikh Zayed: The Politics of Succession in Abu Dhabi and the United Arab Emirates' in *Middle East Policy* (vol. 13, no. 1, 2006).
29. Said bin Zayed of the bani Aisha and Hamad bin Zayed of the bani Mouza.
30. Pope. p. 298.
31. *AFP* 1 January 2005.
32. This will be published by the new Abu Dhabi Centre for Information in 2008 or 2009.
33. In December 2008 Sheikh Khalid bin Muhammad Al-Nahyan married a daughter of Sheikh Surur bin Muhammad Al-Nahyan. A greater discussion of this takes place later in this chapter.
34. This reassignment took place in 2003. Kéchichian. p. 304.
35. *Reuters* 31 October 2008.
36. E.g. the aforementioned Al-Mibar International.
37. Sheikha Manal bint Muhammad Al-Maktum.
38. See chapter 4.
39. Sheikh Shakhbut bin Diab Al-Nahyan appears to have had no brothers, while Sheikh Zayed bin Khalifa Al-Nahyan only had one brother.
40. Sheikha Latifa bint Zayed Al-Nahyan.
41. Van der Meulen. p. 132.
42. E.g. He offered gifts alongside Muhammad bin Zayed at the 2008 Liwa date festival. *Gulf News* 3 August 2008.
43. Sheikh Hamdan bin Hamdan Al-Nahyan.
44. Rush, Alan (ed). *Ruling Families of Arabia: The United Arab Emirates* (Slough: Archive Editions 1991). p. 211; Rugh. p. 67.

45. Pope. p. 198.
46. Rugh. p. 88. E.g. Muhammad bin Zayed, Hamdan bin Zayed, and Said bin Zayed all married daughters of Hamdan bin Muhammad. Abdullah bin Zayed married a daughter of Saif bin Muhammad, and both of Fatima's daughters married into the bani Muhammad bin Khalifa.
47. Van der Meulen. pp. 110–111.
48. Al-Fahim, Muhammad. *From Rags to Riches: A Story of Abu Dhabi* (London: Centre for Arab Studies, 1995). p. 137.
49. Wilson, Graeme. *Rashid's Legacy: The Genesis of the Maktoum Family and the History of Dubai* (Dubai: Media Prima, 2006). p. 390.
50. Heard-Bey. p. 110.
51. Anthony, John Duke. *Arab States of the Lower Gulf: People, Politics, Petroleum* (Washington DC: Middle East Institute, 1975). p. 147.
52. Peterson 1988. pp. 204–205.
53. Ibid. p. 204.
54. His eldest son was Sheikh Ahmad bin Mubarak Al-Nahyan.
55. Presently Sultan bin Zayed and Hamdan bin Zayed.
56. The ADNOC chairmanship was switched to Yousef bin Omar Al-Mazrui.
57. Saif bin Zayed.
58. Pope. p. 295.
59. Rugh. p. 90. Sultan bin Khalifa married Sheikha Sheikha bint Saif Al-Nahyan (repetition intended: 'Sheikha' being both her title and name). Muhammad bin Khalifa married the daughter of Sultan bin Zayed, who in turn was a granddaughter of Muhammad bin Khalifa, as Sultan bin Zayed had married one of Muhammad's youngest daughters.
60. Davidson 2006. p. 56.
61. A deputy inspector general at the federal ministry for the interior.
62. *The National* 16 December 2008.
63. Hawley, Donald. *The Trucial States* (London: George Allen and Unwin, 1970). p. 294.
64. See chapter 1.
65. In summer 2008 he was appointed to another four year term.
66. Van der Meulen. p. 142.
67. Heard-Bey. p. 206.
68. Ibid. p. 104.
69. Ahmad bin Khalaf was also deputy director of Abu Dhabi Municipality.
70. The aforementioned Sheikha Salama bint Buti Al-Qubaisi.
71. Heard-Bey. p. 104.
72. Fadhil bin Khadem Al-Muhairbi.
73. E.g. Rahma bin Muhammad Al-Masud.
74. Atiq Al-Hamili and Ahmad bin Khamis Al-Hamili respectively.

75. Ahmad bin Musa Al-Hamili.
76. Abdullah bin Said Al-Hamili.
77. Khalfan bin Mudar Al-Rumiathi. Van der Meulen. pp. 145–146.
78. Said Al-Rumaithi.
79. Thani bin Obaid Al-Rumaithi.
80. Khamis bin Buti Al-Rumaithi.
81. Juma bin Obaid Al-Rumaithi, former director of immigration.
82. Muhammad Al-Murar was a board member of the General Industries Corporation (GIC).
83. Pope. pp. 212, 235.
84. Including the Al-Bu Mundir section's aforementioned departure in the early 1950s to Saudi Arabia.
85. Zahlan. p. 52.
86. Heard-Bey. pp. 120–121.
87. Said bin Muhammad Al-Mansuri. Van der Meulen. pp. 153–156.
88. Khalifa bin Nasser Al-Mansuri.
89. Ahmad bin Hassan Al-Mansuri.
90. Muhammad bin Nasser Al-Mansuri.
91. Ali bin Mubarak Al-Mansuri was ambassador to France and then to South America.
92. Mouza bint Suhail Al-Khalili.
93. *Oxford Business Group* 'Abu Dhabi: The Report 2007.' p. 213.
94. Kelly. pp. 188–189.
95. Amna bint Salah Al-Badi.
96. Aisha bint Ali Al-Darmaki.
97. Harib bin Masud Al-Darmaki. Van der Meulen. pp. 156–160.
98. Muhammad bin Said Al-Badi.
99. Ahmad bin Surur Al-Dhaheri.
100. Ali bin Khalfan Al-Dhaheri.
101. Matar bin Salim Al-Dhaheri.
102. Abdullah bin Said Al-Badi.
103. Said bin Sultan Al-Darmaki.
104. Hamad bin Sultan Al-Dhaheri.
105. Asri bin Said Al-Dhaheri.
106. Ibid. p. 162.
107. Ibid. p. 162.
108. Muhammad bin Salim Al-Amiri, director of training in the UAE Armed Forces. Ibid. pp. 160–163.
109. Mabkhut bin Said Al-Amiri. Ibid. pp. 160–163.
110. The section has many other branches elsewhere in the lower Gulf.
111. Salim bin Hamed al-Shamsi.
112. Abdullah Al-Shamsi, director of roads and infrastructure at Abu Dhabi Municipality.

113. Van der Meulen. p. 369.
114. E.g. Rashid bin Salim Al-Qitbi was director of soldiers' affairs in the UAE Armed Forces. Ibid. pp. 167–169.
115. Obaid bin Salim Al-Zaabi. Ibid. pp. 163–167.
116. Abdullah bin Isa Al-Zaabi.
117. Ahmad bin Juma Al-Zaabi.
118. Mouza bint Ahmad Al-Otaibi. Rugh. p. 60.
119. Khalaf bin Ahmad Al-Otaibi.
120. Davidson, Christopher M. *Dubai: The Vulnerability of Success* (London: Hurst, 2008). p. 292.

6. LEGITIMIZING THE MONARCHY

1. See for example Hudson, Michael. *Arab Politics: The Search for Legitimacy* (New Haven: Yale University Press, 1977), p. 199.
2. Huntington, Samuel P. *Political Order in Changing Societies* (New Haven: Yale University Press, 1968), p. 142
3. The Dubai Executive Council is very informal. Davidson, Christopher M. *Dubai: The Vulnerability of Success* (London: Hurst, 2008). pp. 158–159. The Sharjah Executive Council is considered quite strong—the ruler claims he cannot make decisions without a consensus from the Council.
4. Said bin Zayed, Hamad bin Zayed, Tahnun bin Zayed, and Diab bin Zayed.
5. Sultan bin Tahnun and Ahmad bin Saif.
6. Nasser bin Ahmad Al-Suwaidi and Hamad Al-Hurr Al-Suwaidi.
7. Ahmad bin Mubarak Al-Mazrui.
8. Mugheer Al-Khaili.
9. Jouan bin Salem Al-Dhaheri.
10. Obaid Al-Hairi Salem Al-Qitbi.
11. Abdullah bin Rashid Al-Otaibi.
12. Although there were discussions in 2003, no such body has been set up in Dubai yet. Davidson 2008. p. 159.
13. Law number 2 of 1971 concerning the establishment of the National Consultative Council.
14. Law number 2 of 1971 and Emiri decree number 39 of 1972.
15. Fifty-five members is the maximum as per article 2 of amendments made in 1990 to Law number 2 of 1971.
16. Law number 2 of 1971.
17. Personal interviews, Exeter, July 2008.
18. See Al-Nabeh, Najat Abdullah. 'United Arab Emirates: Regional and Global Dimensions' (PhD thesis. Claremont Graduate School, 1984).
19. Personal interviews, Abu Dhabi, March 2007; Al-Gurg, Easa Saleh. *The Wells of Memory* (London: John Murray, 1998). p. 140; Kéchichian, Joseph

A. *Power and Succession in Arab Monarchies: A Reference Guide* (Boulder: Lynne Rienner, 2008). pp. 284.

20. Taryam, Abdullah. *The Establishment of the United Arab Emirates, 1950–1985* (London: Croom Helm, 1987), p. 118.
21. Ibid. p. 206.
22. Hadef bin Jouan Al-Dhaheri.
23. Sultan bin Said Al-Mansuri.
24. Muhammad bin Dhaen Al-Hamili.
25. Although Dubai-dwelling, the minister for education—Hanif Hassan Al-Qassimi—had previously been the deputy of Sheikh Nahyan bin Mubarak Al-Nahyan at the ministry for higher education. Possibly also Maryam Al-Roumi, the minister for social affairs, and Maitha bint Salem Al-Shamsi, minister of state without portfolio.
26. Kéchichian. p. 285.
27. Rizvi, S. N. Asad. 'From Tents to High Rise: Economic Development of the United Arab Emirates' in *Middle Eastern Studies* (vol. 29, no. 4, 1993). p. 665
28. These have normally been over concerns that were already shared by the COM, such as the need for tightening anti-drug legislation and the need for further modifying the UAE's property laws. Al-Nahyan, Shamma bint Muhammad. *Political and Social Security in the United Arab Emirates* (Dubai: 2000). pp. 122–123.
29. Especially in cases where the FNC's views were likely to diverge from the relevant minister's outlook, such as over the price of petrol or the cultural content of terrestrial television. Ibid p. 121.
30. There have been examples of the FNC's letters to ministers having remained unanswered for several months, and occasions when the FNC has been unable to persuade ministers to attend their sessions and answer basic questions on their policies. Ibid. pp. 178–179, 188.
31. Author's estimates. See Davidson, Christopher M. 'After Sheikh Zayed: The Politics of Succession in Abu Dhabi and the United Arab Emirates' in *Middle East Policy* (vol. 13, no. 1, 2006)
32. Personal interviews, Abu Dhabi, August 2007.
33. *The National* 4 August 2008.
34. *Oxford Business Group* 'United Arab Emirates: the Report 2000.' p. 70.
35. Personal interviews, Abu Dhabi, December 2005.
36. *The National* 10 July 2008.
37. *Economist Intelligence Unit* May 2005.
38. The number of public sector jobs has been streamlined from 65,000 to 28,000. And it is anticipated that the number will eventually drop to around 8000. *Oxford Business Group* 'Abu Dhabi: The Report 2007.' p. 16.
39. Heard-Bey, Frauke. *From Trucial States to United Arab Emirates* (London: Longman, 1996). p. 397.

40. Federal Commercial Companies Law of 1984, article 22.
41. The fertility rate for all women resident in the UAE is 2.43, but the fertility rate for nationals is likely to be much higher as they marry earlier and can expect greater socio-economic benefits per child. *CIA World Factbook 2008*; Personal interviews, Abu Dhabi, August 2007.
42. Well sourced 1994 estimates put the tribal population of Abu Dhabi at 100,000. Van der Meulen, Hendrik. 'The Role of Tribal and Kinship Ties in the Politics of the United Arab Emirates' (PhD thesis. The Fletcher School of Law and Diplomacy, 1997). This will have excluded other naturalized families. Applying fertility rates since this period there should be at least 200,000 Abu Dhabi nationals today.
43. The UAE total population in 2008 was estimated at 4.6 million, of which about 2.2 million are in Dubai. Of the remainder, perhaps 1.5 million are resident in Abu Dhabi. *CIA World Factbook 2008*; Personal interviews, Abu Dhabi, April 2008; Davidson 2008. p. 191.
44. *The National* 26 September 2008.
45. *The National* 7 September 2008.
46. *The National* 26 September 2008.
47. Personal interviews, Exeter, July 2008.
48. Dresch, Paul, and Piscatori, James P (eds). *Monarchies and Nations: Globalisation and Identity in the Arab States of the Gulf* (London: IB Tauris, 2005). p. 151.
49. *Gulf News* 26 July 2008.
50. Personal interviews with employees of the Ministry of Labour and Social Affairs, Abu Dhabi, March 2002.
51. Emirates News Agency (WAM) 21 October 2002.
52. *Gulf News* 26 July 2008.
53. See for example Khalaf, Sulayman. 'Poetics and Politics of Newly Invented Traditions in the Gulf: Camel Racing in the United Arab Emirates' in *Ethnology* (vol. 39, no. 3, 2000)
54. This festival takes place in Madinat Zayed in the western region and is held every December. *Gulf News* 26 December 2008.
55. *The National* 12 August 2008.
56. *The National* 2 August 2008; Personal interviews, Abu Dhabi, April 2008.
57. See www.sheikhmohammed.co.ae
58. *New Statesman* 5 March 2007; Personal observations.
59. *The National* 22 July 2008; Personal observations.
60. *The National* 7 August 2008.
61. Foreign Office 371/185560/35716. This was one of Zayed's very first acts upon succeeding in 1966.
62. *The National* 2 August 2008.
63. E.g. On Futaisi Island.

64. By issuing ulema with identity cards and approving their sermon content the authorities can also prevent radical preachers from operating. See Davidson, Christopher M. *The United Arab Emirates: A Study in Survival* (Boulder: Lynne Rienner, 2005). p. 275.

65. *Khaleej Times* 10 August 2007.

66. Interestingly, many residents of Bethany are frustrated, with some claiming that their city needs a hospital before it needs a grand mosque. *The National* 27 July 2008.

67. *Gulf News* 27 October 2004.

68. Dr Mahmoud Zaqzouq.

69. Sheikh Ahmed Hassoun.

70. *The National* 25 August 2008.

71. E.g. Salman Al-Odeh.

72. E.g. Sir Christopher Patten, Britain's last governor of Hong Kong.

73. Personal correspondence, September 2008; *The National* 4 September 2008.

74. *AME Info* 3 March 2007; Personal interviews with Derek Kennet, Durham, October 2008. A Nestorian church and monastery was discovered on Sir Bani Yas Island in the mid-1990s.

75. Van der Meulen. p. 166.

76. Sheikh Al-Habib Ali Al-Jifri.

77. *The National* 31 July 2008.

78. *Islamica* 17 April 2006.

79. *Gulf News* 20 February 2008.

80. See chapter 3.

81. (*in Arabic*) Al-Otaibi, Manna Said. *The Economy of Abu Dhabi: Ancient and Modern* (Beirut: Commercial Industrial Press, 1973). p. 175.

82. Wheatcroft, Andrew. *With United Strength: Sheikh Zayed bin Sultan Al-Nahyan, the Leader and the Nation* (Abu Dhabi: Emirates Centre for Strategic Studies and Research, 2005). p. 204.

83. Peck, Malcolm. *The United Arab Emirates: A Venture in Unity* (Boulder: Westview, 1986). pp. 107–108.

84. EAD press release June 2008.

85. The AGEDI was founded in 2002.

86. Wheatcroft. p. 256.

87. *The National* 4 August 2008.

88. *Gulf News* 14 August 2008.

89. Personal correspondence with TDIC spokesperson, September 2008.

90. *Gulf News* 14 August 2008.

91. Wheatcroft. p. 185.

92. Heard-Bey reports this as being 28 percent of Abu Dhabi's GDP. Probably temporarily skewed by massive gifts to Egypt and Syria. Heard-Bey. p. 381.

93. Wheatcroft. p. 334.
94. Wheatcroft. pp. 240–241.
95. Heard-Bey. p. 390.
96. Maitha bint Salem Al-Shamsi.
97. Sir John Holmes.
98. Abdul Haq Amiri.
99. *The National* 11 July 2008.
100. ADFD press releases 2008.
101. This was a gift from Zayed to the Palestinian Authority's Ministry of Public Works and Housing in 2004. *Khaleej Times* 23 October 2004; *(in Arabic)* Hamza, Kamal. *Zayed: A Mark on the Forehead of History* (Abu Dhabi, 2005). pp. 162–163.
102. *(in Arabic)* Mutawwa, Khalid. *The Arabic Falcon* (Sharjah, 2005). pp. 214–215.
103. Hamza. p. 166.
104. *The National* 18 July 2008.
105. Personal interviews, Abu Dhabi, April 2008.
106. *The National* 12 July 2008.
107. *The National* 5 August 2008.
108. *The National* 23 June 2008.
109. *The National* 18 December 2008.
110. Mutawwa. p. 99.
111. *Islamic Republic News Agency* 16 January 2004.
112. Nuri Al-Makili.
113. *The National* 28 July 2008.

7. UNRESOLVED PROBLEMS: EXTERNAL AND STRUCTURAL

1. See chapter 4.
2. *Jane's Defense Weekly* 7 February 2007; Personal interviews, London, May 2008. At least $2.5 billion per annum, but likely to be much more.
3. Personal interviews, Abu Dhabi, April 2008; Abdulla, Abdulkhaleq. 'Political Dependency: The Case of the United Arab Emirates' (PhD thesis. Georgetown University, 1985). p. 208.
4. Zayed had had bad experiences equipping the Abu Dhabi Defence Force force with British aircraft whereas his negotiations with French arms companies always seemed more straightforward. Wheatcroft, Andrew. *With United Strength: Sheikh Zayed bin Sultan Al-Nahyan, the Leader and the Nation* (Abu Dhabi: Emirates Centre for Strategic Studies and Research, 2005). p. 338.
5. *Janes Defense Weekly* 7 February 2007.
6. *Oxford Business Group* 'United Arab Emirates: The Report 2000.' pp. 58–59.

7. *Janes Defense Weekly* 7 February 2007

8. Personal interviews, Dubai, January 2007; *Counterpunch* 4 December 2004.

9. Many Yemenis and Egyptians serve in the UAE Armed Forces. Perhaps over 20,000.

10. Al-Hakeem precision guided missiles.

11. MBDA Corporation.

12. *The National* 12 August 2008; *Gulf News* 30 July 2008; *AFP* 9 September 2008.

13. Manufactured by Northrop Grumman.

14. The submarine system is being set up by Germany's Konigsberg Corporation. Personal interviews, London, May 2008.

15. *Oxford Business Group* 'United Arab Emirates: The Report 2000.' pp. 58–59. The agreement may involve 75,000 troops being promised to the UAE in the event of an invasion.

16. (*in Arabic*) Obaid, Nayef. *The Foreign Policy of the United Arab Emirates* (Abu Dhabi: 2004). pp. 155–156.

17. *Jane's Defense Weekly* 7 February 2007; personal interviews, London, July 2006. Perhaps over 100 US personnel are stationed at Dhafrah airbase.

18. *International Herald Tribune* 22 June 2005. RQ-4 Global Hawk unmanned reconnaissance aircraft have been stationed there. KC-10 tanker aircraft also use the base to support operations in Afghanistan.

19. Davidson, Christopher M. *Dubai: The Vulnerability of Success* (London: Hurst, 2008). pp. 270–271.

20. *Workers World* 17 May 2007.

21. Anthony, John Duke. *Arab States of the Lower Gulf: People, Politics, Petroleum* (Washington DC: Middle East Institute, 1975). p. 152.

22. Obaid. p. 155.

23. Personal interviews, Kuwait, November 2005; Heard-Bey, Frauke. *From Trucial States to United Arab Emirates* (London: Longman, 1996). pp. 388–391.

24. Heard-Bey. pp. 511–513.

25. Hawley, Donald. *The Emirates: Witness to a Metamorphosis* (Norwich: Michael Russell, 2007). p. 30.

26. *Jane's Defense Weekly* 7 February 2007.

27. Amr Moussa.

28. The National 28 July 2008; (*in Arabic*) Mutawwa, Khalid. *The Arabic Falcon* (Sharjah, 2005). p. 99.

29. *Oxford Business Group* 'Abu Dhabi: The Report 2007.' p. 25.

30. *Reuters* 11 May 2007; *BBC News* 13 May 2007.

31. In contrast, Jordan's soldiers are restricted to base camp security duties.

32. *BBC News* 28 March 2008.

33. *Gulf News* 18 July 2008.

34. Abdullah Ibrahim Al-Shehhi (the UAE's former ambassador to India). *AFP* 6 July 2008.
35. *The National* 8 August 2008.
36. Van der Meulen, Hendrik. 'The Role of Tribal and Kinship Ties in the Politics of the United Arab Emirates' (PhD thesis. The Fletcher School of Law and Diplomacy, 1997). p. 238.
37. *Oxford Business Group* 'United Arab Emirates: The Report 2000.' pp. 98–99.
38. *Telegraph* 5 August 2008.
39. Davidson 2008. pp. 289–297.
40. Ibid. pp. 296–297.
41. See for example the joint venture between Mubadala and MGM Mirage discussed later in this chapter. *LA Times* 8 November 2007.
42. See for example the warnings posted by Britain's Foreign and Commonwealth Office in June 2008. *Telegraph* 16 June 2008; *Financial Times* 17 June 2008.
43. If anything, the federation would perhaps become a little tighter; as Dubai's current economic autonomy would likely weaken.
44. Saif Said bin Ghubash.
45. Wilson, Graeme. *Rashid's Legacy: The Genesis of the Maktoum Family and the History of Dubai* (Dubai: Media Prima, 2006). p. 431.
46. Khalifa bin Ahmad Al-Mubarak.
47. Davidson 2008. p. 292.
48. The revolution was being planned from the safety of the UAE. 200 plotters were arrested and jailed, but were soon released and reintegrated into Omani society. Personal interviews, Durham, June 2008; *BBC News* 26 January 2005.
49. *Reuters* 1 July 2008.
50. Personal interviews, Dubai, December 2003; *The Times* 24 December 2002. Al-Nashiri had been apprehended while in the final planning stages of attacks on 'vital economic targets' in the emirate that were aiming to inflict 'the highest possible casualties among nationals and foreigners.
51. *Telegraph* 16 June 2008; *Financial Times* 17 June 2008.
52. *The National* 12 July 2008.
53. *Privacy International* 'Silenced UAE' 21 September 2003.
54. *The National* 14 July 2008; *The National* 20 July 2008; *Gulf News* 20 July 2008.
55. Personal interviews, London, May 2008.
56. In summer 2008 the Al-Mudeef crossing between Al-Ayn and Buraimi was temporarily shut, requiring all to pass through the Khatam Al-Shakla border point, some 20km away from the city. Only GCC nationals (and a few Buraimi-based businessmen who were been issued special ID cards

by the federal ministry for the interior) could pass through the remaining city centre border point at Al-Hili. *The National* 20 July 2008.

57. In 1995 Sheikh Zayed bin Sultan Al-Nahyan remarked of Abu Dhabi nationals that he 'could not understand how physically fit young men can sit idle and accept the humiliation of depending on others for their livelihood.' Wilson. p. 528.

58. A labour law was introduced in 2002 in an effort to regulate the employment of nationals in the private sector. As part of the law, nationals were to benefit from a special pensions fund and were to be 'guaranteed better rights as employees' including a maximum number of working hours per week and a guaranteed finishing time of four o'clock in the afternoon for women with children of school age.

59. Notably banking and insurance companies. *Gulf News* 23 September 2004; *Gulf News* 8 December 2006.

60. *Oxford Business Group* 'Abu Dhabi: The Report 2007.' p. 51.

61. *The National* 27 July 2008.

62. *Gulf News* 8 December 2006.

63. *Gulf News* 28 July 2008.

64. *Oxford Analytica* February 2007.

65. *The National* 3 June 2008.

66. *Masdar Research Journal* (vol. 5, no. 2, 2007).

67. *CIA World Factbook 2007*.

68. *UAE Yearbook 2006* states an average of 10 percent: 9 percent for females, 16 percent for males.

69. Jordan's illiteracy rate is believed to be less than 1 percent. UNESCO 2006.

70. Federal ministry for higher education report 'Educating the next generation of Emiratis' (Abu Dhabi: 2007).

71. *Oxford Business Group* 'Abu Dhabi: The Report 2007.' p. 51.

72. *The National* 14 July 2008 states 38 percent. However a former director at the federal ministry for higher education states 28 percent. See Davidson, Christopher M., and Mackenzie-Smith, Peter (eds). *Higher Education in the Gulf States: Shaping Economies, Politics, and Culture* (London: Saqi, 2008). p. 120.

73. CIA World Factbook 2008; Personal interviews, Abu Dhabi, April 2008. 1.3 percent on education, which is about one third of military expenditure. This compares badly with Jordan, which spends 4.9 percent on education.

74. Federal ministry for higher education report 'Educating the next generation of Emiratis' (Abu Dhabi: 2007).

75. Ibid. Interestingly, a federal government white paper has predicted that the HCT institutions across the UAE may have to turn away 3000 students in 2007 in order to maintain the quality of their programs.

76. Ibid.
77. Personal interviews, Dubai Knowledge and Human Development Authority, August 2007.
78. *Khaleej Times* 23 November 2007.
79. *The National* 30 April 2008.
80. *The National* 11 July 2008.
81. *The National* 20 April 2008.
82. *Gulf News* 13 July 2008.
83. *Zawya Dow Jones* 14 April 2006.
84. NYU-AD was announced in August 2007. It will have over 2000 undergrads and 800 postgrads, and will be launched in 2010. *New York Times* 31 August 2007.
85. Personal interviews, Abu Dhabi, April 2008.
86. *The National* 28 July 2008.
87. *Gulf News* 8 March 2008.
88. See chapter 6.
89. Growth rates for the UAE national population are estimated to be between 4.5 and 6 percent. A 2005 report by the National Human Resource Development and Employment Authority (Tanmia) estimated it to be 5.6 percent.
90. In 2002 it was estimated that 85 percent of the UAE's population was urbanised, and it was predicted that by 2030 over 96 percent would be urbanised. Emirates News Agency (WAM) 9 April 2002.
91. In 2005 the National Human Resource Development and Employment Authority (Tanmia) estimated that female participation in the labour force had risen to over 16 percent. This compares with just 5 percent in 1995.
92. Most notably the Qatar election law, which was passed in May 2008 and is likely to lead to 30 of the 45 positions in the Consultative Assembly being elected in 2009 or 2010.
93. Personal interviews with employees of the Dubai Chamber of Commerce and Industry, Dubai, February 2006.
94. For a discussion of anthropological reality in the region see Roy, Olivier. *The Politics of Chaos in the Middle East* (London: Hurst, 2008). p. 43.
95. *The National* 6 August 2008.
96. *Gulf News* 27 March 2008; *Oxford Business Group* 'Abu Dhabi: The Report 2007.' p. 16.
97. *Gulf News* 7 August 2008.
98. *Oxford Business Group* 'Abu Dhabi: The Report 2007.' p. 16.
99. Anwar bin Muhammad Gargash from Dubai. *Khaleej Times* 10 February 2006.
100. 6689 in total, of which 1189 were women.
101. Davidson 2008. pp. 165–166.

102. Jamal bin Sanad Al-Suwaidi.
103. *Gulf News* 21 March 2007.
104. Anwar bin Muhammad Gargash was reassigned to being federal minister of state for foreign affairs, under Sheikh Abdullah bin Zayed Al-Nahyan.
105. *Oxford Business Group* 'Abu Dhabi: The Report 2007.' p. 17.
106. Personal interviews, Dubai, January 2007.
107. *Gulf News* 21 December 2006.
108. *Gulf News* 26 June 2008.
109. Ibid.
110. *Gulf News* 7 May 2008.
111. Sheikh Hamdan bin Rashid Al-Maktum.
112. *Gulf News* 26 June 2008; Personal interviews, Abu Dhabi, April 2008.
113. *AMEInfo* 14 April 2008.
114. *Associated Press* 9 January 2009.
115. Personal interviews, Abu Dhabi, April 2008.
116. *The National* 28 June 2008.
117. Ibid. This interview was with the Lebanese newspaper *Al-Nahar* in June 2008.
118. Seznec, Jean-François. 'The Gulf Sovereign Wealth Funds: Myths and Reality' in *Middle East Policy* (vol. 15, no. 2, 2008). pp. 102–103.
119. Abu Dhabi Law 14 of 2008 was confirmed by Emirates News Agency (WAM) 20 December 2008.
120. *Censorship RMIT* 10 June 2008.
121. *Gulf News* 5 September 2008; *Times Higher Education* 25 September 2008.
122. US Bureau for Democracy, Human Rights, and Labor 2007 report on the United Arab Emirates.
123. *New Statesman* 5 March 2007.
124. In September 2007 Sheikh Muhammad bin Rashid Al-Maktum overturned jail sentences for two journalists accused of libel. *Gulf News* 24–25 September 2007.
125. Fines can go up to 20,000 dirhams. Censorship RMIT 10 June 2008.
126. *Wall Street Journal* 22 January 2009.
127. US Bureau for Democracy, Human Rights, and Labor 2007 report on the United Arab Emirates.
128. *Guardian* 16 June 2008. The interview took place on *National Public Radio* 22 January 2008.
129. E.g on Iran's trade relationship with Dubai.
130. E.g. *The National* 15 September 2008. 'Media Council Denies Book Ban.'
131. *New York Times* 29 April 2008.
132. *Privacy International* 'Silenced UAE' 21 September 2003.

133. Internet Content Filtering Policy and Procedure. Telecommunications Regulatory Authority 24 September 2006.
134. Including Amnesty International and Human Rights Watch.
135. US Bureau for Democracy, Human Rights, and Labor 2007 report on the United Arab Emirates.
136. US Bureau for Democracy, Human Rights, and Labor 2007 report on the United Arab Emirates.
137. The 'Secret Dubai' blog is authored by an anonymous Canadian expatriate and was temporarily blocked in July 2005. *Gulf News* 19 July 2005; US Bureau for Democracy, Human Rights, and Labor 2007 report on the United Arab Emirates.
138. Notably Emaar and Nakheel.
139. Syria, Egypt, Hezbollah in Lebanon, etc. Roy. p. 96.
140. Ibid. p. 96.
141. Federal Law 15 of 1971.
142. See Hall, Marjorie J. *Business Laws of the United Arab Emirates* (London: Jacobs, 1987).
143. The suffix: dot.il.
144. In practice it is possible to enter the UAE with Israeli passport stamps, but no effort has been made to clarify the situation.
145. Davidson 2008. pp. 199–200. The ZCCF hosted a number of anti-semitic speakers including members of the International Progress Organisation and authors that had already received international condemnation for their work.
146. US Bureau for Democracy, Human Rights, and Labor 2007 report on the United Arab Emirates.
147. See *Gulf News* 11 January 2009 'Israel's War of Deceit, Lies, and Propaganda.'
148. See *Gulf News* 4 January 2009 'Zionists are the New Nazis.'
149. *Gulf News* 2 November 2007.
150. *Boston Globe* 31 August 2003; *Jewish Week* 30 May 2003.
151. Davidson 2008. p. 200.
152. The US Department for Commerce's Bureau for Industry and Security has an Office of Antiboycott Compliance.
153. Amnesty International 27 September 1995; *Los Angeles Times* 10 February 1996.
154. Davidson. pp. 282–285.
155. Ibid. p. 285.
156. Anti-slavery.org 29 March 2005.
157. Federal Law 51 of 2006.
158. Combating Human Trafficking UAE Annual Report 2007.
159. US Bureau for Democracy, Human Rights, and Labor 2007 report on the United Arab Emirates.

160. US Annual Trafficking in Persons Report 2007.
161. *Financial Times* 10 December 2008.
162. *The National* 9 December 2008.
163. *Financial Times* 10 December 2008.
164. Ibid.
165. For a general discussion of civil society in the UAE see Davidson 2008. pp. 209–218; Krause, Wanda. *Women in Civil Society: The State, Islamism, and Networks in the United Arab Emirates* (New York: Palgrave, 2008).
166. *Gulf News* 9 April 2006.
167. *Gulf News* 1 April 2007.
168. Jamal bin Sanad Al-Suwaidi.
169. *Gulf News* 27 March 2008.
170. Amnesty International 2007 report on the United Arab Emirates.
171. US Bureau for Democracy, Human Rights, and Labor 2007 report on the United Arab Emirates.
172. As per new anti-terrorism legislation. US Bureau for Democracy, Human Rights, and Labor 2007 report on the United Arab Emirates.
173. Amnesty International 5 October 2007.
174. Amnesty International 30 May 2008.
175. Amnesty International 17 January 2008.
176. Amnesty International 2007 report on the United Arab Emirates.
177. Amnesty International 28 June 2008.
178. Amnesty International 2007 report on the United Arab Emirates.
179. Amnesty International 23 August 2005.
180. *Zawya Dow Jones* 24 December 2008.
181. Amnesty International, 5 October 2007.
182. Amnesty International 11 October 2005.
183. US Bureau for Democracy, Human Rights, and Labor 2007 report on the United Arab Emirates.
184. *Gulf News* 14 July 2008.
185. *The National* 20 July 2008.
186. US Bureau for Democracy, Human Rights, and Labor 2007 report on the United Arab Emirates.
187. Personal correspondence with ITP Publishers, September 2008.
188. *New York Times* 1 November 2007.
189. Personal interviews, Abu Dhabi, August 2008.
190. *People's Daily Online* 26 March 2007.
191. In Ghantoot.
192. *AFP* 26 November 2006.
193. Taryam, Abdullah. *The Establishment of the United Arab Emirates, 1950–1985* (London: Croom Helm, 1987). p. 199.
194. The aforementioned Supreme Petroleum Council manages Abu Dhabi's oil affairs, while the Abu Dhabi-based deputy supreme commander and

the commander-in-chief of the UAE Armed Forces are the two key military positions.

195. *Gulf News* 20 July 2008.
196. Personal interviews, Dubai, August 2007.
197. Al-Sharhan International Consultancy. 'United Arab Emirates Country Report' (Dubai: 2001). p. 41; *Oxford Business Group* 'United Arab Emirates: The Report 2000.' p. 75; Hakim, Iqbal Ismail. *United Arab Emirates Central Bank and 9/11 Financing* (New York: GAAP, 2005). pp. 2, 187.
198. *Financial Times* 7 July 2008; *The National* 14 July 2008.
199. Davidson 2008. p. 181.
200. Ibid. p. 119.
201. *Oxford Business Group* 'United Arab Emirates: The Report 2000.' p. 115.
202. In March 2006 a sentence was passed in Ra's al-Khaimah requiring a man's hand to be cut off. US Bureau for Democracy, Human Rights, and Labor 2007 report on the United Arab Emirates.
203. US Bureau for Democracy, Human Rights, and Labor 2007 report on the United Arab Emirates.
204. *Oxford Analytica* May 2008.
205. *The National* 4 August 2008.
206. Article 13.
207. Wheatcroft. p. 202.
208. Ibid.
209. *Oxford Business Group* 'Abu Dhabi: The Report 2007.' p. 35.
210. *The National* 28 July 2008.
211. It is estimated that over the past decade the four poorest emirates have only accounted for between 6 and 15 percent of the UAE's GDP. Crown Prince Court Department of Research and Studies. 'Statistical Book' (Abu Dhabi: 1996). p. 54; Personal interviews, Dubai, January 2007; Encyclopaedia of the Nations, December 2008.
212. Sheikh Saqr bin Muhammad Al-Qasimi has ruled Ra's al-Khaimah since 1948.
213. Davidson 2008. p. 262.
214. See www.sheikhkhalidrak.com and California Strategies press release 14 November 2008.
215. *The National* 19 July 2008.
216. *Khaleej Times* 7 February 2008.
217. See for example *The Daily Telegraph* 15 January 2005; Davidson 2008. p. 189.
218. *Bloomberg* 4 December 2008 quoting EFG-Hermes; *Daily Telegraph* 21 November 2008 claiming villas on Palm Jumeirah had lost 40 percent of their value.

219. *Financial Times* 23 November 2008.

220. *Financial Times* 10 November 2008.

221. *Guardian* 5 December 2008.

222. *Guardian* 21 November 2008.

223. *Financial Times* 13 November 2008.

224. Tamweel and Amlak were merged into the Real Estate Bank, which is a unit of the federal ministry for finance. *Financial Times* 23 November 2008.

225. See chapter 6.

226. *The National* 15 December 2008; *Financial Times* 15 December 2008.

227. *Wall Street Journal* 25 November 2008.

228. See chapter 4.

229. *Times* 29 November 2008.

230. Excerpts from a speech delivered by Muhammad Ali Al-Abbar on 24 November 2008 at the Dubai International Financial Centre.

BIBLIOGRAPHY

Abdekarim, Abbas (ed). *Change and Development in the Gulf* (London: Macmillan, 1999).

Abdulghani, Abdulhamid Muhammad. 'Culture and Interest in Arab Foreign Aid: Kuwait and the United Arab Emirates as Case Studies' (PhD thesis. University of California at Santa Barbara, 1986).

Abdulla, Abdulkhaleq. 'Political Dependency: The Case of the United Arab Emirates' (PhD thesis. Georgetown University, 1985).

Abdullah, Muhammad Morsy. *The United Arab Emirates: A Modern History* (London: Croom Helm, 1978).

(*in Arabic*) Abdullah, Muhammad Morsy. *Between Yesterday and Today* (Abu Dhabi, 1969).

Abu-Baker, Albadr. 'Political Economy of State Formation: The United Arab Emirates in Comparative Perspective' (PhD thesis. University of Michigan, 1995).

Al-Akim, Hassan Hamdan. *The Foreign Policy of the United Arab Emirates* (London: Saqi, 1989).

Anthony, John Duke. *The United Arab Emirates: Dynamics of State Formation* (Abu Dhabi: Emirates Centre for Strategic Studies and Research, 2002).

——— *Arab States of the Lower Gulf: People, Politics, Petroleum* (Washington DC: Middle East Institute, 1975).

(*in Arabic*) Al-Ayderus, Muhammad Hassan. *The State of the United Arab Emirates* (Kuwait: Zat Al-Salasil, 1989).

(*in Arabic*) Al-Ayderus, Muhammad Hassan. *Political Developments in the United Arab Emirates* (Kuwait: Zat Al-Salasil, 1983).

(*in Arabic*) Badawi, Jamal. *Supporting the Federal System* (Abu Dhabi: Al-Ittihad Press, 1975).

(*in Arabic*) Bashir, Iskander. *The United Arab Emirates* (Beirut: Al-Khayats, 1982).

(*in Arabic*) Batikh, Ramadban Muhammad. 'The Development of Political and Constitutional Thought in the United Arab Emirates' (PhD thesis. University of the UAE, 1997).

Beblawi, Hazem, and Luciani, Giacomo (eds). *The Rentier State* (New York: Croom Helm, 1987).

BIBLIOGRAPHY

Belgrave, Charles. *The Pirate Coast* (London: G.Bell and Sons, 1966).

Bhargava, Pradeep. *A Political Economy of the Gulf States* (New Delhi: South Asian Publishers, 1989).

Bhutani, Surendra. The *Contemporary Gulf* (New Delhi: Academic Press, 1980).

(*in Arabic*) Bilal, Muhammad. *Changes in Population and Power Among Immigrants and Citizens of the United Arab Emirates, 1976–1980* (Sharjah: Sociologist Society, 1990).

Brown, Gavin. *OPEC and the World Energy Market* (London: Longman, 1998).

Bulloch, John. *The Gulf* (London: Century, 1984).

Buxani, Ram. *Taking the High Road* (Dubai: Motivate, 2003).

Chubin, Sharam (ed). *Security in the Persian Gulf: Domestic Political Factors* (Montclair: Allenheld Osman, 1981).

Clements, Frank A. *United Arab Emirates: World Bibliographical Series Volume 43* (Oxford, Clio, 1998).

Codrai, Ronald. *The Seven Sheikhdoms: Life in the Trucial States Before the Federation of the United Arab Emirates* (London: Stacey International, 1990).

Collard, Elizabeth. 'Economic Prospects for the United Arab Emirates' in *Middle East International* (no.21, 1973).

Cordesman, Anthony H. *Bahrain, Oman, Qatar, and the United Arab Emirates: Challenges of Security* (Boulder: Westview, 1997).

Cotrell, Alvin (ed). *The Persian Gulf States* (Baltimore: John Hopkins University Press, 1980).

Crystal, Jill. *Oil and Politics in the Gulf: Rulers and Merchants in Kuwait and Qatar* (New York: Cambridge University Press, 1995).

Davidson, Christopher M. 'Dubai: The Security Dimensions of the Region's Premier Free Port' in *Middle East Policy* (vol. 15, no. 2, 2008).

—— *Dubai: The Vulnerability of Success* (London: Hurst, 2008).

—— 'The Full Extent of Arab Nationalism and British Opposition in Dubai, 1920–1966' in *Middle Eastern Studies* (vol. 43, no. 6, 2007).

—— 'The Emirates of Abu Dhabi and Dubai: Contrasting Roles in the International System' in *Asian Affairs* (vol. 38, no. 1, 2007).

—— 'After Sheikh Zayed: The Politics of Succession in Abu Dhabi and the United Arab Emirates' in *Middle East Policy* (vol. 13, no. 1, 2006).

—— *The United Arab Emirates: A Study in Survival* (Boulder: Lynne Rienner, 2005).

Davidson, Christopher M, and Mackenzie-Smith, Peter (eds). *Higher Education in the Gulf States: Shaping Economies, Politics, and Culture* (London: Saqi, 2008).

Davies, Charles E. *The Blood Red Arab Flag: An Investigation into Qasimi Piracy, 1797–1820* (Exeter: Exeter University Press, 1997).

224

Dresch, Paul and Piscatori, James P (eds). *Monarchies and Nations: Globalisation and Identity in the Arab States of the Gulf* (London: IB Tauris, 2005).

Ehteshami, Anoushivaran. 'Reform From Above: The Politics of Participation in the Oil Monarchies' in *International Affairs* (vol. 79, no. 1, 2003).

El-Din, Amin Badr. 'The Offsets Program in the United Arab Emirates' in *Middle East Policy* (vol. 5, no. 1, 1997).

Al-Fahim, Muhammad. *From Rags to Riches: A Story of Abu Dhabi* (London: Centre for Arab Studies, 1995).

Fairhall, D. *Russia looks to the sea* (London: 1971), p.234.

Fenelon, Kevin. The *United Arab Emirates: An Economic and Social Survey* (London: Longman, 1973).

———— *The Trucial States: A Brief Economic Survey* (Beirut: Al-Khayats, 1969).

Field, Michael. *The Merchants: The Big Business Families of Arabia* (London: John Murray, 1984).

Findlow, Sally. 'The United Arab Emirates: Nationalism and Arab-Islamic Identity' in *Emirates Centre for Strategic Studies and Research Occasional Papers* (no.39, 2000).

Foley, Sean. 'The United Arab Emirates: Political Issues and Security Dilemmas' in *Middle East Review of International Affairs* (vol. 3, no. 1, 1998).

Gause, F. Gregory. *Oil Monarchies: Domestic and Security Challenges in the Arab Gulf States* (New York: Council on Foreign Relations Press, 1994).

Ghanem, Shihab. *Industrialisation in the United Arab Emirates* (London: Avebury, 1992).

(*in Arabic*) Ghubash, Moza. *Human Development in the United Arab Emirates* (Abu Dhabi: Cultural Foundation, 1996).

Graham, G. S. *Great Britain in the Indian Ocean, 1810–1850* (Oxford: Stevenson, 1967).

Al-Gurg, Easa Saleh. *The Wells of Memory* (London: John Murray, 1998).

Hall, Marjorie J. *Business Laws of the United Arab Emirates* (London: Jacobs, 1987).

Hakim, Iqbal Ismail. *United Arab Emirates Central Bank and 9/11 Financing* (New York: GAAP, 2005).

(*in Arabic*) Al-Hamid, Muhammad Ahmad. 'Gulf Security and its Impact on the Gulf Cooperation Council' in *Emirates Centre for Strategic Studies and Research Occasional Papers* (no.16, 1997).

(*in Arabic*) Hamza, Kamal. *Zayed: A Mark on the Forehead of History* (Abu Dhabi, 2005).

Hawley, Donald. *The Emirates: Witness to a Metamorphosis* (Norwich: Michael Russell, 2007).

———— *The Trucial States* (London: George Allen and Unwin, 1970).

Hay, Rupert. 'The Impact of the Oil Industry on the Persian Gulf Sheikhdoms' in *Middle East Journal* (vol. 9, no. 4, 1955).

BIBLIOGRAPHY

Heard-Bey, Frauke. 'The United Arab Emirates: Statehood and Nation-Building in a Traditional Society' in *Middle East Journal* (vol. 59, no. 3, 2005).

——— *From Trucial States to United Arab Emirates* (London: Longman, 1996).

——— 'The Gulf States and Oman in Transition' in *Asian Affairs* (vol. 3, no. 1, 1972).

Henderson, Edward. *This Strange Eventful History: Memoirs of Earlier Days in the United Arab Emirates* (London: Quartet, 1988).

Herb, Michael. *All in the Family: Absolutism, Revolution, and Democracy in the Middle Eastern Monarchies* (New York: State University of New York Press, 1999).

Holden, David. 'The Persian Gulf after the British Raj' in *Foreign Affairs* (vol. 49, no. 4, 1971).

——— *Farewell to Arabia* (New York: Faber and Faber, 1966).

Hopwood , Derek. *The Arabian Peninsula* (London: 1972).

Hudson, Michael (ed). *Middle East Dilemma: The Politics and Economics of Arab Integration* (London: IB Tauris, 1999).

——— *Arab Politics: The Search for Legitimacy* (New Haven: Yale University Press, 1977).

Huntington, Samuel P. *Political Order in Changing Societies* (New Haven: Yale University Press, 1968).

Hvidt, Martin. 'Public-Private Ties and their Contribution to Development: The Case of Dubai' in *Middle Eastern Studies* (vol. 43, no. 4, 2007).

(*in Arabic*) Ibrahim, Abdul-Aziz. *Britain and the Emirates of the Omani Coast* (Baghdad: Matba'at al-Irshad, 1978).

(*in Arabic*) Ibrahim, Muhammad. *Foundations of the Political and Constitutional Organisation of the United Arab Emirates* (Abu Dhabi: 1975).

(*in Arabic*) Isa, Shakir Musa. *The Experience of the United Arab Emirates* (Beirut: Al-Khayats, 1981).

Ismael, Jacqueline. *Kuwait: Dependency and Class in a Rentier State* (Gainesville: University of Florida Press, 1993).

Johns, Richard. 'The Emergence of the United Arab Emirates' in *Middle East International* (vol. 21, 1973).

Joyce, Miriam. 'On the Road Towards Unity: The Trucial States from a British Perspective, 1960–1966' in *Middle Eastern Studies* (vol. 35, no. 2, 1999).

(*in Arabic*) Kawari, Ali Khalifa, and Al-Sadun, Jasim. The *Gulf Cooperation Council Countries: A Futuristic View* (Kuwait: Girttas, 1996).

Kazim, Aqil. *The United Arab Emirates: A Socio-Discursive Transformation in the Arabian Gulf* (Dubai: Gulf Book Centre, 2000).

Kéchichian, Joseph A. *Power and Succession in Arab Monarchies: A Reference Guide* (Boulder: Lynne Rienner, 2008).

BIBLIOGRAPHY

Kelly, John B. *Arabia, the Gulf, and the West: A Critical View of the Arabs and their Oil Policy* (New York: Basic Books, 1986).

——— *Britain and the Persian Gulf* (Oxford: Oxford University Press, 1968).

——— *Eastern Arabia Frontier* (New York: Praeger, 1964).

Khalaf, Sulayman. 'Poetics and Politics of Newly Invented Traditions in the Gulf: Camel Racing in the United Arab Emirates' in *Ethnology* (vol. 39, no. 3, 2000).

——— 'Gulf Societies and the Image of Unlimited Good' in *Dialectical Anthropology* (vol. 17, no. 1, 1992).

Khalifa, Ali Muhammad. *The United Arab Emirates: Unity in Fragmentation* (Boulder: Westview, 1979).

Khoury, Enver M. *The United Arab Emirates: Its Political System and Politics* (Maryland: Institute for Middle Eastern and North African Affairs, 1980).

Kostiner, Joseph (ed). *Middle East Monarchies: The Challenge of Modernity* (Boulder: Lynne Rienner, 2000).

Krause, Wanda. *Women in Civil Society: The State, Islamism, and Networks in the United Arab Emirates* (New York: Palgrave, 2008).

Al-Kuwari, Ali Khalifa. *Oil Revenues in the Gulf Emirates: Patterns of Allocation and Impact on Economic Development* (Essex: Bowker, 1978).

Laquer, Walter. *The Struggle for the Middle East* (London: Routledge, 1969).

Lienhardt, Peter. *Sheikhdoms of Eastern Arabia* (Oxford: Palgrave, 2001).

——— 'The Authority of Sheikhs in the Gulf: An Essay in Nineteenth Century History' in *Arabian Studies* (vol. 2, no. 1, 1975).

Long, David. *The Persian Gulf* (Boulder: Westview, 1978).

Lorimer, John G. *Gazetteer of the Persian Gulf, Oman, and Central Arabia* (London: Gregg International Publishers, 1970).

Luce, Margaret. *From Aden to the Gulf: Personal Diaries, 1956–1966* (Salisbury, Michael Russell, 1987).

Maitra, Jayanti, and Al-Hajji, Afra. *Qasr Al-Hosn: The History and Rulers of Abu Dhabi, 1793–1966* (Abu Dhabi: Centre for Documentation and Research, 2001).

(*in Arabic*) Al-Majd, Kamal Abu. *The Constitutional System of the United Arab Emirates* (Cairo: 1978).

El-Mallakh, Ragi. Economic *Development in the United Arab Emirates* (New York: St. Martin's, 1981).

Mann, Clarence. *Abu Dhabi: Birth of an Oil Sheikhdom* (Beirut: Al-Khayats, 1969).

Mellamid, Alexander. 'The Buraimi Oasis Dispute' in *Middle Eastern Affairs* (vol. 7, no. 2, 1956).

Mobley, Richard A. 'The Tunbs and Abu Musa Islands: Britain's Perspective' in *Middle East Journal* (vol. 57, no. 4, 2003).

BIBLIOGRAPHY

Moyse-Bartlett, Hubert. *The Pirates of Trucial Oman* (London: Macdonald, 1966).

Al-Musfir, Muhammad Salih. 'The United Arab Emirates: An Assessment of Federalism in a Developing Polity' (PhD thesis. State University of New York and Binghamton, 1985).

(*in Arabic*) Mutawwa, Khalid. *The Arabic Falcon* (Sharjah, 2005).

(*in Arabic*) Mutawwa, Muhammad A. *Development ad Social Change in the Emirates* (Beirut: Al-Farabi, 1991).

Al-Nabeh, Najat Abdullah. 'United Arab Emirates: Regional and Global Dimensions' (PhD thesis. Claremont Graduate School, 1984).

Al-Nahyan, Shamma bint Muhammad. *Political and Social Security in the United Arab Emirates* (Dubai: 2000).

Al-Nahyan, Sultan bin Khalifa. *National Security of the United Arab Emirates: A Perspective in Light of Global Changes to the New World Order* (London: Rivermill, 2003).

Niblock, Tim (ed). *Social and Economic Development in the Arab Gulf* (London: Croom Helm, 1980).

Nonneman, Gerd. 'Rentiers and Autocrats, Monarchs and Democrats, State and Society: The Middle East between Globalisation, Human Agency, and Europe' in *International Affairs* (vol. 77, no. 1, 2001).

(*in Arabic*) Obaid, Nayef. *The Foreign Policy of the United Arab Emirates* (Beirut: Majd, 2004).

Onley, James. *The Arabian Frontier of the British Raj: Merchants, Rulers, and the British in the Nineteenth Century Gulf* (Oxford: Oxford University Press, 2007).

———— 'Britain's Native Agents in Arabia and Persia, 1758–1958' in *Comparative Studies of South Asia, Africa, and the Middle East* (no.33, 2003).

Al-Otaibi, Manna Said. *The Petroleum Concession Agreements of the United Arab Emirates* (London: Croom Helm, 1982).

(*in Arabic*) ———— *Petroleum and the Economy of the United Arab Emirates* (Kuwait: Al-Qabas Press, 1977).

(*in Arabic*) ———— The Economy of Abu Dhabi: Ancient and Modern (Beirut: Commercial Industrial Press, 1973).

Overton, J. L. 'Stability and Change: Inter-Arab Politics in the Arabian Peninsula and the Gulf' (PhD thesis. University of Maryland, 1983).

Pal, Dharm. 'British Policy Towards the Arabian Tribes on the Shores of the Persian Gulf, 1964–1868' in *Journal of Indian History* (vol. 24, no. 1, 1945).

Peck, Malcolm. *The United Arab Emirates: A Venture in Unity* (Boulder: Westview, 1986).

Peterson, John E. 'The United Arab Emirates: Economic Vibrancy and US Interests' in *Asian Affairs* (vol. 34, no. 2, 2003).

BIBLIOGRAPHY

———— 'The Nature of Succession in the Gulf' in *Middle East Journal* (vol. 55, no. 4, 2001).

———— 'The Arab Gulf States: Steps Towards Political Participation' in *Washington Papers* (no.131, 1988).

Peterson, John E and Sindelar, Richard (eds). *Crosscurrents in the Gulf* (London: Routledge, 1988).

Philips, C. *The East Indian Company 1784–1834* (Manchester: Manchester University Press, 1961).

Pope, M. T. G. *Businessman's Guide to the United Arab Emirates* (Sharjah: Dar al-Fatah, 1996).

Pridham, B (ed). *The Arab Gulf and the West* (London: Croom Helm, 1975).

(*in Arabic*) Al-Qadir, Mustafa. *Contemporary Studies on the History of the Arabian Gulf* (Cairo: 1978).

(*in Arabic*) Qasim, Jamal Zakariyya. *Old Emirates and New State* (Cairo: 1978).

(*in Arabic*) Al-Qasimi, Nora Muhammad. *The Indian Existence in the Arabian Gulf, 1820–1947* (Sharjah: Department of Education, 2000).

Al-Qasimi, Sultan bin Muhammad (ed). *The Journals of David Seton in the Gulf, 1800–1809* (Exeter: Exeter University Press, 1995).

———— *The Myth of Arab Piracy in the Gulf* (London: Croom Helm, 1986).

Ramahi, Saif, and El-Wady, A. *Economic and Political Evolution in the Arabian Gulf States* (New York: Carlton, 1973).

(*in Arabic*) Al-Rahman, Abdullah Abd. *The Emirates in the Memory of its Children* (Dubai: Dubai Printing Press, 1990).

(*in Arabic*) Rashid, Ali Muhammad. *Political and Economic Agreements Made Between the Oman Coast Emirates and Britain, 1806–1971* (Sharjah: UAE Writer's Union Publications, 1989).

Reynolds, David. *Britannia Overruled: British Policy and World Power in the Twentieth Century* (Harlow: Longman, 1991).

Rizvi, S. N. Asad. 'From Tents to High Rise: Economic Development of the United Arab Emirates' in *Middle Eastern Studies* (vol. 29, no. 4, 1993).

Roy, Olivier. *The Politics of Chaos in the Middle East* (London: Hurst, 2008).

Rugh, Andrea B. *The Political Culture of Leadership in the United Arab Emirates* (New York: Palgrave Macmillan, 2007).

Rugh, William A. 'The United Arab Emirates: What are the Sources of its Stability?' in *Middle East Policy* (vol. 5, no. 3, 1997).

(*in Arabic*) Al-Rumaithi, Muhammad G. *The Impediments to Development in the Contemporary Arab Societies of the Gulf* (Kuwait: Matabi Dar al-Siyasah, 1977).

(*in Arabic*) ———— *Petroleum and Social Change in the Arabian Gulf* (Cairo: Dar al-Shab, 1975).

Rush, Alan (ed). *Ruling Families of Arabia: The United Arab Emirates* (Slough: Archive Editions 1991).

BIBLIOGRAPHY

Sadiq, Muhammad, and Snavely, William. *Bahrain, Qatar, and the United Arab Emirates: Colonial Past, Present Problems, and Future Prospects* (Lexington: Heath, 1972).

Al-Sagri, Saleh Hamad. 'Britain and the Arab Emirates, 1820–1956' (PhD thesis. University of Kent at Canterbury, 1988).

Al-Sayegh, Fatma. 'The United Arab Emirates and Oman: Opportunities and Challenges in the Twenty-First Century' in *Middle East Policy* (vol. 9. no. 3, 2002).

———— 'Merchants' Role in a Changing Society: The Case of Dubai, 1900–1990' in *Middle Eastern Studies* (vol. 34, no. 1, 1998).

(*in Arabic*) ———— *The United Arab Emirates: From Tribe to State* (Dubai: Al-Khaleej Books, 1997).

Seznec, Jean-François. 'The Gulf Sovereign Wealth Funds: Myths and Reality' in *Middle East Policy* (vol. 15, no. 2, 2008).

Al-Shamsi, Said Muhammad. 'The Buraimi Dispute: A Case Study in Inter-Arab Politics' (PhD thesis. American University, 1986).

(*in Arabic*) Sharabah, Naji Sadiq. *The United Arab Emirates: Politics and Rulership* (Abu Dhabi: Al-Kitab al-Jamiy, 1995).

(*in Arabic*) ———— 'The Federal Experiment of the United Arab Emirates, 1971–1977' (PhD thesis. University of Cairo, 1980).

(*in Arabic*) Sharaf, Muhammad Yasir. *United Arab Emirates Society* (Abu Dhabi: Al-Mutanabi Books, 1997).

Suwaidi, Jamal S (ed). *The Gulf: Challenges of the Future* (Abu Dhabi: Emirates Centre for Strategic Studies and Research, 2005).

(*in Arabic*) Tabatabai, Adil. *Comparative Studies in the Emirates* (Cairo: 1978).

Tammam, Hamdi. *Zayed bin Sultan Al-Nahyan: The Leader on the March* (Tokyo: Dai Nippon, 1983).

Taryam, Abdullah. *The Establishment of the United Arab Emirates, 1950–1985* (London: Croom Helm, 1987).

Teitelbaum, Joshua (ed). *Political Liberalization in the Persian Gulf* (London: Hurst, 2009).

Thesiger, Wilfred. *Arabian Sands* (London: Penguin, 1991).

Tomkinson, Michael. *The United Arab Emirates* (London: Jarrold and Sons, 1975).

Van der Meulen, Hendrik. 'The Role of Tribal and Kinship Ties in the Politics of the United Arab Emirates' (PhD thesis. The Fletcher School of Law and Diplomacy, 1997).

Wheatcroft, Andrew. *With United Strength: Sheikh Zayed bin Sultan Al-Nahyan, the Leader and the Nation* (Abu Dhabi: Emirates Centre for Strategic Studies and Research, 2005).

Wilson, Graeme. *Rashid's Legacy: The Genesis of the Maktoum Family and the History of Dubai* (Dubai: Media Prima, 2006).

Wriggins, Howard (ed). *The Dynamics of Regional Politics: Four Systems on the Indian Ocean Rim* (New York: Columbia University Press, 1992).

Yorke, Valerie. *The Gulf in the 1980s* (London: Royal Institute of International Affairs, 1980).

Zahlan, Rosemarie Said. *The Making of the Modern Gulf States* (London: Unwin Hyman, 1989).

——— *The Origins of the United Arab Emirates* (New York: St. Martin's, 1978).

INDEX